Bryan, Ford R. (Ford Richardson)
    Henry's lieutenants / Ford R. Bryan. --
Detroit : Wayne State University Press,
c1993.

    321 p. : ill. -- (Great Lakes books)

    ISBN 0-8143-2428-2: $24.95

                                27615   JUL '93

    1. Ford Motor Company--History.   2.
Automobile industry and trade--United States
--Biography.   3. Industrialists--United
States--Biography   I. Title.   II. Series.

HENRY'S
LIEUTENANTS

Henry Ford, 1863–1947.

HENRY'S LIEUTENANTS

Ford R. Bryan

Wayne State University Press   Detroit

GREAT LAKES BOOKS

*A complete listing of the books in this series can be
found at the back of this volume.*

Philip P. Mason, Editor
Walter P. Reuther Library, Wayne State University

Dr. Charles K. Hyde, Associate Editor
Department of History, Wayne State University

Library of Congress Cataloging-in-Publication Data

Bryan, Ford R. (Ford Richardson)
    Henry's lieutenants / Ford R. Bryan.
        p.   cm.—(Great Lakes books)
    Includes bibliographical references.
    ISBN 0-8143-2428-2   (alk. paper)
    1. Ford Motor Company—History.   2. Automobile industry and
trade—United States—Biography.   3. Industrialists—United States—
Biography. I. Title. II. Series.
HD9710.U54F534   1993
338.7'6292'0922—dc20
[B]   92-31789

Book design by Mary Primeau
Frontispiece: Henry Ford, 1863–1947.

To my late wife, Ellen Juntunen Bryan,
an avid reader and constructive critic.

Contents

Contents

Acknowledgments

The author gratefully acknowledges David R. Crippen of the Ford Archives for his encouragement and guidance in finding sources of information for this book. The entire staff of the Archives and Library of the Edison Institute (Henry Ford Museum & Greenfield Village) were consistently helpful over my nearly three years of research.

Archives and Library administrators Steven K. Hamp, Judith Endelman, Cynthia Read-Miller, Jeanine Head, and Jennifer Heymoss were all very supportive of my work. Joan Klimchalk and Winthrop Sears, Jr., helped especially in obtaining photographs.

These establishments also contributed materially: the Bentley Historical Library of the University of Michigan, the Cranbrook Archives and Historical Collections of the Cranbrook Educational Community, the Burton Historical Collection of the Detroit Public Library, General Motors Corporation Public Relations, the Lawrence Technological University, and the Dearborn Historical Museum Research Department.

Several close relatives of biography subjects were especially helpful in supplying photographs and otherwise unavailable information pertaining to their families. However, unless otherwise noted, the photographs are from the collections of the Henry Ford Museum & Greenfield Village and are reproduced with permission—and my thanks.

And, as usual, the rallying spirits of my close friends Rylma I. La-Chance and Hubert J. Beudert is most appreciated.

Introduction

Henry Ford had the innate power to motivate and control people. As a boy he had two younger brothers over which he ruled. As a young man he was able to induce others into helping with mechanical projects believed to border on the ridiculous. And at age thirty-three, he obtained considerable free technical help in building his first automobile. From the very beginning of the Ford Motor Company, Henry Ford attracted the talents needed to spur it on to success. During the course of this success, Ford gathered a most notable array of professionals, many of them self-trained as was he. These individuals vastly differed in character, but together completed the pattern required to launch the largest productive enterprise in the world.

The breadth of Ford's needs ranged from engineering the world's largest manufacturing plant to measuring a piece of steel within an accuracy of two-millionths of an inch. He employed people who could manage a 2.5 million acre rubber plantation in Brazil, remove a human kidney stone, direct fleets of ships, operate coal mines, and play violins. Henry Ford recognized a need for essentially every profession. The people who carried out Henry Ford's instructions are in themselves significant personalities worthy of individual attention. Some made their greatest contributions under Ford's direction; others reached the apexes of their careers after escaping from Ford's dominance. Of the people described in this book, the greater number were employed by Ford Motor Company. A lesser number were Ford's personal employees, satisfying concurrent needs of a more private nature—his farming, educational, and sociological ventures.

Although Henry Ford gloried in the limelight of highly publicized achievement, he privately admitted, "I don't do so much, I just go around lighting fires under other people." These other people were allowed very little public recognition by Ford.

It is well known that Ford frowned upon Ford Motor Company employees' publishing technical papers, speaking before technical groups, or even attending such meetings on their own initiative. Company affairs were not to be discussed outside work. Henry alone controlled announcements of company plans and accomplishments either directly to the press or through a delegated personal representative such as Ernest Liebold or William Cameron. For years, Ford Motor Company patents were in the name of Henry Ford as inventor, rather than being assigned by the actual inventor to Ford Motor Company.

Henry Ford was fond of announcing grandiose plans, some of which did and some of which did not materialize. Those projects that succeeded were realized through the efforts of his key employees. Considering the combined contributions of his many "lieutenants" leaves less and less attributable to Henry Ford himself. And, noting the many books that have heaped praise upon Henry Ford, perhaps it is time to acknowledge the contributions of some of those people who elevated Ford to his honored position.

Although these biographies can be read together with enjoyment as a book, their primary purpose is for library reference. The series is admittedly incomplete; it would require far more than this number of talented people to provide all of the business and sociological achievements attributed to Henry Ford. An extended list of biographies could well include the people listed in Appendix I.

The order in which the biographies appear is alphabetical. There is no reliable way to assign a relative value to the contributions of each person. Each biography subject was important at one time or another to Henry Ford. And some people of considerable importance are not included here because information about them is too obscure.

Much help in preparing this series of biographies was provided by more than two hundred oral reminiscences of Ford associates collected and transcribed by Owen Bombard in the early 1950s and more recently by David R. Crippen. These reminiscences are now on file in the Archives of the Henry Ford Museum & Greenfield Village. Although many of the people interviewed had not been especially vital to Ford's success, each presents an interesting facet of Ford activities. People who have submitted oral reminiscences are listed in Appendix II.

It was difficult sometimes to determine where credit for a given Ford development is primarily due. Sometimes more than one employee in their reminiscences have claimed credit for the same accomplishment. In such cases, both individuals are acknowledged as contributors.

Assuming this book will be used most frequently to obtain data concerning only one biography subject at a time, major references are located at the end of each biography even though there is considerable repetition from one biography to another. Particularly the extensive works of Allan Nevins and Frank Ernest Hill can be applied to many of the personalities associated with the Ford Motor Company.

HENRY'S
LIEUTENANTS

Clarence Williard Avery, 1882–1949.

Clarence Williard Avery

1882–1949

"Mr. Avery was Edsel Ford's schoolteacher,
and Edsel liked him very much."
—William C. Klann*

Clarence Avery was a major contributor to the techniques of mass production; however, it seems he gained little credit from Henry Ford for his accomplishments. Avery was a socially responsible person and a close friend of Edsel Ford. It was a severe blow to Edsel when Avery decided to leave Ford Motor Company for opportunities elsewhere.

Clarence Williard Avery was born in Dansville, Michigan, on February 15, 1882. He was educated at Dansville High School, continued his education at Ferris Institute in Big Rapids, Michigan, and completed a two-year manual training course at the University of Michigan. After teaching for one year in a rural school, Avery became manual training supervisor in the Battle Creek, Michigan, public schools in 1903.

While at Battle Creek, Avery married Lura Warner of nearby Doster. Warner was a 1904 graduate of the University of Michigan. They were to have two daughters, Eloise and Anabel.

In 1904, Avery accepted the position of principal of the Michigan Manual Training School at Ishpeming. In 1907, Avery became director of manual training at Detroit University School.

In Detroit, the family first lived at 671 Hurlbut; in 1911, they moved to 364 Montclair Avenue.

Avery was one of young Edsel Ford's instructors in manual training at Detroit University School. Edsel was in his teens, Avery in his twenties. Edsel was greatly impressed with Avery's mechanical ingenuity. In 1912, in casual conversation, Avery mentioned to Edsel his desire to enter the automobile business, and it was arranged by Edsel. Avery was classified at Ford Motor Company as a "student worker" and was paid twenty-five cents an hour as Charles Sorensen's assistant at the Highland Park plant. Although the pay was very low to start, Avery recognized the opportunity and made the most of it.

*From the oral reminiscences of William C. Klann, assistant to Clarence W. Avery.

15

Within a year, Avery, Sorensen, and others were involved in establishing the moving final assembly line for automobiles. Although Henry Ford is usually credited with its initiation, the idea quite definitely originated far below him. Several who were there at the time testify it was Avery who was the guiding light. He determined the optimal rate of line speed and the distribution of workers along the line. Avery became the company expert on time study and introduced time standards throughout the plant.

By December 1913, the moving final assembly line allowed the Model T, which had required 12.5 man-hours of labor to assemble, to be assembled using 2.7 man-hours. Later it would take only 1.5 man-hours. This was just the beginning for Avery. He next designed subassembly operations feeding the final assembly. Engines, transmissions, and magnetos all yielded to the system. Later, Henry Ford declared, "Every piece of work in the shop moves. It may move on hooks on overhead chains going to assembly in the exact order in which the parts are required, it may travel on a moving platform, or it may go by gravity, but the point is that there is no lifting or trucking of anything other than materials."

Avery's star was rising, and the family moved to a new home at 50 Puritan Avenue in Highland Park. By 1918, the Averys were at 460 Boston Boulevard, in an area only recently vacated by Henry Ford himself. Six years later, still working for Ford, Avery purchased a house at 1560 Wellesley, in exclusive Palmer Woods very close to the home of his Ford associate Peter E. Martin. This was the family's Detroit address for the rest of Avery's life.

Closed automobiles were rather rare until about 1915. The window glass in early cars was usually cut from by-products of the architectural plate-glass industry. As closed autos became more popular, the amount of by-product became insufficient to supply the auto industry. Prices had risen from twenty-two cents to ninety cents per square foot because of the greater demand. The auto industry had to look for other sources. In 1918, Henry Ford spotted a Model T backlight window exhibiting conspicuous optical distortion, and he decided he needed better as well as less expensive glass and considered manufacturing it himself.

Avery was aware of the problem, had studied the glass manufacturing process, and had some ideas. The usual procedure consisted of pouring molten glass from a melting furnace into clay pots, which were transferred to fixed flat tables where the glass was rolled, ground, and polished. Avery, with helpers, started experiments in 1919, in cooperation with Pilkington, a British concern. By November 1921, Ford had a system whereby a tank furnace poured molten glass continuously through rolls onto a moving table, which carried the glass under a series of grinders and polishers to be cut to size at the end of the line, the continuous line of tables returning again to the furnace. This novel procedure was such a success that glass manufacturers in Europe as well as America came to see it in use and put it into practice themselves. Henceforth, Avery was Ford's glass manufacturing expert. Using Avery's process, Ford Motor Company had three large glass plants producing 33 million square feet of quarter-inch plate glass annually by 1926.

In 1920, Avery was put in charge of organizing Ford's Northern Michigan Iron, Land and Lumber Company. This operation was to include 400,000 acres in four counties of Upper Michigan, holdings which by 1925 were valued at $23 million. The heart of the system was a huge lumber mill and chemical plant at Iron Mountain where sound wood was processed into auto body parts and scrap wood converted to charcoal briquets and useful chemicals. Supplying this plant with wood were several logging operations and several smaller mills. By 1921, the Rouge plant was receiving body frame parts from Iron Mountain, and until 1951 the Iron Mountain plant built all of Ford's wooden station wagon bodies.

For a time, Avery was in charge of the Ford Village Industries—small plants using water power to manufacture small auto parts. The Waterford plant on the Rouge River was equipped with a turbine which during certain seasons of the year fell a bit short of the power required. Avery added a Lincoln engine for occasional auxiliary power. Henry Ford didn't like his using the engine, though, and he ordered it removed and delivered to Avery's front porch. Working for Henry was not always easy.

In 1922, the Ford Motor Company purchased the Lincoln Motor Company, in which Edsel Ford took special interest. The Lincoln operations were to be "Fordized" for greater efficiency. Avery was involved in this process and worked closely with Edsel. Lincoln drivetrains were excellent, but the bodies were obsolete, requiring special attention. From 1922 to 1927, Edsel and Avery worked together on both vehicle design and manufacture. During this period, Avery was considered chief development engineer for Ford Motor Company.

In 1927, when Model T assembly at Highland Park was terminated and the planned Model A was to be assembled at the Rouge, there was a strong management clique at the Rouge headed by Sorensen and Harry Bennett, who were not receptive to executives coming from other locations within the company. Avery knew he was not welcome at the Rouge. In a letter to Edsel Ford on August 29, 1927, he expressed his desire to retire, mentioning the situation at the Rouge, which Edsel

Founders of Henry Ford Trade School: Avery, Frederick E. Searle, Samuel S. Marquis, and Hubert E. Hartman. This photograph was taken at a Trade School reunion July 1, 1946.

could do little to correct because Sorensen and Bennett were then favorites of Henry Ford. Edsel replied by letter expressing his regrets. It is doubtful Henry regretted Avery's leaving; he had not approved Edsel's close, continuing friendship with Avery.

Before the end of that year, Avery joined Murray Corporation, a supplier of automobile bodies and parts to the automotive industry. After one year as chief engineer and manufacturing manager, Avery became president and chairman of the board of directors, positions he held for the next twenty years. Murray became a major supplier of quasi-custom bodies for the Model A Ford and a few full-custom bodies for the Lincoln. Standard "Tudor" and "Fordor"—high-volume Ford bodies— were manufactured at the Rouge. More stylish, low-volume bodies were purchased by Ford from such suppliers as Murray and Briggs. Murray also produced automotive frames, fenders, and seat springs.

18

The Averys were still living in Palmer Woods. The daughters, Eloise and Anabel, graduated from the University of Michigan in 1930 and 1940, respectively. Avery was named president of the Detroit Board of Commerce in 1941 and belonged to a host of organizations such as the Detroit Club, the Recess Club, the Detroit Athletic Club, the Economic Club of Detroit, the Engineering Society of Detroit, and two prominent golf clubs. He was a director of the Federal Reserve Bank of Chicago, was a member of the Automotive Council for War Production, and was active in the Detroit Bureau of Governmental Research.

In December 1944, Ford Motor Company hosted a dinner for their thirty-five-year employees. To be speaker of the evening, they called on Avery, whom they highly regarded and with whom some of these employees had worked years before. Of the entire party at the dinner, only Avery was a non–Ford employee. In June 1944, the University of Michigan presented Avery with an honorary Doctor of Engineering degree.

Avery gave up the presidency of Murray Corporation in 1948 but continued as chairman of the board of directors. On May 13, 1949, at age sixty-seven, he had a fatal heart attack. He died at the family retreat in Doster. Attending his funeral in Detroit were such automotive notables as K. T. Keller, Loyd Maxwell, Joseph Galamb, Ernest Liebold, William C. Cowling, Peter Martin, Logan Miller, T. B. Zeder, W. Cole, Frederick Searle, Ernest Kanzler, and Henry Ford II.

On October 3, 1990, Avery was inducted into the Automotive Hall of Fame, based on his being designer of the first moving assembly line for mass production of automobiles.

Major References

Avery, Clarence W. "The Glass Industry." Speech, American Society of Mechanical Engineers, May 3, 1929. Accession 433, Henry Ford Museum & Greenfield Village Archives.

Clarence W. Avery collection. Bentley Historical Library, University of Michigan, Ann Arbor.

Clarence Avery—Lincoln Production, 1922–1927. Accession 814, Henry Ford Museum & Greenfield Village Archives.

Klann, W. C. Reminiscences. Accession 65, Henry Ford Museum & Greenfield Village Archives.

Lewis, David L. *The Public Image of Henry Ford.* Detroit: Wayne State University Press, 1976.

Nevins, Allan. *Ford: The Times, the Man, the Company.* New York: Charles Scribner's Sons, 1954.

Nevins, Allan, and Frank Ernest Hill. *Ford: Expansion and Challenge.* New York: Charles Scribner's Sons, 1957.

Irving Ruben Bacon, 1875–1962. (Photo courtesy of Gretchen Bacon Chaddock.)

Irving Ruben Bacon

1875–1962

*"Miss Jones was drawing teacher for all public school chil-
dren. Irving used to help her by drawing the lessons on the
blackboard, and there was a faint suspicion, which no one
dared to utter, that he was better than she."*
*—George W. Stark**

Irving Bacon lead a charmed life as Henry Ford's "court
painter." He did paintings of every aspect of Ford's life,
from frivolous childhood scenes to mature portraits. Ford
expressed satisfaction with Bacon's paintings; Clara Ford,
however, was not quite as generous with her praise.

Irving Ruben Bacon was born November 29, 1875, in Fitchburg,
Massachusetts. He came to Detroit with his family when he was five
years old. He was the son of Joseph and Caroline Bacon. His father is
listed in 1880 in the *Detroit City Directory* as a pattern maker working
at the Detroit Stove Works. The Joseph Bacon family is said to have first
taken up residence at the home of Rebecca Flaherty on Mt. Elliott
Street in Detroit. Flaherty was an older sister of Henry Ford's father,
William. Her son, John, later married Joseph Bacon's sister, Rhoda. In
1879, when Ford first left his home on the farm, he stayed at his aunt
Rebecca's boardinghouse in Detroit. So some of the Fords knew the
Bacon family at a very early date. Irving Bacon states in his reminiscences that he first became well acquainted with Henry Ford in 1898,
when he was given a ride in Henry's first automobile.

Bacon attended public grade schools in Detroit and excelled in art.
About 1888, he won several awards in a drawing contest conducted by
the *Detroit News*. In 1889, his parents moved to Montana, where Irving, then a teenager, reveled in horseback riding, cowpunching, and
the wild ways of the West. The family soon decided Irving had had
enough of the Western influence and moved back to Detroit.

Bacon finished high school in Detroit, meanwhile drawing some
cartoons for Detroit newspapers. Henry Ford is said to have enjoyed
Bacon's cartoons. In 1895, Bacon is listed in the *Detroit City Directory*

*From "Town
Talk—by Stark,"
Detroit News,
November 29, 1942.

as a draftsman at the Detroit Boat Works, boarding at 311 Sheridan Avenue. In 1903, he is listed in the same directory as an artist working for the Book-Keeper Publishing Company, Ltd., with his home address as 703 Stanley Street in Detroit. It is thought his parents moved to Cleveland that same year.

The West was still in Bacon's blood. He went out to North Dakota, to Fort Yates on the Standing Rock Reservation, where he completed a painting of Buffalo Bill and sold it to Buffalo Bill when the popular Wild West show appeared there. Bacon received $350 for the painting. Buffalo Bill later commissioned Bacon to paint him a Western scene titled "The Life I Love," now in the Buffalo Bill Historical Center in Cody, Wyoming. Bacon next went to New York, where he studied at the Chase School of Art and sold his work to various newspapers and magazines.

When Bacon was twenty-one, he married Elfleda Louise Wheeler, daughter of Mr. and Mrs. Charles Henry Wheeler, owners of the Banner Laundry Company of Detroit. After marriage, the couple lived on Avery Street at Calumet Avenue. Daughters Dorothy, Virginia, and Janice were born in Detroit. In 1907, Bacon sold some of his paintings to the Wheelers and left Detroit with a scholarship to study at the Royal Art Academy in Munich, where a fourth daughter, Gretchen, was born. His daughters say they greatly enjoyed their leisure days with their father in Germany. While in Munich, Bacon painted "Conquest of the Prairie," which now also hangs in the Buffalo Bill Historical Center. After Bacon had spent more than three years at the Royal Art Academy, he returned to Detroit.

Henry Ford suggested to Edsel, "Let's go down and buy one of Bacon's paintings for the house." Henry selected a farm stable scene with a horse standing and cows lying down. (Bacon thought Henry had picked one of the poorest of the lot.) Henry Ford truly believed Bacon had talent, and in later years took art lessons from Bacon.

About this time, the Bacons moved their now sizable family into a large home in Redford, on the outskirts of Detroit.

C. Harold Wills, with whom Bacon was acquainted, also thought Bacon's paintings were very attractive and provided Bacon, his wife, and two of the five children with funds of $625 every three months so they could return to the Royal Art Academy for another two years between 1913 and 1915. As repayment, upon Bacon's return, Wills selected twenty-seven canvases from Bacon's collection.

Bacon was forty years old in 1915 when he joined the Photographic Department of Ford Motor Company. Bacon had just returned from a Europe at war, and Henry Ford asked Bacon to draw some antiwar cartoons. These were published in the *Ford Times* beginning on October 15, 1915. Bacon became afraid that his high ideals concerning serious art might be completely squelched by Ford. Bacon, who could paint very lifelike portraits, became busy during World War I drawing Liberty Bond and Thrift Stamp posters. He also was asked to design an army tank, but his design did not please Ford because bullets would not be deflected properly from the surfaces.

Ford's Photographic Department included elaborate motion picture operations. Bacon traveled with others throughout the United States and elsewhere filming waterpower plants, Seminole Indians, the Big Cypress Swamp, sponge fishing, and Jamaican plantation scenes. Other documentaries depicted such operations as Ford's Detroit, Toledo and Ironton Railroad and Ford's coal-mining properties in Kentucky and West Virginia. These films were distributed to schools throughout the country. At that time, around 1920, Ford is said to have had the largest photographic facilities in the United States. Bacon stated that at that time he had recommended George Ebling to Henry Ford as his private photographer.

Other assignments included filming a trip in a Lincoln automobile on a tour over the Lincoln Highway to deliver a letter from the mayor of New York to the mayor of San Francisco. On another tour, Bacon accompanied the ten-millionth Model T across the country.

In 1925, Bacon's first article with illustrations appeared in the *Dearborn Independent,* its title "On the Road with Buffalo Bill."

It was Bacon who designed the greyhound radiator ornament for the Lincoln automobile and also the quail for the Model A Ford. The company sold 240,000 quail ornaments for a profit of $240,000.

On Bacon's fiftieth birthday, he suffered an attack of angina. Henry Ford Hospital doctors warned him that he could suffer another attack at any time. Within three months, he did have another attack and then spent a month in the hospital and a month at home. But on his first day back at work, he had still another attack, which kept him from work for nine months. He was admonished to watch his eating, his exercise, and especially his emotions. He was then restricted to sedentary occupations—no more lugging cameras. Ernest Liebold wanted Bacon to do all the *Dearborn Independent* illustrations, but Bacon refused because of the monotony of such a job.

Bacon's wife, Elfleda, died in 1931 while he was on vacation in the Maritime Provinces in Canada doing some painting. She had been an invalid for some twenty-five years. In 1933, Bacon married Bessie Huss of Grosse Pointe Woods.

Bacon now spent more of his time at Greenfield Village painting village scenes, stage scenery for the Museum Theater, and portraits of the Fords. He stated that Henry Ford was impatient when asked to pose, and Clara Ford was difficult to satisfy. His best portrait of Henry

Ford, he admitted, was painted from a photograph snapped by Ebling. Bacon also taught art to Edison Institute students, but "Professor Bacon" was unhappy with that assignment.

Six years after the October 29, 1929 "Light's Golden Jubilee" celebration was held at the Henry Ford Museum, Bacon was asked to provide a painting showing those present at the large banquet. This was no simple undertaking. No photographers had been allowed. So Bacon had only a list of some 500 guests and blueprints of the table layout. His method was to find individual photographic portraits of the majority of attendees and paint their likenesses on a large canvas. Bacon managed to paint 266 recognizable portraits on an eight-by-twenty-foot canvas. But this didn't solve the problem entirely. Clara Ford

Bacon family (circa 1920): Irving, second from left, Elfleda, far right.
Children: Joseph, Caroline, Dorothy, Carol, Virginia, Janice, Gretchen, Lewis.

Irving Ruben Bacon

Portrait of Henry Ford as painted by Bacon.

wanted women shown although they had not been in attendance. She also wanted her grandchildren in the painting. This project required a good portion of Bacon's time for the next eight years. The enormous scene was completed in 1945 and is now on display in the main concourse of the Henry Ford Museum.

Bacon belonged to the Detroit Yacht Club, was cofounder of the Adcraft Club, and was especially fond of swimming and playing bridge.

After Henry Ford's death in 1947, Irving Bacon did very little painting. He abandoned his art studio in Greenfield Village, leaving dozens of valuable paintings there and in the Henry Ford Museum.

Light's Golden Jubilee Banquet scene upon which Bacon worked for several years following the 1929 banquet. Photograph taken January 12, 1938.

With his second wife, Bacon moved first to Coral Gables, Florida, and later to El Cajon, California. It was in El Cajon that Bacon died on November 21, 1962, at age eighty-six. Funeral services were held in Detroit on November 26, with burial in Woodmere Cemetery.

Major References

Bacon, Irving R. *Reminiscences.* Accession 65, Henry Ford Museum & Greenfield Village Archives.

Chaddock, Gretchen Bacon, and Janice Bacon McDonald, daughters of Irving R. Bacon. Personal communication, 1991.

Detroit City Directory. Detroit: R. L. Polk, 1875–1910.

"Irving Bacon, Ford Artist, Dies; Memory Lives in Museum and Village." *Greenfield Villager,* Dearborn, December 1962.

Stark, George W. "Town Talk—by Stark." *Detroit News,* November 29, 1942.

Irving Ruben Bacon

Harry Herbert Bennett, 1892–1979.

Harry Herbert Bennett

1892–1979

"Bennett was merely following instructions."
—Charles E. Sorensen*

Harry Bennett has always been a controversial figure. Friends insist his reputation was the result of Henry Ford's demand that Bennett play the role of villain in the Ford-directed super-drama. Bennett had close associates who were gentlemen and close associates who were crooks.

Harry Herbert Bennett was born on Wall Street in Ann Arbor, Michigan, on January 17, 1892. His father, Verne C. Bennett, was of Irish-English extraction, and his occupation was sign painting. His mother, Imogene Bangs Bennett, was of Scotch-Irish ancestry, a native of Plainwell, Michigan, and a schoolteacher. Harry had a brother, Haze Bennett, four years older than himself. When Harry was two, his father died from injuries occurring in a brawl.

Within a few years of her husband's death, Imogene Bennett married Robert Winslow, a professor of engineering at the University of Michigan. Harry was a somewhat unruly child and did not get along too well with his parents, especially his stepfather. Harry sang with the St. Andrews Episcopal Church choir for a time. His parents later transferred to the Church of All Creeds, with a congregation made up of Protestants, Catholics, and Jews.

His stepfather died just a few years after his marriage to Harry's mother, and Harry was sent to live for a while with an uncle in Saginaw, Michigan. When he was fifteen, he and his mother moved to Detroit, where he felt quite restricted at home and decided to join the Navy in 1909, at age seventeen. The sailor's life was much to his liking—a life of activity, adventure, comradeship, and a chance to excel in his favorite sport of boxing.

It was quite by accident that Bennett left the Navy. He was in New York, planning to reenlist, when by chance he met Henry Ford. In civilian garb, Bennett and a buddy had got into a scuffle at the Customs House in Battery Park when Arthur Brisbane, the noted journalist,

*From Charles E. Sorensen, *My Forty Years with Ford,* (New York: W. W. Norton, 1956), p. 314.

29

happened by. Brisbane, witnessing the police grappling with Bennett, saw a possible story for himself and obtained permission from the police to interview Bennett. It happened that Brisbane was on his way to an appointment with Henry Ford at the Ford Sales Office; he took Bennett along, and Ford heard Bennett's story. Ford was impressed with Bennett's fearless spirit and told Bennett he could use his talents to help keep order in his new Rouge manufacturing complex. This was in 1916, when Bennett was twenty-four.

But young Bennett was not on the Ford payroll immediately. After returning to Detroit, he could not reach Henry Ford but found a job as an artist in the Ford Motion Picture Department through Ernest Liebold, Henry Ford's secretary. Bennett had inherited considerable artistic talent from both his father and his mother, as well as having had formal instruction in art. But he was not satisfied in the art department. Finally, after several months, Henry Ford called and made the offer Bennett had been waiting for.

His assignment was to be Ford's private "eyes and ears" at the new and bustling Rouge plant. Evidently, Bennett could not be fired by anyone but Henry Ford himself. Charles Sorensen was production manager at the Rouge, and the two got along remarkably well. Both were intensely loyal to Ford and ready to carry out, without question, any order Ford issued.

About this time, shortly after World War I, Bennett married Eileen McClellan of Ann Arbor, the first of his three wives. From this union, two daughters, Billie and Gertrude, were born. But Bennett's extreme loyalty to Henry Ford prevented him from having a normal family life. Eileen divorced him, and in 1928 he married Margaret MacKensie, an attractive college graduate. With Margaret, he planned a quiet family home on the Huron River near Ann Arbor. Henry Ford furnished the money, and Ford and Bennett together constructed a veritable fortress. The life-style was oppressive to Margaret, and after bearing one child, Harriet, Margaret divorced Bennett in 1933, taking Harriet with her. Within a few years, Bennett married Esther Beattie, a vivacious, fun-loving nurse who worked in the Rouge Administration Building. Apparently, Esther could cope with the obstreperous Bennett. She bore still another daughter, Esther Rae, and she long outlived Bennett.

Bennett seems not to have had a formal title or set salary, but he received pay from Liebold in what Bennett considered miserly amounts. Nevertheless, Bennett became Henry Ford's chief troubleshooter, taking charge of "Ford Service," said to have been the largest private police force in the world. Under Bennett's direction, Ford Service grew to a force of 3,000 men.

Bennett's success under Ford was a result not only of his quick responses to Ford's orders but also of Bennett's growing connections with Detroit's underworld. A cunning Henry Ford was convinced the safety of his grandchildren was dependent on having high-level friends in the underworld, and Bennett became his agent. These connections were fostered by lucrative food concessions at the Rouge plant given to such characters as Chester LaMare and Joe Tocco, notorious gang leaders, in trade for protection. Now and then, a Ford dealership was offered. This was during Prohibition, and the city was rife with crime. Ford was convinced that Bennett's connections were successful in preventing the kidnapping of members of his family—and perhaps himself.

Bennett soon managed the Rouge Employment Office, where in 1921 he eliminated the Sociological Department which had earlier been both criticized and applauded in its efforts to watch over employee home life. Now, with his authority to hire and fire, Bennett's prestige outside Ford Motor Company became enormous. The Rouge plant became especially known for its desire to hire ex-criminals and athletes. A letter from a judge or a college coach was very helpful in obtaining a job. Henry Ford was known to favor rehabilitation of convicts and was also particularly desirous of giving employment to black employees and handicapped men. During the 1920s, more than 10,000 blacks and several hundred handicapped people were employed.

Bennett's office was in the basement of the Rouge Administration Building. It had a private outside entrance, apparently to accommodate callers who might be considered crackpots. But Henry Ford, too, spent a great deal of time there, discussing problems and target shooting with .32-caliber pistols. Ford also had a target box in his private garage at Fair Lane. Both Ford and Bennett were dead shots.

Although Bennett was getting no specific salary, he was handsomely paid in gifts of property—quite likely possessions worth a million dollars or more. But Bennett states they were gifts with rubber bands attached. His chief residence, locally known as the Castle, was located at 5668 Geddes Road near Ann Arbor between the road and the Huron River. Its design, incorporating suggestions from Ford, included towers, secret passages, tunnels, and tiger cages—all for protection. During his career with Ford, Bennett was threatened many times, shot at several times, and hit at least once—so he himself said. Ford was apparently aware of the dangers to which Bennett was subjected, just as Bennett was concerned with Ford's vulnerability. Whether Bennett caused more trouble than he alleviated is not at all certain. Ford, however, thought highly of Bennett; he believed Bennett saved both the company and the Ford family from serious criminal consequences.

Another piece of property, 2,800 acres in Clare County, Michigan, was given to Bennett as a hideaway in the woods. An 8,400-square-foot, four-bedroom concrete "cabin" built in 1942 on Lost Lake provided Bennett and friends with utmost seclusion. This property later sold for $350,000. Still another property, on the Detroit River at Grosse Ile, was given to Bennett by Ford. Bennett later traded it for a 290-acre ranch at Desert Hot Springs, California. A lodge on Harsens Island on Lake St. Clair is estimated to have been worth $200,000.

The Bennett family—his third wife, Esther, and their children, Billie, Gertrude, and Esther Rae—were well guarded at the Castle. Billie and Gertrude, however, regularly attended Roosevelt School in Ypsilanti, a public teacher training school associated with Michigan State Normal College. Not far from the Castle, Bennett had built a home on a farm for his mother, Imogene. She died in that home in 1936.

The Bennett home is said to have taken on the character of a night club in entertaining Bennett's many friends and would-be friends. Bennett could do some entertaining himself by playing saxophone or clarinet. He had been a member of the American Federation of Musicians union for twenty-five years.

Only five feet, five inches tall, 150 pounds, always wearing a bow tie, Bennett was sometimes labeled "the little guy." He rode horseback and was a physical fitness adherent. He had three yachts at his disposal, furnished by Henry Ford for the purpose of entertaining Bennett's friends and consequently friends of Ford Motor Company. The S-Star (Esther), a seventy-five-foot steel cruiser, was used not only for Great Lakes outings but also occasionally for Caribbean vacations.

In the 1930s, when unions threatened the Ford organization, Henry Ford saw no reason for unions in his shops. Bennett was given responsibility for keeping the unions out. During the winter of 1932, when 5,000 of Detroit's unemployed demanded jobs by storming the gates of the Rouge plant, members of either Ford Service (under Bennett) or Dearborn Police, or both, fired shots into the crowd, killing four. (Accounts of who fired differ.) In the crowd was Bennett himself, trying to quell the melee. He was battered by stones and taken to Ford Hospital.

On May 26, 1937, the memorable "Battle of the Overpass" took place. This involved an attempt by the United Automobile Workers to distribute prolabor handbills to Ford employees leaving and entering the main gates of the Rouge plant. Labor leaders, standing on the road overpass with their leaflets, were beaten and mauled by Service Department employees. Labor literature is now commonly distributed at plant gates, placing the "Battle of the Overpass" prominently in the annals of labor history.

While Henry Ford insisted he would sell his factories before allowing a union, Edsel and Clara Ford wanted him to negotiate. On April 2, 1941, when a strike closed the Rouge steel mill, the entire Rouge plant

Henry Ford talking with Bennett during the early 1940s in Bennett's office,
Administration Building, Dearborn.

was closed down. No help came from the state capital or from Washington, and after persistent insistence by Edsel Ford, Henry Ford agreed
to settle by negotiation. Bennett was then appointed negotiator, and
during June 1941, a very liberal contract was signed with the United
Automobile Workers.

Being a Navy veteran with responsibility for perhaps 150,000 war
contract employees at Ford Motor Company, Bennett was awarded the
rank of lieutenant commander in the United States Naval Reserve during World War II. At Ford's Willow Run bomber plant, Bennett was
taught to fly by Charles Lindbergh.

The year Edsel Ford died, 1943, Henry Ford put Bennett on the
board of directors of Ford Motor Company. By 1944, Bennett was general supervisor of all personnel, labor relations, and public relations, as 33

well as aiding Henry Ford in formulating general company policy. At this same time, Henry Ford II had been elected executive vice president. The elder Henry Ford thought of Bennett almost as his own son and favored Bennett over his grandson as president of Ford Motor Company. But with the backing of Eleanor (Mrs. Edsel) Ford and Clara Ford, Henry II compelled his somewhat senile grandfather to resign the presidency. With the departure of the senior Henry Ford from the presidency, Bennett was left without support and resigned from Ford Motor Company in September 1945.

Bennett's comparatively bad reputation can be blamed on Henry Ford to a substantial extent. Ford gave the orders; Bennett took the blame when they were carried out. His role, he said, was to protect Ford from himself, from his own follies. Among Ford executives, Bennett limited his respect largely to Henry Ford and Sorensen, although he admitted Ford was at least eccentric if not a scalawag, and Sorensen had a brusque manner. Bennett's relationship with Edsel Ford was very strained, and with Liebold it was definitely belligerent.

After Bennett's retirement, the family moved to their winter home at Desert Hot Springs, California. In 1969, they relocated to a ranch near Las Vegas, Nevada. Bennett died January 4, 1979, in a nursing home in Los Gatos, California.

Major References

Bennett, Harry (as told to Paul Marcus). *We Never Called Him Henry*. New York: Fawcett Publications, 1951.

Lewis, David L. "Harry Bennett, Ford's Tough Guy, Breaks Thirty Years of Silence and Tells His Side of Story." *Detroit Free Press*, January 20, 1974.

———. "Harry Bennett's Mysterious, Legendary Castle," *Detroit Free Press*, June 18, 1972.

———. "Harry Bennett's Story of his Ford Years." *Detroit Free Press*, January 27, 1974.

Nevins, Allan, and Frank Ernest Hill. *Ford: Decline and Rebirth, 1933–1962*. New York: Charles Scribner's Sons, 1963.

———. *Ford: Expansion and Challenge, 1915–1932*. New York: Charles Scribner's Sons, 1957.

Fred Lee Black, 1891–1972. (Photo courtesy of Tara B. Gnau.)

Fred Lee Black

1891–1972

"People like Fred Black would call him Edsel, but of course that's Black, you know. He was a man who was an individual type and one with a very genial nature."
—*A. J. Lepine**

A highly intelligent extrovert, Fred Black could work well with anyone, but he could accomplish more working *with* Edsel Ford than working *for* Henry Ford. He was a showman, and with Edsel he raised Ford Motor Company's public image through subtle advertising to its most elegant plane.

Fred Lee Black was born in Battle Creek, Michigan, on January 26, 1891, son of John Black and Mary Yonte Black. His father operated a general store and did some preaching. Fred was the oldest of eleven children. When he was three, the family moved to Kenton, Ohio, where he attended grade school and high school. He could not read well but had a remarkable memory. For a while, he dropped out of high school to work in a silk mill, but he returned to finish high school in 1911.

Black entered Miami University in Oxford, Ohio, where he received a bachelor of arts degree in 1915. Immediately following college, in June 1915, he married Maude Thomas, a college acquaintance from Gunpowder Creek, Kentucky. The marriage took place in nearby Lexington. For a while, the couple lived in a student rooming house in Oxford.

Black's first job after marriage was with the Whitaker Paper Company of Cincinnati. He traveled as a salesman for a year before being transferred to Detroit as a salesman and advertising manager. The only child of Fred and Maude Black was Joyce Elizabeth, born in Detroit on April 17, 1916. In Detroit, the Blacks lived at 807 Maybury until 1918, when they were listed as living at 246 Hogarth.

While working for Whitaker, Black became well acquainted with Gaylord Pipp, who owned a printing plant on Grand River Avenue. Pipp's father was E. G. Pipp, editor of the *Detroit News* and a close friend of Henry Ford. Black helped Ford find a $5,000 printing press.

*From the oral reminiscences of A. J. Lepine, secretary to Edsel Ford.

37

This was a circa 1890 press at the Franklin Press, publisher of *American Boy.* Ford could use this press for printing the *Dearborn Independent.* Black's first contact with Ford was during the November 1918 Peace Parade, when Ford asked Black, "Say, let's go out and see where we are going to put this press." Black met Ford at the tractor plant in Dearborn, and they measured off some space. Ford's next pronouncement was "We've got to have somebody to run the business end of the thing. How would you like to come out and work on it?"

Black was anxious to accept the position, and he wired Whitaker in Cincinnati asking to be released. He became business manager of the *Dearborn Independent,* an old newspaper Ford had bought from Marcus Woodruff, who was finding in quite unprofitable as a local newspaper anyway. The *Independent* would be published under the auspices of the Dearborn Publishing Company owned by Henry Ford.

The initial *Independent* staff included E. G. Pipp as editor in chief, with William J. Cameron (also from the *News*) and Marcus Woodruff as writers. The *Independent* was inaugurated January 1919, and until June 1919, Black devoted full time to the Dearborn Publishing Company, which also printed the *Ford News* with Black as an editor.

On May 12, 1919, the *Chicago Tribune* sued Henry Ford for libel, and the trial was held in Mt. Clemens, Michigan. Black was asked to organize a news bureau to cover the trial and present "the straight story" to the press. This office was set up in Mt. Clemens, and the various press associations gladly accepted its releases. Pipp and Cameron were the principal writers. Ford's statement during the trial, "History is bunk," brought extreme ridicule from the *Tribune* people.

Ford was so annoyed by the reaction to his statement that he vowed to prove it. A book titled *The Escape and Suicide of John Wilkes Booth,* published in 1907 by Finis L. Bates, came to Ford's attention. Ford told Black to find Bates and investigate the validity of his book. The book stated that Booth had escaped and settled in Texas and had become a saloon keeper under the name of John St. Helen. Bates was found and invited to Dearborn to tell his story, whereupon Bates promised to furnish Booth's body for a price. But after several months of research, Black concluded he could not support the Bates story. Black described his Booth research in the March and April 1925 issues of the *Independent.*

In the fall of 1919, Ford and Black had the following conversation:

"Fred, what do you know about wireless?"

"I don't know anything, Mr. Ford, just the stories published in the newspapers."

"Well, I think it would be a damned good time to learn. You make me one of those wireless receiving outfits."

Black was ready to quit working for Ford. He knew essentially nothing about wireless. However, he found out he could take an evening class at Detroit's Cass Technical High School. With this training and the help of a young signal corps officer, he built a breadboard receiving set in his friend's bedroom. Next, a battery-operated transmitting set was built in Black's bedroom a few blocks away. The two could communicate with each other in Morse code.

Using the abandoned Ford waterworks pumphouse, with an aerial attached to the nearby water tower, commercial equipment was installed and a limited commercial license obtained. Station KDEN inaugurated transmission on March 22, 1920, between Dearborn and Cleveland.

With additional staff, Ford wireless telegraph developed into interplant radio telegraphy and, later, public broadcasting, with Ford forecasting a 400-station private system. Black had a good radio voice and did much of the announcing on the Ford Wednesday-night broadcasts. However, federal regulations favored commercial monopolies such as the National Broadcasting Corporation and Columbia Broadcasting System. Although Black was involved for a while in Ford's radio exploits, he soon became assigned to other projects.

When Henry Ford was being pushed to become a candidate for president of the United States, Black was asked to investigate the various Ford clubs that had sprung up throughout the United States. Using the name Fred Newman, Black interrogated leaders of these clubs to determine for Ford the kind of people they were and whether they were substantial individuals. Ford did not necessarily support the clubs, nor did he campaign for the presidency; he did, however, remark to Black, "I'd like to be down there [in Washington] about six weeks to throw monkey wrenches into the machinery."

When Ford was considering the development of a dam across the Mississippi River at St. Louis, Black was sent to investigate the St. Louis committee that had approached Ford. Black's report convinced Ford he should ignore their proposition because the committee was made up of speculators.

When the new Engineering Laboratory was built to replace the tractor plant in 1923, Black was asked to work with Albert Kahn to lay out the various departments. Black was well acquainted with the department heads, and with some help from Charles Sorensen's draftsmen, he was able to combine newspaper publishing, radio broadcasting, automotive engineering, old-fashioned dancing, and Henry Ford's rapidly growing antique collection all in the same building. By this time, the Blacks had moved to Dearborn and were living at 448 Nona Street (now 22608 Nona).

Circulation of the *Dearborn Independent* grew to 900,000, at an annual subscription price ranging from $1.00 to $1.50 for the fifty-two issues. Black helped Cameron with the writing of "Mr. Ford's Page" and often read the copy to Ford. Ford could read, but he preferred to have someone read to him; he would then interrupt the reader to make comments. When the *Independent* was discontinued at the end of 1927, Black became head of the Ford Motor Company Advertising Department. As advertising manager, Black, with an office close to Edsel Ford, found Edsel was interested in the subtleties of advertising, whereas Henry Ford was a born publicist. While the advertising department reported to Edsel, Henry Ford obtained free advertising with exciting headlines. Black had found Henry difficult to work with. He did not listen much; he made decisions without being fully informed. As did many others, Black preferred to work for Edsel, and they were the same age.

In advertising the new Model A in December 1927, Black spent $1 million in one week, mostly in newspapers and magazines. Advertising philosophy was: "Put Model A into the best garages and the best families. If you sell the classes, the masses will follow." Black's responsibilities also included the Lincoln automobile and the Ford Trimotor aircraft accounts, not to mention by-product Benzol fuel, ammonium sulfate fertilizer, and charcoal briquets. In 1929, Black was on the committee with Ernest Liebold and Frank Campsall to organize *"Light's Golden Jubilee,"* a tribute to Thomas A. Edison.

During the depression year of 1933, all Ford advertising was cancelled. Black was alone in his department. Considering the situation, he took a position with E. R. Squibb as assistant to the vice president in charge of advertising. But within a year, Edsel Ford asked Black to return to take charge of the Ford exhibit at the Chicago World's Fair, *"A Century of Progress."* When Black returned, Henry Ford commented, "It's all a mistake, your leaving here."

At Chicago, Black employed about 800 people. He went to universities for much of his help—the University of Chicago, Northwestern University, the University of Illinois, and Armour Institute. Students were used as guides, lecturers, and exhibit operators; there were no salesmen. Edsel Ford employed the Detroit Symphony Orchestra at the Chicago fair, and the Ford Rotunda was a featured attraction. Following the fair, Edsel Ford retained the symphony for his "Ford Sunday Evening Hour" radio broadcast, and Black worked with Kahn to move the Rotunda to Dearborn at a cost of $2.5 million. The Rotunda was placed directly across the road from the offices of Edsel Ford and Black, where it was dubbed "Black's Folly." But the building served remarkably well as a very attractive tourist destination and starting point for visitors to

Black in his office in the Engineering Building at Dearborn in 1934.

the famous Rouge plant, until 1962, when the Rotunda accidentally burned.

The year 1939 was an exceptional one for fairs. Black was in charge at both the New York World's Fair and the San Francisco Golden Gate Exposition. He made his headquarters in New York and assigned an assistant, Clarence Olmstead, to the West Coast event. At New York, Black had a total of 920 employees, including 320 college people. After the fair was under way, his work during his seven months at New York consisted primarily of entertaining dignitaries at lavish parties. Presenting a bill totaling $250,000 to Burt Craig, Ford Motor Company treasurer, drew the question, "Hey, Fritzie, does Mr. Ford know about this?" Black replied that Edsel knew about it. Black stated that during

41

At the opening of the Chicago World's Fair in May, 1934. From left: Black, Col. Bell of Fair management, Henry Ford, Edsel Ford, Benson Ford and Henry Ford II.

two summers in New York he served 49,000 free meals. Expenditures in New York were six times those in San Francisco.

In the early years of World War II, Black was in charge of Ford public relations. This was during the period when Harry Bennett was head of Ford personnel. With Henry Ford nearly eighty years old and bordering senility and Edsel Ford no longer in the picture, Bennett made a number of major personnel decisions designed to eliminate several of Henry Ford's closest associates. Bennett wanted full control of the company. Black was on Bennett's list to go. Along with Albert Wibel and H. C. Doss, Black was terminated in June 1943. Other key men such as Sorensen and Liebold were dismissed in 1944 because of Bennett's destructive influence. Black was quickly picked up by Nash Kelvinator (American Motors) as head of advertising.

In 1938, the Black family had moved into a new, stately home at 21551 Cherry Hill Road in Dearborn. But in 1949, the Blacks were divorced, leaving the house to Maude Black while Fred Black moved to 4331 Orchard Trail, Orchard Lake, Michigan. He then married Ruth Crane, a widow and the daughter of a Hawaiian missionary.

Black retired from American Motors in 1955 at the mandatory retirement age of sixty-five and joined the faculty of the University of Michigan as professor of business administration. During his tenure, Black was given charge of a student exchange program with Taiwan and spent two years in that country.

During much of his adult life, Black had done extensive traveling in the southwestern United States and Central America in researching pre-Columbian history. In later years, he spent considerable time at Sedona, Arizona. It was in Sedona that Black died on March 23, 1972. His ashes were scattered over the Grand Canyon. Joyce Elizabeth Black, daughter of Fred and Maude Black, had died December 31, 1966, in Detroit. Maude Thomas Black died on January 4, 1982, in Dearborn.

Major References

Black, Fred L. Reminiscences. Accession 65, Henry Ford Museum & Greenfield Village Archives.

Gnau, Tara, granddaughter of Fred L. Black. Personal communication, 1990.

Lewis, David L. *The Public Image of Henry Ford.* Detroit: Wayne State University Press, 1976.

Nevins, Allan, and Frank Ernest Hill. *Ford: Decline and Rebirth, 1933–1962.* New York: Charles Scribner's Sons, 1963.

———. *Ford: Expansion and Challenge, 1915–1932.* New York: Charles Scribner's Sons, 1957.

Robert Allen Boyer, 1909–1989. (Photo courtesy of Mrs. Robert Boyer.)

Robert Allen Boyer

1909–1989

"At the time Greenfield Village was being developed by Mr. Ford, he brought Bob Boyer out of the trade school and decided to set him up in an experimental laboratory in Greenfield Village."
—J. L. McCloud*

With a vigorous start via Henry Ford Trade School, followed by the Edison Institute— Ford's "School for Inventors"—Robert Boyer quickly became well known for his "plastic car" and his "soybean suits." After leaving Ford, and with much less publicity, Boyer contributed significantly to the production of the many soybean food products now on worldwide markets.

Robert Allen Boyer was born on September 30, 1909, in Toledo, Ohio. He was the son of Earl Boyer and Ruth Harris Boyer. His parents moved to Royal Oak, Michigan, in 1916, where Robert attended grade school while his father worked in the accounting department of Ford Motor Company in nearby Highland Park. When Robert was in the seventh grade, his father transferred from Ford Motor Company to the Henry Ford Hospital business department. Frank Campsall, Henry Ford's secretary, became acquainted with Earl Boyer at the hospital, and when Henry Ford bought the Wayside Inn in Massachusetts in 1923, it was Campsall who suggested that Earl Boyer would be an appropriate business manager for the inn. So the Boyers, including young Robert and his three sisters, moved into a Ford-owned house near the inn. For several weeks until their house was ready, Robert slept in the Longfellow room at the inn. He then attended high school at Framingham, Massachusetts, and graduated in 1927.

Young Robert enjoyed skating on the mill pond near the inn. So did Henry Ford on his winter visits there. It was at the pond that Ford, with skates in hand, asked Robert, "Mind if I skate?" They were soon playing hockey on the ice with two stones for goal posts. Robert was privileged also to meet Harvey Firestone, John Burroughs, and Thomas Edison at the inn while he was in high school. One day, Ford asked Robert what

*From the oral reminiscences of J. L. McCloud, chemical engineer at Ford Motor Company.

45

he was going to do after high school. He was a senior and planned to attend Dartmouth. Ford suggested that he come to Dearborn for some work experience before going to college. Soon Robert's father was saying, "It's all settled; you're going to Dearborn."

So, in September 1927, Boyer arrived in Dearborn, where Campsall arranged his enrollment in the Henry Ford Trade School at the Rouge plant. There he received classwork in mathematics and mechanics along with a job operating a boiler at the powerplant, receiving pay of twenty cents an hour. With his family still at Wayside, Boyer lived at the YMCA. He was now eighteen and had his own Model T roadster, but he was homesick.

Ford had taken recent trips to Europe and had been impressed with the agricultural prosperity in some of those countries. In Dearborn, he wanted to set up an experimental agricultural chemical factory to determine what products could be obtained from plants. The experimental chemical factory became a one-quarter-size model of Ford's mammoth wood distillation plant at Iron Mountain, Michigan. The model was constructed at Iron Mountain and moved to Greenfield Village in late 1928. About then, Ford asked Boyer, "Bob, how would you like to supervise this model plant, stay another year or two, and live at the Sarah Jordan boarding house in Greenfield Village?"

Boyer had had little formal training in chemistry, but he was provided with tutors from the University of Michigan, and from 1929 to 1933 he attended the Edison Institute of Technology, a school for inventors founded by Ford and Edison. For assistants, he was given twelve to fifteen permanent helpers, boys from the trade school. With their distillation apparatus, Ford wanted them to distill destructively all sorts of other plant materials as well as wood. A great variety of vegetables was tried, including turnips, tomatoes, lettuce, and carrots. At one point, Ford ordered several truckloads of carrots dumped outside the laboratory. When Boyer acted surprised at such a quantity, Ford replied, "I can't look at anything smaller than an elephant." These vegetables were mostly water, and very little valuable material was extracted. Ford's purpose was to find industrial uses for farm crops; a farm depression was imminent.

In 1931, Boyer married Elizabeth Szabo of Detroit. They had three children: Nancy, Robert Jr., and Thomas. Their residence was at 1036 Washington Street in Dearborn.

In 1931, soybeans became one of the plants investigated at the chemical laboratory. The seed, especially, was of much interest. Soybeans were relatively unknown in this country at that time. Usually the beans were pressed to obtain the oil, and the remaining "cake" was fed to animals. The Boyer group, however, developed a solvent extraction procedure whereby soy protein as well as oil could be produced. Ford

realized he could use the soy oil in automotive lacquers and made good
use of that product. He also found markets for the protein and the
remainder of the meal in plastics.

By this time, Ford was growing rather old, approaching seventy. Design of the V-8 Ford engine in 1931 seems to have been his final great
interest in automobile mechanics. His Edison Institute schools, Greenfield Village, and soybean research now occupied much of his time. In
1932, he began to plant hundreds of acres of soybeans on his Dearborn
farm lands and began procuring thousands more acres in southeastern
Michigan. Several additional processing plants were located in outlying
towns, where he promised to buy even more soybeans from local farmers to use in automotive paints and plastics. Boyer was largely responsible for Ford's advancement in soybean technology.

Ford's vegetarian eating habits led him to hire his old grade-school
friend, Dr. Edsel Ruddiman, an organic chemist, to devise tasty dishes
containing soybean ingredients for the dining room. And Ford's executives, including Boyer, were coaxed by Ford to try them—soybean
milk, soups, bread, croquets, simulated meats, butter, and ice cream.
Most were not very palatable, however, because of the tendency of the
soy oil to be slightly rancid.

In 1934, at the Chicago World's Fair, one of the most interesting of
Ford's displays was the "Industrialized American Barn," where Edison
Institute boys demonstrated to the public how soybeans could be pro-
cessed on a small scale into gearshift knobs and horn buttons. The
demonstration was carried on in a small wooden barn moved to Chicago from Ford's homestead in Dearborn. Boyer was in charge of the
demonstration, and Ford was very pleased that farmers could see how
easy it could be to become small-scale industrialists.

The First Joint Conference of Representatives of Agriculture, Industry and Science, a group of some 300 prominent chemists and industrialists, was invited by Ford to meet at his Dearborn Inn in May 1935.
Boyer was in charge of arrangements. This was the first of the famous
"Chemurgy" conferences. The second, in 1936, was also held in Dearborn and hosted by Ford. The purpose of these meetings was to help
farmers pull out of the depression by raising crops useful to industry.
Boyer led the groups of participants through his soybean laboratory at
Greenfield Village, explaining the procedures and describing the products produced and utilized by Ford Motor Company.

Another use for soybean protein, besides in foods, was as a substitute
for animal products such as leather, mohair, and wool, which were expensive as automobile upholstery material. Boyer's soy leather was
relatively stiff, lacking the flexibility required, but the soy protein,
when subjected to extrusion as a fiber, held better prospects. Soy protein threads were sent east, where the soy fiber was blended with wool

(35% soy, 65% wool) and woven into cloth. The cloth was given to Ford's own tailor, and suits of soy fiber were worn by Ford on occasions that were highly publicized. According to the news media, the future of soybean clothing was firmly established. Boyer and his children were also outfitted with soy clothing. Boyer admitted that the tensile strength of soy fiber was only 85% that of wool, however, behooving the wearer to avoid strenuous movements, bending down, for example, very cautiously.

Boyer's fiber was ideal for felt hats, however. All of the fiber Boyer could produce was wanted by the Hat Corporation of America. The soy fiber blended well with rabbit fur and was less expensive and much cleaner to work with. To produce fiber in larger amounts and to develop fiber of higher tensile strength, a modern air-conditioned laboratory was built on Village Road in Dearborn. In this plant, not only fiber producing equipment was installed but complete weaving equipment as well.

Ford had dreams of an automobile built from soybean plastic. He had Boyer fabricate plastic panels to substitute for steel. A rear deck panel, for example, was installed by Boyer on a 1939 Ford car. Ford, with great glee, was photographed vigorously striking the panel with an axe. The photo caption, however, did not mention that Ford was using the blunt end of the axe.

Perhaps the most exciting plastics news event was in 1941, when, at Ford's request, Boyer constructed a plastic car. Ford reveled in the publicity it provided. Although the car was sometimes dubbed the "soybean car," there was little, if any, soybean in it. Its body was constructed of conventional phenol formaldehyde plastic pressed into panels of appropriate shape to form a car body. Mounted on a conventional metal chassis, the car operated as expected. After many photographs were taken and great publicity achieved, Boyer drove the car for a few weeks before it was abandoned. People still wonder what became of it. A major defect never corrected, according to Boyer, was the strong odor reminiscent of a mortuary.

The soy protein fiber facility was operating nicely when, in 1943, the U.S. Air Force took over the air-conditioned building for precision measurement of aircraft engine parts. When his building was thus usurped, Boyer was out of a soybean job. He transferred to Ford's Willow Run bomber plant at Ypsilanti, where, because of his knowledge of plastics, he was given responsibility for protecting the plastic windshields on the B-24's during assembly of the planes. These methyl methacrylate panes were easily scratched when handled. The panes were so vulnerable to sand abrasion that when the B-24's operated in North Africa, windshields often had to be replaced after a single sortie.

Boyer was involved for a short time in Ford research contracts with

The Chemical Laboratory building at Greenfield Village at Dearborn in 1930.

the Air Force concerning the feasibility of plastic wings for planes, but he had other, more interesting ideas in mind pertaining to edible soy fibers. He took a much better-paying position with Drackett Products Company of Cincinnati, the concern that had purchased the Ford fiber processing equipment in 1943. The Boyers left their home at 700 Clairmont in Dearborn and moved to Cincinnati. Boyer was never again in direct contact with Henry Ford. When H. R. Drackett died in 1949, Boyer left the Drackett company so he could pursue his goal of receiving a pioneer patent for texturizing vegetable protein. He was granted this patent in 1949. As many as thirty corollary patents were subsequently obtained.

Boyer had developed methods for producing soy fiber that was thoroughly washed and tasteless. In 1951, he became a consultant to several food processors that were licensed to use his patents in their operations. These firms included Worthington Foods, Swift and Company, Ralston Purina, Unilever Company of England, National Biscuit Company, General Foods, and General Mills. Dozens of high-volume foods were, and still are, produced using Boyer's procedures. The feeding of undernourished populations worldwide is dependent largely on the use of vegetable proteins.

Boyer worked as a consultant to several food manufacturers that sold edible protein in bulk to markets worldwide. As a food extender, soy protein is now commonly used in baked goods, hot dogs, sausages and other products ranging from Touche in the dog's bowl to Bacos in salad. Boyer worked full-time for Ralston Purina in St. Louis from 1962 until 1971.

49

In February 1963, Elizabeth Szabo Boyer died, and in April 1965, Boyer married Nancy Ann Miller, a recent widow living in St. Louis. Boyer retired from general consulting work in 1971 after his patents had expired in 1966, but he continued consulting with Worthington Foods until 1977. In 1973, the Boyers retired to Dunedin, Florida.

The Boyers did considerable traveling. But in the early 1980s, Robert's eyes began to fail, and then his chief hobby became baking, an occupation he had always enjoyed. In 1985, he dictated his oral reminiscences as requested by the Henry Ford Archives. Boyer died in Dunedin on November 11, 1989. The body was cremated and the ashes scattered over the Gulf of Mexico.

Henry Ford discussing soybean work with Boyer in the Chemical Laboratory on Ford's birthday, July 30, 1937.

Boyer and Henry Ford with the "plastic car" at Dearborn in 1941.

Major References

Boyer, Nancy. Personal communication, 1991.

Boyer, Robert A., "Resumé of Robert A. Boyer" (unpublished). Vertical file, Henry Ford Museum & Greenfield Village Archives.

Boyer, Robert A., Reminiscences. Accession 65, Henry Ford Museum & Greenfield Village Archives.

———. Unpublished reminiscences in possession of the Boyer family.

"The Industrialized American Barn." Chicago World's Fair pamphlet. Ford Motor Company, Dearborn, 1933.

Lewis, David L. *The Public Image of Henry Ford.* Detroit: Wayne State University Press, 1976.

Nevins, Allan, and Frank Ernest Hill. *Ford: Expansion and Challenge, 1915–1932.* New York: Charles Scribner's Sons, 1957.

Proceedings: First Dearborn Conference, Joint Conference of Agriculture, Industry and Science, May 7–8, 1935. Printed and distributed by the Chemical Foundation, New York.

Smith, Robert. Reminiscences. Accession 65, Henry Ford Museum & Greenfield Village Archives.

Wik, Reynolds W. *Henry Ford and Grassroots America.* Ann Arbor: University of Michigan Press, 1972.

William John Cameron, 1878–1955.

William John Cameron

1878–1955

"Cameron, for instance, had a personality of his own, but he was one man that Henry Ford absolutely trusted. If it hadn't been for Cameron, Henry Ford would have gotten into some of the damnedest holes you can imagine, politically and nationally, and Cameron saved him time after time."
—H. M. Cordell*

As spokesman for Henry Ford, William Cameron translated Ford's thoughts into coherent statements suitable for press and radio releases to the public. His voice on the "Ford Sunday Evening Hour" was heard as gospel by millions during radio's heyday.

William John Cameron was born in Hamilton, Ontario, on December 29, 1878. He went to school in Hamilton, and when he was nine years old his family moved to the United States, to Detroit, where his Scotch father worked as a molder in a foundry. William had five sisters and three brothers. He attended Webster School in Detroit, working during vacations as delivery man for a grocery store, driving a wagon and taking orders. For college, he went back to Hamilton to the Collegiate and also took courses at the University of Toronto.

As a boy, William had listened to phonograph records of famous orators such as William Jennings Bryan and Robert Ingersoll. He greatly admired these men and felt he would like to be a great speaker himself. His first real position, however, was as timekeeper for the engineers and firemen at the Michigan Central Railroad yards in Jackson. Not far from Jackson was the little town of Brooklyn, where a relative invited him to speak at the local People's Church on Sunday mornings. He readily accepted this opportunity, giving many people the impression he was indeed a minister. It was in Brooklyn that he met Eleanor Maud Clough, whom he married in 1900.

Back in Detroit, Cameron did some "preaching," although he later insisted, "I was never a minister, never ordained." He also insisted he was "not a natural speaker, and while speaking is easy enough, the preparation is killing." Nonetheless, Cameron was in considerable demand as a speaker in the Detroit area at a relatively early age.

*From the oral reminiscences of H. M. Cordell, a secretary to Henry Ford.

53

In Detroit, Cameron began to write editorials for the *Detroit News*. By 1904, he had become a reporter and staff writer. He started at fifteen dollars per week, and when he left fifteen years later he was getting eighty-five dollars, a high salary for a newspaper writer. His early assignments were the usual reporting tasks—fires, accidents, murders, and so on. He later wrote a column, "Reflections," which was of a thoughtful nature. On May 17, 1909, Cameron wrote his famous editorial, "Don't Die on Third."

Cameron left the *Detroit News* shortly after his managing editor, E. G. Pipp, had taken a position in 1918 as editor of the new Ford-sponsored weekly newspaper, the *Dearborn Independent*. Pipp needed Cameron as a writer. Henry Ford was then embroiled in a lawsuit with Robert McCormick of the *Chicago Tribune*. A Ford news agency was set up at the site of the trial in Mt. Clemens, Michigan, and Cameron became the ghost writer who provided the Ford viewpoint. Thus, he became well acquainted with Henry Ford. When Pipp left the *Dearborn Independent* in 1920, Ford named Cameron editor.

Cameron and his family of six had moved into a Ford-built home on Nona Street in Dearborn. In 1922, Ford furnished the Camerons with a larger home at 262 Morley Avenue (now 22362 Morley), built of cypress from the plantations of Richmond Hill, Georgia. Three of the Cameron children—Donald, John, and Jean—attended Dearborn public schools. The oldest child, Marian, was married by that time.

As editor of the *Dearborn Independent,* Cameron had the duty, under general manager Ernest Liebold, to express Ford's beliefs. It was Cameron's task to interpret and present Ford's offhand remarks in much expanded form in a manner agreeable to Ford and likewise acceptable to the readers of the *Independent*. One particular page in the newspaper was reserved as "Mr. Ford's Page," which Cameron wrote, Liebold reviewed, and Ford may or may not have seen prior to publication.

The *Dearborn Independent* got into trouble because of anti-Semitic articles. When Ford was sued for libel in the *Aaron Sapiro* case, Cameron testified as Ford's chief witness, taking full responsibility and stating that Ford did not receive advance copies. There is considerable evidence, however, that Cameron himself did not foster the anti-Jewish articles. The case was settled out of court, with Ford issuing a public apology. Cameron remained editor until the *Independent* was discontinued shortly after the settlement of the *Sapiro* case. By this time, he was handling much of Ford's public relations, usurping some of Liebold's influence with the press. In 1926, Cameron wrote the well-known Ford-attributed article "Mass Production," published in the thirteenth edition of the *Encyclopedia Britannica.*

Cameron stated in his reminiscences, "I never had an official function with Ford Motor Company. After the *Independent* closed, I just went on doing what I had been doing. I never knew what I was." Cameron was regarded as a public relations man, but there was no public relations department. He just acted as interpreter for Ford.

With his weekly newspaper behind him, Ford was turning to radio as a major means of expression. As early as 1920, he was employing radio in intraplant communication, and between 1922 and 1926 he operated a broadcasting station from which he transmitted programs for public consumption. Thereafter, government regulations forced him to utilize large commercial networks. After Ford dealers had proved the benefits of national radio programs featuring such entertainers as Fred Waring and his Pennsylvanians and World Series baseball, at Edsel Ford's suggestion the Ford Motor Company decided in 1934 to sponsor the Detroit Symphony Orchestra and its guest artists as the "Ford Sunday Evening Hour." This program was broadcast for eight years over eighty-six stations of the CBS network. The audience of an estimated 10 million was unusually large for a symphonic orchestral program.

Cameron was Ford's personal representative on these programs. Here again, Cameron became prominent as interlocutor and spokesman for the principles of Henry Ford—without direct reference to Henry Ford or to Ford products. Cameron's evangelical voice, intoned with religious eloquence, became well known to a national audience. There was never an audible hint that Cameron was inclined toward chronic inebriation. Ford was well aware of Cameron's propensity for "the juice" but forgave one who could nonetheless perform so well. Cameron's own assessment: "When I was on the radio, it was like having a baby every week." Cameron's babies were born on the stage of the Masonic Temple in Detroit.

Cameron's talks, delivered as intermissions to the concerts, were followed as closely as were the renderings of the orchestra. His speeches emphasized straight thinking and common sense regarding problems of the day. Cameron had no group of advisers; he was on his own in choosing subjects and addressing them. Occasionally, he might meet with Ford for a moment to discuss a particular topic. And Cameron was delighted to find Mr. and Mrs. Ford frequently in their private box above and to his left during his inspirational declamations. Ford must have been pleased, because he had 45 million copies of Cameron's 285 speeches published and distributed in booklet form. An honorary doctor of law degree was conferred on Cameron by Washington-Jefferson College on June 20, 1935.

In March 1942, with World War II in progress, Ford cancelled the "Sunday Evening Hour." Other, less dignified programs followed without Cameron. But Cameron stayed on with Ford, continuing to write and speak for Ford. From 1943 to 1945, Cameron delivered biweekly

Henry Ford with Cameron in Cameron's office at Dearborn in 1933.

talks at Greenfield Village chapel services, continued to speak at college commencements, and spoke before organizations as diverse as the National Shade Tree Conference and the national meeting of the Foundrymen's Society of America. He also wrote speeches for Henry Ford II.

Harry Bennett was envious of Cameron's closeness to the Fords and attempted to persuade Ford to dismiss Cameron. Ford, however, was very tolerant of Cameron, perhaps partly because of Cameron's very beneficial testimony at the 1927 *Sapiro* trial. Cameron did not retire from Ford Motor Company until April 1946, at age sixty-seven after twenty-seven years as Ford's spokesman. This was two years after Bennett's abrupt departure.

In 1952, the Camerons moved from Dearborn to Oakland, California, where Cameron died at his home on August 4, 1955, at age seventy-six. Burial was in Northview Cemetery at Dearborn, Michigan.

Major References

56   Baggerman, Jean, daughter of William J. Cameron. Personal communication, 1989.

William John
Cameron

Cameron (right) with CBS announcer Truman Bradley at a Detroit "Ford Sunday Evening Hour" broadcast.

Bryan, Ford R. *Beyond the Model T: The Other Ventures of Henry Ford*. Detroit: Wayne State University Press, 1990.

Cameron, William J. Reminiscences. Accession 65, Henry Ford Museum & Greenfield Village Archives.

Lewis, David L. *The Public Image of Henry Ford*. Detroit: Wayne State University Press, 1976.

Nevins, Allan, and Frank Ernest Hill. *Ford: Expansion and Challenge, 1915–1932*. New York: Charles Scribner's Sons, 1957.

———. *Ford: Decline and Rebirth, 1933–1962*. New York: Charles Scribner's Sons, 1963.

"W. J. Cameron, Voice on the Sunday Evening 'Mike,'" *Ford Digest*, November 6, 1936.

Frank Charles Campsall, 1884–1946.

Frank Charles Campsall

1884–1946

*"Frank, I imagine, was the most faithful servant a man
ever had. He was at Mr. Ford's beck and call
night and day."*
—*Irving R. Bacon**

As private secretary to Mr. and Mrs. Henry Ford, Frank
Campsall ministered to their every wish. He took care
of their personal business, answered Henry's mail, arranged
travel plans, and accompanied the Fords on trips. He was
faithful to the extent that his wife is said to have felt somewhat neglected at times.

Frank Charles Campsall was born January 2, 1884, in Essex, Ontario. His father, William Campsall (earlier spelled Campsale), had im-
migrated from the village of Campsall near Yorkshire, England, in
the year Frank was born. Frank's mother was Susannah Thornton
Campsall.

In 1892, the family, with four children—Frank, Arthur, Frederick,
and Dorothy—moved to Detroit and settled in a predominantly French
section of the city. Frank became a citizen of the United States as a
minor child. His father operated a building contracting business in
Detroit.

Frank attended public schools in Detroit and, after graduating from
Central High School, did office and secretarial work for various business establishments. He married Florence Valliere of Detroit on
June 21, 1908. The Campsalls had three children: Madeline, Eleanore,
and Frank Jr.

In the *Detroit City Directory,* Campsall is listed in 1911 as living at
654 Porter Street. He was at 98 23rd Street in 1912 and 1913, and
designated "clerk" at Ford Motor Company. His home was at 729 Porter Street from 1914 to 1917, when the family moved to 1254 Taylor
Avenue, and Campsall is listed as "secretary." This Taylor Avenue address remained their home until 1925, when the Campsalls occupied
their Dearborn residence at 705 South Military Avenue.

*From the oral remi-
niscences of Irving R.
Bacon, artist em-
ployed by Henry Ford.

Campsall first worked in the Ford purchasing department at Highland Park. Because of his secretarial experience, he was transferred to Henry Ford's office. From 1922 until about 1938, Campsall spent considerable time supervising the purchase of property and the restoration of historic Wayside Inn in South Sudbury, Massachusetts, where he represented Henry and Clara Ford. When they were not on the scene, weekly reports of operations of the inn, adjoining farmlands, gristmill, and schools were sent to Campsall, who reported items of importance to the Fords. The Wayside Inn was the motivation for Ford's establishment of Greenfield Village in Dearborn. Wayside Inn was headquarters for a collection of antiques from the New England area during the late 1920s and early 1930s.

From 1925 until his death twenty-one years later, Campsall represented Ford in the purchase of plantations and the operation of the Ford Farms (70,000 acres) at Richmond Hill (Ways Station), Georgia. From Dearborn, Campsall arranged shipments of materials to and from Richmond Hill plantation and escorted the Fords on their winter sojourns there.

As Henry Ford's private secretary, Campsall not only had to be thoroughly familiar with Ford's varied activities, but he had to execute his every wish relating to them. Ford's control of such enterprises as Henry Ford Hospital, Dearborn Country Club, Greenfield Village Schools, Wayside Inn, and Richmond Hill plantation was exercised largely through Ernest Liebold and Campsall. Just answering the voluminous stacks of mail addressed to Ford involved several under-secretaries in addition to more than fifty types of form letters.

Campsall's office records are filled with details of travel plans for which he was responsible down to the last detail, all as favored by Henry and Clara. In 1928, Campsall made arrangements for a European trip for Mr. and Mrs. Ford and accompanied them on that trip. Their passports specified both business and pleasure, and their destinations were given as England, Scotland, Ireland, and France. This was the Fords' first trip to Europe since 1912, when, with Edsel, they had visited France, England, and Ireland. They had located their ancestral homes—his in Ireland, hers in England. The 1928 trip, limited to England, extended from March 31 until May 8. Passage was on the steamer *Majestic*. Campsall's expense account reveals he provided British currency almost daily to Clara Ford, and he bought for himself a set of golf clubs.

During the period when Liebold was losing authority, from 1933 to 1944, Campsall's responsibilities to the Fords were increasing. As secretaries, the two men's positions were considerably different, however, inasmuch as Liebold's duties were largely legal and financial, while the more gracious Campsall handled personal affairs. Campsall's office was very close to Henry Ford's in the Engineering Laboratory at Dearborn. Almost every morning, there was a discussion between the two in Campsall's office regarding the day's activities and future plans. Ford had a favorite chair in Campsall's comfortable location. Under the glass covering Campsall's desk and facing him was the old Indian prayer, "Great Spirit, help me not criticize my neighbor until I have walked a mile in his moccasins."

The Ford homestead, which Henry Ford owned and restored years before he moved it to Greenfield Village, required attention by Campsall. He also monitored the condition of the Ford cemetery, where Ford's parents and grandfather were buried. Although Ford never owned the cemetery, he instructed Campsall to see that it was well kept. When a derelict friend of Ford's known as Bismark was buried in a far corner of the cemetery at Ford's instigation, it was Campsall from whom the Ford relatives demanded removal of the body. The body was exhumed within twenty-four hours. Henry and Clara Ford are now buried in this same cemetery.

Someone had to arrange for the old-fashioned dances in which Henry and Clara Ford loved to participate. This was another of Campsall's duties. Selection and notification of guests were his tasks after consultation with the Fords. In most cases, an invitation was essentially a mandate; guests were usually people whose livelihood depended on the Fords. Although many disliked the dances, Charles Sorensen was one of the very few who refused to attend.

Ford's gifts of automobiles and tractors to individuals and to institutions were arranged by his personal secretary. Campsall was involved, for example, with the generous and prolonged assistance to the Berry Schools of Rome, Georgia, and rehabilitation camps for disabled war veterans. Ford's close friendship with George Washington Carver of the Tuskegee Institute was maintained over the years by Campsall's planning trips to and from Tuskegee and conducting Ford's correspondence with Carver. Ford very seldom wrote or signed a letter himself. Nor did he dictate the wording to be used. Campsall composed and signed the letters on Ford's private stationery.

The Ford Foundation was organized on January 15, 1935, and by 1942 it had assets of more than $30 million. Edsel Ford was president, and Campsall was a member of the board of directors and continued on the board until his death in 1946.

When Edsel Ford died on May 26, 1943, at age fifty, there was great anxiety about the future of Ford Motor Company. Edsel had been president for twenty-four years, and his son Henry II was only twenty-five years old and serving in the U.S. Navy. Because the company was im-

Campsall at work at his desk in Dearborn Engineering Laboratory, July 1941.

mersed in huge war contract commitments, the government in Washington threatened to take over Ford plants. Some in Washington wanted to put Sorensen in charge. Henry Ford, however, at age eighty, unhesitatingly became president of Ford Motor Company once again. With the return of Henry Ford to the presidency, the following statement was given to the newspapers on June 1, 1943:

As is well known, the Ford Motor Company has never created a General Managership, although in a way this position was filled by Mr. Edsel Ford up to the time of his death. The duties of this position will be taken over by Mr. Henry Ford in addition to his duties as President. However, the position of Assistant General Manager has been created and the appointment of Mr. Frank Campsall has been made to fill this position. Part of his duties will be to coordinate the Administration and Manufacturing Departments.

Campsall was named to the board of directors of Ford Motor Company on December 24, 1943, and also became a member of the board of trustees of the Ford Foundation.

Campsall's work was not at all easy. Particularly during the three years following Edsel Ford's death until his own in 1946, Campsall had to please the aged Henry Ford while others in the Ford family were fighting for the complete expulsion of Henry's friend and confidant Harry Bennett in order to clear the way for Henry Ford II. Although Campsall himself was not coveting power in this game for high stakes, he was certainly in the midst of the fray.

Henry Ford knew there needed to be a plan for future management of the company. Although Sorensen was on the board of directors, Ford in his dotage was very partial to Bennett. Henry Ford had not been well satisfied with Edsel's gentlemanly management methods. He preferred Bennett's tactics.

In June 1943, Henry Ford is supposed to have added a secret codicil to his will, appointing both Sorensen and Bennett as trustees to manage the company. Ford apparently thought Bennett could handle company affairs better than either Sorensen or Henry Ford II, who had very recently been made a vice president of the company. And because of Sorensen's rather harsh treatment of Edsel Ford over the years, both Clara Ford and Eleanor Ford, Edsel's wife, would be pleased to have Sorensen leave the company.

The situation became difficult for Campsall, who was committed to carry out the senior Ford's wishes and was apparently a party to the codicil. Ford, not only at Bennett's suggestion but with the concurrence of others in the Ford family, requested Campsall to ask Sorensen for his resignation. (Ford is not known to have fired people directly.) This was a particularly difficult assignment for Campsall, considering that Sorensen was so well respected in both Detroit and Washington. By phone on March 2, 1944, Sorensen, who was on vacation at his Florida home, was asked by Campsall to resign. He agreed without much argument.

At the crucial board of directors meeting on September 21, 1945, when the Ford family insisted that Henry Ford II displace his grandfather as president of the company, it was Campsall who prepared the letter of resignation at the request of Henry Ford II. And it was Campsall who handed the document to Henry Ford and obtained his signature.

Campsall was with the Fords in the winter of 1946 on their annual

Campsall (left) walking with Henry Ford, about 1943.

vacation at Richmond Hill, Georgia. On March 5, he felt ill and was taken to a Savannah hospital. He died of previously undiagnosed colon cancer on March 16. Henry Ford was with Campsall when he died. Campsall was buried in Holy Sepulchre Cemetery in Southfield, Michigan. His wife, Florence, lived until June 28, 1971.

Major References

Henry Ford Office—Miscellany, Frank Campsall files, 1922–1944. Accession 292, Henry Ford Museum & Greenfield Village Archives.

Lewis, David L. *The Public Image of Henry Ford*. Detroit: Wayne State University Press, 1976.

Liebold, Ernest G. Reminiscences. Henry Ford Museum & Greenfield Village Archives.

Nesbith, Madeline, daughter of Frank C. Campsall. Personal communication, 1990.

Nevins, Allan, and Frank Ernest Hill. *Ford: Decline and Rebirth, 1933–1962.* New York: Charles Scribner's Sons, 1963.

———. *Ford: Expansion and Challenge, 1915–1932.* New York: Charles Scribner's Sons, 1957.

Obituary. *Detroit News,* March 17, 1946.

Public Relations General File. Accession 536, Henry Ford Museum & Greenfield Village Archives.

Frank Charles Campsall

James Joseph Couzens, 1872–1936.

James Joseph Couzens

1872–1936

*"The paradox is that but for Couzens and his organization
and domination of sales and finance Ford Motor Company
would not have lasted long."*
—*Charles E. Sorensen**

T he role of James Couzens as an officer of Ford Motor
Company has been almost totally eclipsed by Couzens's
later role in city and national politics. Ford Motor Company's success in its very early years was publicized as Henry
Ford's achievement. The vital business functions necessary
for success during those crucial formative years must be
credited, however, to Couzens.

Born in Chatham, Ontario, James Joseph Couzens was son of James
Joseph Couzens, Sr., who had come from London, England, in 1870
and had married Emma Clift of Chatham in 1871. James Jr. was born
August 26, 1872, and grew up in Chatham, where his father had held a
rather miserable job in a soap factory. But the father soon became a
soap salesman, and James Jr., at a young age, often accompanied his
father in his business rounds, thus learning about simple and not so
simple business transactions. James's parents were strict and frugal
Presbyterians, his father very dignified in appearance and very demand-
ing in discipline. James grew up somewhat like his father, although he
had extremely resented his father's strict orders. Young James liked his
mother better; she was under the same strict discipline as he.

In 1891, James Sr. went into the soap-making business on his own,
organizing the Chatham Steam Soap Works. The family had by that
time enlarged, and now, with James the oldest, there were also two
brothers, Albert and Homer, and two sisters, Rosetta and Alice. At about
age twelve, James attempted a job as bookkeeper, but was not successful and returned to finish high school. He also completed courses at a
business college in Chatham before deciding to leave home for a larger
city—Detroit. He did not want to work under his father's dominance.

*Charles E. Sorensen,
*My Forty Years with
Ford* (New York: W. W.
Norton, 1956), p. 43.

67

In Detroit, he was hired as a car checker by the New York Central Railroad. He worked at this position for three years, from 1890 to 1893.

While working for the New York Central, at age twenty-six, Couzens married Margaret Manning on August 31, 1898. Their first child, a son, died an infant in 1899. A second child, Homer, was born in 1900, and another son, Frank, in 1902.

In the railroad freight office, young Couzens's exactitude was observed by one of the railroad's steady customers, Alexander Y. Malcolmson, who operated a large coal dealership in Detroit. Couzens was hired by Malcolmson as an assistant bookkeeper and general office employee at seventy-five dollars per month. He remained with Malcolmson for the next eight years.

During this same interval, Henry Ford was attempting to market an automobile. Ford had failed twice (the Detroit Automobile Company and the Henry Ford Company), primarily because of Ford's slowness in perfecting a machine that would meet his own goals as well as those of his sponsors. But in 1902, Ford was successful in races with cars he and his mechanical assistant, C. Harold Wills, had built to their own specifications. Ford was organizing a third venture in 1902. Malcolmson was interested in this.

Couzens also became interested in the success of the Ford-Malcolmson venture, because Malcolmson had insinuated that if the auto business should become a success, Couzens would manage Malcolmson's coal business. It soon became apparent that producing the Ford-Wills-designed car in quantity would require more money than Malcolmson could furnish. Ford was not to invest any money for the 50-percent interest he would obtain. So, rather than having the company be owned 50-50 by Malcolmson and Ford, other stockholders were solicited. One of the investors was Malcolmson's cousin, John Wendell Anderson, a lawyer who invested $5,000; another was Malcomson's uncle, John S. Gray, a banker who invested $10,500. Other major stockholders included the Dodge brothers, John and Horace, who accepted stock in payment for auto parts such as engines to be used in the vehicles. Couzens struggled to raise $2,500, based considerably on promissory notes accepted by Malcolmson. Couzens induced his sister, Rosetta, a teacher in Chatham, to invest $100.

The Ford Motor Company was founded on June 16, 1903, with Gray as president, Ford as vice president, Couzens as secretary, and Malcolmson as treasurer. Ford took charge of production, and Couzens ran the business affairs. The other stockholders did not participate in operations. Ford's salary was fixed at $3,600 per year, and Couzens was paid $2,400.

Ford and Couzens worked long hours, one in the shop and the other in the office, each with independent responsibilities. Ford had difficulty facing up to seasoned businessmen, so he would depend on Couzens as his ally and spokesman. It can be presumed that Ford, by himself, could not have managed a small grocery store, and Couzens could not have assembled a child's kiddie car. Yet together they built an organization that astounded the world. Couzens took charge of purchases, sales, personnel (including wages), advertising, and customer relations as the company grew and profits began to roll in.

By 1904, the Couzenses had a daughter, Madeline, and dividends from the Ford Motor Company allowed Couzens to pay off his notes to Malcolmson and invest $7,500 in a new house at 80 Chandler Avenue in Detroit. At that same address in 1910, their daughter, Margo, was born; quite soon after, their last child, Edith Valerie (Betty), arrived.

A serious business difficulty arose during the early years of the Ford Motor Company because of a patent held by George B. Seldon. This patent, controlled by the Association of Licensed Automobile Manufacturers, could have put the company out of business if it did not pay a royalty on each car it built. By 1904, Ford Motor Company had to either concede to the royalty or put up a fight to prove the patent void. While other stockholders favored paying the royalty, Couzens and Ford demanded they go to court. The costly trial lasted seven years, but during that time, Ford Motor Company sold cars at a greater rate than ever. The publicity was of much greater value than the cost of trial expenses. The case was won by Ford together with other independent manufacturers in 1911 with much fanfare.

Since Malcolmson had largely lost out to Couzens in managing the company, in 1905 Malcolmson organized a company of his own—the Aerocar Company—of which he was president. This gave Couzens and Ford an excuse to ease Malcolmson completely out of Ford Motor Company management because he was now a competitor. After buying Malcolmson's stock, Henry Ford had now accumulated more than 50 percent. In 1906, Gray died, and Ford became president of Ford Motor Company. Couzens was now made general manager. For practical purposes, Couzens was boss.

With the introduction of the Model T in 1908, troubles mounted. The early Model T's had their share of difficulties. The Model T was an Edsel introduced at just the right moment. The clamor for inexpensive automobiles far overrode the problems of initial defects. Couzens answered these complaints and initiated many management techniques required by the unusually high production volumes; among them were the financing of dealerships, the instigating of just-in-time delivery of parts, and efficient shipping methods. He was making use of his railroad experience.

Tremendous dividends allowed the Couzens family to move into an elegant home at 610 Longfellow, Detroit, and to purchase a large summer home and farm, "Wabeek," in the Bloomfield Hills suburban area. Couzens had induced his parents to occupy a new home he had purchased for them in Highland Park, near his own city home. His older son, Homer, died in an automobile accident near Wabeek in 1914. Frank, the younger son, grew up to be mayor of Detroit in 1933.

With wealth, Couzens seemed to adopt a liberal political ideology. Biographers say it was Couzens who proposed the eight-hour, five-dollar profit-sharing plan to Henry Ford. The idea was sold to Ford on the basis of improvement of worker initiative, much less labor turnover, and great positive publicity rather than pure philanthropy. Public credit for these generous worker benefits naturally went to Ford so that the company name would gain in reputation. Along with worker benefits, Couzens implemented the program of monitoring employee homes and instituting a "welfare work" program to provide jobs for needy people. These humanitarian programs put Ford Motor Company in the limelight, and sales continued to rise.

Both Couzens and Ford were now multimillionaires from Model T profits, and they began to look outside the company for other fields to conquer. Ford became especially interested in farming and the development of a tractor. Couzens began to take part in other businesses and in civic matters. He organized the Highland Park State Bank and became active in the Bank of Detroit and in Detroit's municipal affairs. As these men accumulated wealth, they became staunchly independent, each assuming himself omnipotent in nearly all situations. They began to find fault with each other, first in little matters, then more fundamentally.

As World War I developed, Couzens openly declared Ford to be a simpleton in thinking a "Peace Ship" to Europe could end the war. Ford accused Couzens of taking far too much time from his work for various activities outside the company. Other major differences annoyed them. The crucial break came on October 12, 1915, when Couzens resigned his job as general manager but remained on the board of directors.

Politics became Couzens's second career. A better term would be *social service,* because he was not the typical politician. He was fiercely independent in this thinking and actions. Although he was nominally a Republican, his socialistic views often frightened his conservative colleagues.

Couzens had already been active in Detroit banking circles and municipal affairs, somewhat to the annoyance of Ford. Both gentlemen, however, were susceptible to the notoriety of public office. In 1918,

Couzens (left) with Henry Ford, about 1910.

Ford ran for the U.S. Senate and Couzens ran for mayor of Detroit. Ford lost; Couzens won. As mayor, Couzens worked hard for municipal ownership of the privately owned city electric railways. Ford, perhaps out of jealousy, fought the plan by announcing electric streetcars were obsolete. He had a gasoline-driven streetcar he said was better. Ford, in 1919, wanting complete control of Ford Motor Company and its dividends, bought out his minority stockholders. Couzens received $29,308,857 from Ford. His sister Rosetta received $641,142.

When Ford's senatorial opponent, Truman S. Newberry, resigned from his post in 1922, Couzens was appointed senator from Michigan. Couzens, supposedly a conservative Republican, often fought feverishly on the side of the liberals. For example, he proposed an amendment to the Volstead Act to allow sale of beer and light wines. While Ford denounced the proposal as a sorry step backward, Couzens was denouncing Ford's filing his name as candidate for president of the United States, saying it was ridiculous. Neither was successful in his effort. Couzens remained in the Senate for fourteen years and became an enthusiastic supporter of Franklin D. Roosevelt for president in 1936, 71

Couzens (far left) with his son, Frank K. Couzens, and Henry and Edsel Ford in 1933.

whereas Ford had little use for Roosevelt. But despite their political differences, Ford and Couzens remained substantially friends. Each, no doubt, realized he owed his success to a considerable extent to the other.

Couzens announced his candidacy for reelection to the Senate in early June 1936. But instead of conducting a vigorous campaign, he spent the summer cruising the Great Lakes on a chartered yacht, *The Buccaneer*. Couzens was unenthusiastic. He favored Roosevelt over Landon as president but was running himself on the Republican ticket. Under political pressure, he admitted he was for Roosevelt, and the campaign was over.

Couzens's health was poor. He was suffering from jaundice, diabetes, and sacroiliac pain. In mid-October 1936, he was in Harper Hospital, but as chairman of the reception committee for Roosevelt's visit to Detroit, he left the hospital to participate in the day's activities. He became exhausted. Back in the hospital, he was diagnosed with uremic poisoning. Couzens died on October 22, 1936. With the city and state in mourning, Couzens was buried in Detroit's Woodlawn Cemetery.

James Joseph Couzens

Major References

Barnard, Harry. *Independent Man: The Life of Senator James Couzens.* New York: Charles Scribner's Sons, 1958.

"Couzens, James." *Who's Who in America.* Chicago: A. N. Marquis, 1928–1929.

Nevins, Allan. *Ford: The Times, the Man, the Company.* New York: Charles Scribner's Sons, 1954.

Nevins, Allan, and Frank Ernest Hill. *Ford: Expansion and Challenge, 1915–1932.* New York: Charles Scribner's Sons, 1957.

Burt John Craig, 1885–1954. (Photo courtesy of Phyllis Manuel.)

Burt John Craig

1885–1954

"There were certain individuals with whom Edsel Ford used the first name, but he'd never call Mr. Craig anything but 'Mister.'"
—A. J. Lepine*

As treasurer of Ford Motor Company, B. J. Craig signed checks amounting to millions of dollars. It was also his responsibility to see that there was cash on hand to fill the envelopes of the thousands of workers who went to the cashier windows for their crisp new bills and shiny coins each payday.

Burt John Craig was born in Detroit on August 7, 1885. He was the son of John G. Craig and Harriet Henry Craig. In the year of his birth, the Craigs lived at 96 Lewis Street, and his father was clerk at Gillett and Hall, merchants in grain, flour, and seeds. By 1888, John G. Craig had become manager of Star Elevator Company, and the family had moved to 312 Hancock Avenue West. But on June 20, 1890, John G. Craig died at the age of only twenty-eight. Burt, at age five, was sent to live with his grandmother, who also lived in Detroit. Burt had a sister, Frances, and later, when his mother remarried, he had a half-brother, Merrick Coate.

Craig was educated in Detroit public schools and at Montclair Academy in New Jersey. His first position following school was as bookkeeper with the Commercial Milling Company, wholesalers of flour, corn, meal, and feed. The business was located at Randolph and Atwater Streets in Detroit.

Craig joined Ford Motor Company in 1907 at the Piquette Plant as a bookkeeper under Frank L. Klingensmith, company treasurer, and W. C. White, assistant treasurer. On June 17, 1908, Craig married Everil Stone, a Canadian living in Detroit. The couple established residence at 297 Ferry Avenue East in Detroit. In 1910, they had their only child, Phyllis. By 1912, the family was living at 236 Philadelphia Avenue in Detroit. From bookkeeper, Craig progressed to accountant, and when

*From the oral reminiscences of A. J. Lepine, secretary to Edsel Ford.

75

Edsel Ford became treasurer of Ford Motor Company in 1918, Craig became assistant treasurer. This position was paramount to Craig's being treasurer because Edsel Ford had had no formal financial training.

From the time Edsel Ford was made president of Ford Motor Company in 1919, he depended on Craig for financial responsibility. Craig was involved in the Ford financial panic of 1921, when New York banks threatened to take over the company. A crucial $5-million check from Craig to the First National Bank of New York relieved the situation. With finances more normal in 1922, the Fords purchased the Lincoln Motor Car Company from the Lelands, appointing Edsel Ford second vice president and Craig assistant secretary and treasurer under the Lelands.

On May 12, 1925, Craig was appointed controller of Ford Motor Company, and in July of the same year, the Stout Metal Airplane Company of Dearborn was purchased with Edsel Ford as president, William B. Stout and William B. Mayo as vice presidents, and Craig as secretary and treasurer. During this period of prosperity, the Craigs moved to a more prestigious home at 2314 Boston Boulevard in Detroit.

Although Craig did not live in Dearborn, he was associated with two Dearborn corporations besides Ford Motor Company. These were the William Ford Tractor Sales Company, in which he was vice president, and the First Liquidating Corporation of Dearborn. Both firms were related to activities of Henry Ford's brother William D. Ford.

During the Great Depression of the 1930s, "B. J.", as he was called by his associates, almost became a banker. Edsel Ford was trying to keep Detroit banks solvent using Ford Motor Company funds. In December 1932, Craig was told to write a check for $3.5 million to help the Guardian Detroit group of banks. Henry Ford would offer more only with the proviso that Craig be made head of this entire Guardian group. Both Edsel and Henry Ford respected Craig's financial wisdom.

On February 14, 1933, when the governor of Michigan officially closed all the state's banks because of the financial crisis in Detroit, Craig's phone rang all day and all night at home. In financial circles, Craig was known to hold the purse strings of Henry Ford, and according to the newspapers, Ford was expected to bail out the banks. By this time, the Craigs were living at 19595 Canterbury in Detroit, a home they were to occupy for some twenty years.

Craig had been closely associated with Edsel Ford and Ernest Kanzler in forming Universal Credit Corporation in 1928. Craig was named secretary and treasurer. This was a lending institution providing loans to Ford dealers and their customers. In August 1933, with Edsel Ford and Clifford B. Longley, Craig became a cofounder and director of Manufacturers National Bank of Detroit, which with capitalization of $3 million absorbed five faltering banking institutions located in Highland Park and Dearborn. Craig is said earlier to have been offered the presidency of Ford's Highland Park State Bank, but he preferred to stay with Ford Motor Company.

Essentially, all Ford Motor Company funds were paid out by Craig's office under direction of Edsel Ford. These payments included a cash payroll amounting to several million dollars each week. In addition, Albert M. Wibel's purchasing activities required several more millions from Craig's accounts. Craig managed company funds in at least 125 American banks, and during March 1935, for example, he is said to have supervised the payment of $81 million in Ford funds, a record to that time. Diligently working to conserve Ford's resources, Craig was quite annoyed to find executives such as Harry Bennett, Raymond Dahlinger, and Charles Sorensen freely commandeering company property and manpower for personal use—much of this apparently with the approval of Henry Ford.

Whereas Henry Ford's concept of his business was a view of men and materials, Craig was viewing columns of figures on paper. Craig supplied Edsel Ford constantly with a detailed explanation of financial conditions; Henry Ford, on the other hand, wanted merely a simple, direct answer to a question such as "How much money do we have?" Craig often joined the Fords and other executives at the midday luncheon table in the Dearborn Engineering Laboratory. There were no latecomers at these luncheons. All were there at 12:55, with the exception of Henry Ford, who would arrive at 12:59.

In 1937, Craig worked with Edsel Ford, Kanzler, and Longley in organizing the Ford Foundation. Craig then served on the board of directors of that organization. Before long, the Ford Foundation became one of the largest foundations in the United States.

Shortly after Edsel Ford died, and when Henry Ford, Sr., again became president of Ford Motor Company, Craig was elected to the board of directors as vice president and treasurer of the company. This was on June 1, 1943. Other new directors were Eleanor Ford, Mead Bricker, Harry Bennett, and Raymond Rausch. Bennett and Rausch did not remain on the board after Henry Ford II became president in 1945. Henry Ford II trusted Craig, however, and "B. J." continued to serve the Ford family as well as Ford Motor Company. Under the new company management, announced September 27, 1945, Craig was named responsible for accounting, auditing, and finance.

Craig left Ford Motor Company in 1946 to become secretary-treasurer of the Ford Foundation. He retired from that position in 1951. About 1950, the Craigs had moved out of Detroit to 1379 Dor-

From left: John W. Thompson, Craig, Frank Campsall, Charles Sorensen, Henry Ford, Raymond Dahlinger, and Henry Ford II at dedication of the Edsel Ford Memorial Workshop in Greenfield Village, December 24, 1943.

stone Place in Birmingham. Craig retained his membership in the Detroit Club, the Detroit Athletic Club, and the Detroit Golf Club and was for a time a member of the Oakland Hills and Bloomfield Hills country clubs. His chief outside recreation was golf, and most of his playing was at the all-male Detroit Golf Club, where he played with a foursome that did not include Ford Motor Company executives. The family supported All Saints Episcopal Church. The Craigs also enjoyed a winter home on Sunset Island II at Miami Beach, Florida, where they were members of the Surf Club. Craig especially enjoyed relaxing in the Florida sun.

Craig's inside recreation was primarily reading and smoking a cigar or pipe. He was a conservative. He did not believe in installment purchasing and never himself owned mortgaged property. And he would sometimes teasingly recommend a child's portion from a restaurant menu for his teenaged grandchildren.

At age sixty-nine, on September 2, 1954, Craig died at Henry Ford Hospital of a lingering blood disease diagnosed as aplastic anemia. In the hospital, the day before he died, he arranged for his bank to cash his personal check to provide his wife with sufficient money for her impending expenses. At his bedside when he died were his wife, Everil, and his daughter, Phyllis Manuel. He was entombed in the Woodlawn Cemetery Mausoleum on Woodward Avenue in Detroit.

Major References

"Ass't. Treas. B. J. Craig—Guardian of Ford Strong Box." *Ford Digest,* November 1935. Accession 1107, Henry Ford Museum & Greenfield Village Archives.

"Craig, Burt J.," *Encyclopedia of American Corporations.* New York: Publications Institute for Research in Biography, Inc., 1944.

Crimmins, J. C. Reminiscences. Accession 65, Henry Ford Museum & Greenfield Village Archives.

Detroit City Directory. Detroit: R. L. Polk, 1885–1940.

Manuel, Phyllis, and Ann Reed, daughter and granddaughter of B. J. Craig. Personal communication, 1991.

Obituary. *Detroit News,* September 2, 1954.

Edward James Cutler, 1882–1961.

Edward James Cutler

1882–1961

"E. J. Cutler looked after the tearing down and moving of the buildings to the village. He saw that photographs were taken, exact measurement made, and generally looked after the reerection."
—*Ernest G. Liebold**

Henry Ford was a stickler for detail. He could spot a huge wall out of alignment by an inch or detect an unmatched shingle or an imperfectly puttied window at some distance. To satisfy Ford's exacting requirements in restoration architecture was no simple task for Edward J. Cutler.

Edward James Cutler was born in London, Ontario, on August 12, 1882, and attended public schools in London. About 1900, he left London to study art at the Cincinnati Art Academy, at that time an outstanding art school. He attended for two years before being offered a position as artist with the Hobbs Leaded Glass Company in London. His work was designing and painting figure windows. On August 14, 1907, he married Winifred Hyde of Cincinnati. While living in London, their first two children, Edward Malcolm and James Rusling Cutler, were born.

Cutler stayed with Hobbs about five years, until 1908, when he started a similar business of his own, designing and painting leaded glass church windows. He gave up this business in 1912 to go to Vancouver, British Columbia, to work for Begardus-Wiggins and Company. He worked there in the same line—leaded glass—until 1914, when World War I broke out and the glass business subsided. As Cutler phrased it, "There wasn't even a good wind to blow the church windows out. There weren't any repairs to be made." In Vancouver, the Cutlers added a daughter, Sarah Lillian, to their family. At Vancouver, Cutler suffered a very serious head injury when he fell three stories while checking a leaded glass window. The family moved back to Cincinnati to allow Cutler to recover. They occupied a cottage at Milford, Ohio, on a farm belonging to Winifred Cutler's parents. In December 1915, Cut-

*From the oral reminiscences of Ernest G. Liebold, general secretary to Henry Ford.

81

ler visited his brother, who lived in Detroit and who had one of those "high-paying" jobs at the Ford Motor Company Highland Park plant. Using his brother's connections, Cutler was given an interview. When he stated that he had been in the glass business, he was immediately put to work in the windshield department. Ford needed a man to trim the edges of windshield glass to make the glass fit the brass windshield frames. No one else there could handle the job, and Cutler handily demonstrated that he could.

Cutler's glass-cutting capabilities led to his being put in charge of window maintenance for the entire building. That meant overseeing a crew of men maintaining thousands of window panes, replacing hundreds in the fall of the year before cold weather. This was not at all the type of work Cutler wanted. However, he soon found an open position in the drafting department. But the glass department would not let him go until Cutler threatened to quit altogether. He was then transferred to drafting, and he worked on ambulance designs during the balance of World War I.

While he worked at the Ford Highland Park plant, Cutler and his wife, Winifred, and their young children Malcolm, Rusling, and Sarah lived at 938 Lantz Avenue, Detroit, one and a half miles north of the Ford factory. At this address, children Alfred Wylly and Winifred Cutler were born.

In 1922, Cutler's small drafting group was moved to Dearborn, where, in the old Tractor Building, he worked on Model T designs. Henry Ford spent considerable time in the Tractor Building, where he conducted private projects and collected antiques. Tractor operations had been moved to the Rouge in 1920. The organization at Dearborn was not rigid, and Cutler was recommended by his drafting boss to design a windmill for Henry Ford. The windmill was to be built on the Ford homestead property a few miles away. Cutler went with Ford on drives about the countryside, viewing windmills of the type similar to Ford's recollection of the one at his home during his youth.

Cutler had the rare ability to sketch quickly in detail any proposed design. In this manner—on a piece of paper, on a board, or in the sand—Ford was able to grasp Cutler's ideas. Cutler's artistic talent is credited to a large extent for his success in satisfying Ford in his major personal hobby for some twenty-four years.

The windmill Cutler designed for Ford was the first of many structures designed, built, moved, or restored for Ford under Cutler's supervision. Cutler became Ford's antique building architect. In Greenfield Village alone, there would be nearly one hundred such structures. Ford's twenty or more Village Industries in southeastern Michigan required restoration of many of the old waterpowered gristmills and as-

sociated buildings. At the 1702 Wayside Inn site at South Sudbury,
Massachusetts, in 1924, Cutler accompanied Henry Ford to sketch and
measure several buildings for restoration. Next, also in 1924, it was the
1836 Botsford Tavern on the outskirts of Detroit, where Henry Ford
had danced as a youth, that needed restoration.

Ford had bought an old gristmill and an adjoining house at Nankin
Mills, a few miles up the Rouge River from his home at Fair Lane. Cutler was asked to restore them. On their first inspection visit, they were
discouraged by the tenant from looking through the house, for some
of the rooms were filled with chickens. Nevertheless, the house was
restored along with the mill, and Ford suggested to Cutler that he
move his family into the house. Cutler was opposed to this because the
local country school was poor, and he preferred that his children obtain
their education in Detroit. Ford promised there would be very little
rent to be paid, so in the summer of 1924, the Cutlers moved from
Detroit to Nankin Mills, RFD 1, Plymouth, Michigan. Ford later improved the school.

By 1925, Ford was thinking about a historic village at Dearborn.
There were several possible sites on land already owned by Ford. Cutler
accompanied Ford to view some of these locations. The one chosen had
a knoll for a church, a small lake, and a railroad siding—a site ready
for easy development into an old-fashioned village. Ford had been collecting antiques since before 1920 and had stored them at the tractor
plant. The village location was to be near the old tractor plant. According to Cutler, Ford asked him to draw plans for a village. Of course,
Ford modified the plans at will. During the early building of Greenfield
Village, Ford probably spent more time overseeing Cutler than perhaps
anyone else in his employ.

Ford started buying structures for his village in 1927, when he
purchased the thoroughly dilapidated Clinton Inn and the Waterford
General Store. Ford already owned his family homestead, the Scotch
Settlement School where he had been a pupil, and Thomas Edison's
laboratory in Fort Myers, Florida. After Ford had decided to buy a
building, he would say to Cutler, "Measure it up and bring it in." Cutler
would alert his carpenter foreman, William R. Kanack, who immediately set to work with his experienced crew.

Before these buildings could be brought into the village, it was
Cutler's responsibility to measure them and make architectural drawings before they were taken down, then number all major parts—door
frames, window frames, timbers, and trusses—while they were taken
down. Only then could they be moved to Dearborn and reerected.
These buildings, often with associated shrubs, came from such varied
locations as Cape Cod, Massachusetts,; Springfield, Illinois; Savannah,   83

Cutler exploring old house in Macon, Michigan, before restoration begins in October 1944.

Georgia; Santa Rosa, California; and Fort Myers, Florida. The Sir John Bennett Jewelry Store from England, a five-story building, had to be scaled down to a height less than the village church steeple—a New England custom not to be broken.

Cutler designed a chapel and constructed it of bricks taken from Clara Ford's abandoned homestead. He also designed the Village Town Hall. These buildings were constructed around a central green. The largest of the village installations was the Edison Menlo Park compound, a group of six buildings from West Orange, New Jersey, used by

Cutler at his drawing board in Plymouth House of Greenfield Village.

Edison from 1876 to 1885. Remains of the six buildings, together with seven boxcar loads of underlying New Jersey clay, were moved to Greenfield Village in 1928. Considerable archaeology was involved in retrieving Edison's discarded laboratory ware.

In restoring buildings, it was necessary to work from old photographs and pieces of old wood and metal to reconstruct what was original. One of the most difficult problems, according to Cutler, was determining what had been added to the original structure and removing those items without damage to the original building. These additions could be a wing or lean-to, a dormer, porch, pantry, archway, or windows—so-called improvements in the minds of subsequent dwellers. For authenticity, Cutler moved graves to Dearborn with a residence from Maryland, but he admitted he could not move a well.

Aside from Greenfield Village work, there were assignments designing interiors for the Ford Trimotor planes, providing illustrations for Ford's *Dearborn Independent* newspaper, and remodeling Clara Ford's Harbor Beach house on Lake Huron. Cutler stated his work for Ford was very satisfying, with the exception of his few years at Highland

Martha-Mary Chapel in Greenfield Village—designed and built in 1929 by Cutler.

Park. Cutler thoroughly enjoyed his work and put in many volunteer hours of overtime. He continued to work privately for Ford and under Frank Campsall until after Ford's severe stroke in 1945. With little work asked of him in the village, Cutler transferred to the Rouge plant on January 14, 1946, as "architectural engineer." This transfer to the Ford Motor Company payroll allowed him to receive retirement benefits not available from Greenfield Village. However, he was not accustomed to the bureaucracy at the Rouge and retired about the time of Ford's death in 1947.

The Cutler family had moved from their Nankin Mills address to 8869 Ridge Road, Plymouth, in 1937. There, on a pleasantly wooded five acres, Cutler was able to pursue his hobby of painting. Many of his paintings were displayed in Plymouth's Mayflower Hotel. In 1951, Cutler provided the archives of Henry Ford Museum & Greenfield Village with his reminiscences, and in 1957 he presented a talk reviewing his work with Ford before the Plymouth DAR. Cutler passed away on March 8, 1961, at age seventy-eight. His wife died in 1965. They are buried in Riverside Cemetery at Plymouth.

Edward James Cutler

Major References

Cutler, Edward J. Reminiscences. Accession 65, Henry Ford Museum & Greenfield Village Archives.

Hamilton, Winifred Cutler, daughter of Edward J. Cutler. Personal communication, August 1989.

Upward, Geoffrey C. *A Home for Our Heritage*. Dearborn, Mich.: Museum Press, 1974.

Raymond C. Dahlinger, 1885–1969.

Raymond C. Dahlinger

1885–1969

"Between Dahlinger and that ex-pugilist Bennett and all those, Henry Ford had a regular system of reports that he got daily, and there was nothing he didn't know about."
—H. M. Cordell*

Evangeline Cote Dahlinger

1893–1979

"Mr. Ford admired Mrs. Dahlinger a great deal. Mrs. Ford did not."
—Harry Bennett**

The Dahlingers, husband and wife, were quite ordinary employees of Ford Motor Company until Henry Ford decided to employ them both as personal helpers. Their relationship with Henry and Clara Ford extended well beyond that of domestic servants to positions of exceptional influence.

Raymond C. Dahlinger was born in Detroit on July 3, 1885, son of Charles F. Dahlinger, an instrument maker, and Emma Dahlinger. They lived at 12 Chestnut Street, and Raymond attended Detroit grade and high schools. When he was sixteen, he left school to work as a stock boy in the Newcomb Endicott Department Store, one of the best in Detroit. He was eventually elevated to floorwalker but was still earning only thirteen dollars a week. He was interested in higher-paying automotive work, especially with Henry Ford, and his opportunity came when Ford stockholder Horace Rackham came into the store and young Dahlinger had a chance to discuss his wishes with him while

*From the oral reminiscences of H. M. Cordell, secretary to Henry Ford.
**From Harry Bennett, *We Never Called Him Henry* (New York: Fawcett Publications, 1951), p. 105.

89

Mrs. Rackham was busy shopping. As a result of their discussion, Dahlinger was given a job on April 7, 1907, on the Ford factory final assembly line. This job included driving cars from the end of the line and on short final test drives before shipment. Henry Ford often wanted to sample cars as they came from the line, so this is how Ford became acquainted with the twenty-two-year-old Dahlinger.

About 1912, Dahlinger was transferred to the experimental room, where new devices and materials were being tried on the Model T. He became an automotive tester and sometimes shared these test runs with Ford, becoming Ford's personal driver to some extent.

Ford developed considerable confidence in Dahlinger. They were well enough acquainted by 1915 for Ford to choose Dahlinger to accompany him on his peace mission to Europe. Dahlinger acted as personal bodyguard and custodian of large cash funds carried on the trip. After their unsuccessful European voyage, Dahlinger did not return to the factory but instead was retained by Ford as a driver and handyman at Fair Lane. He was soon put in charge of the farmlands adjoining the mansion.

In the meantime, at the factory, Ford had had his eye on Evangeline Cote, secretary to C. Harold Wills. Henry is said to have convinced Dahlinger he should try to marry Evangeline. Henry also may have encouraged Evangeline in the matter. Raymond Dahlinger was then, in 1916, boarding with his widowed mother, Emma, at 12 Chestnut Street, and Evangeline Cote was boarding at her parents' home at 181 Glendale in Highland Park. They were married February 10, 1917, and Ford immediately furnished them with a farm home in Dearborn Township close to his own Fair Lane. Raymond was thirty-two and Evangeline twenty-four.

Raymond Dahlinger's most important position under Ford was as general manager of Ford Farms, consisting of tens of thousands of acres in several counties of southeastern Michigan. Dearborn was the headquarters office. These farmlands included a hundred or more individual farms with homes and families living on them. In most cases, the farmers were supplied with seed, fertilizer, and implements and paid wages by Ford. The produce was marketed by Ford Farms. Overall directions for planting and harvesting were given by Ford to Dahlinger, who in turn passed these instructions to his several area managers. Millions of dollars were lost by these farm operations. They were a very costly hobby of Ford's.

In addition to farm responsibilities, Dahlinger, in 1924, took charge of construction of the Ford Airport and Automotive Proving Grounds in Dearborn. And in 1929, with his workmen, he provided the landscaping of Greenfield Village. When the Model A Ford was introduced in

1927, as a publicity stunt Dahlinger drove from coast to coast for a total of 8,328 miles, gathering inquisitive crowds at each stop. He was chief test driver for the Model A, but his terse reports of the car being either "damn good" or "no damn good" did not exactly pinpoint problems for the engineers.

Dahlinger seems to have spent an hour or so with Ford nearly every day, with Ford often giving instructions while riding somewhere with Dahlinger driving. Almost any kind of chore might have fallen to Dahlinger and his Ford Farms men. They kept the winding Rouge River clean through the Fair Lane estate and maintained Clara Ford's extensive flower gardens. It was Dahlinger who sent the truckloads of Michigan goodies to the Ford winter home in Georgia and had Clara Ford's favorite Rolling Rock beer trucked to Dearborn from Pennsylvania. The luxurious tree house on the Fair Lane grounds was Dahlinger's project, as was the hasty removal of the body of a derelict mistakenly buried in the Ford cemetery.

Dahlinger felt he was in competition with Harry Bennett for the top spot under Ford. Both Bennett and Dahlinger threw lavish parties to gain backing from other Ford executives. When Bennett was ousted by Henry Ford II in 1945, Dahlinger became especially close to Ford, but with the death of "the boss" in 1947, Dahlinger's only remaining tie was with Clara Ford. When she died in 1950, Dahlinger was quickly retired—he knew he was, because he could not gain entrance to his office. Dahlinger died at Dearborn in 1969, age eighty-three.

Evangeline Cote was born in Detroit on October 17, 1893, the daughter of French-Canadian parents, Albert Joseph Cote, an instructor in shorthand at Detroit Business University, and Agatha Reheaume Cote. Evangeline's father became ill when she was sixteen, and being the oldest of four children, she took a position in 1909 as a stenographer at Ford Motor Company in order to support the family. By 1911, she had been appointed head of the stenographic pool, and she became secretary to C. Harold Wills.

Henry Ford was impressed with Evangeline Cote's vivacious personality. He suggested to his friend Raymond Dahlinger that he try to marry her, and he also seemed anxious to recommend Dahlinger to her. This ploy may well have been to attract her away from Wills, who was not yet married and considered somewhat of a playboy. Ford was successful in matching Evangeline Cote with Raymond Dahlinger. Both Ford and Dahlinger were especially attentive to her before the marriage in February 1917.

Ford presented the couple with a well-equipped farmhouse in Dear- 91 born Township, and both were given positions on Ford's private salary roll. Evangeline's position never had a title, nor could it have had an exact one. Ford spent considerable time in the kitchen of the farmhouse discussing both personal and business affairs with the Dahlingers.

Evangeline Dahlinger had only one child, John Cote Dahlinger, born in 1923. He was presumed to be Raymond Dahlinger's child, but there are some who believe he was Ford's. In his autobiography, John Cote Dahlinger insists he is Ford's son. In any case, the Dahlingers, including the son, lived like royalty at Ford's expense. Two of Evangeline's brothers were given Ford dealerships, and one brother of Ray's also was provided with a dealership.

About 1927, Evangeline Dahlinger acquired land and built a sum-

Henry Ford with Dahlinger at Willow Run plant in 1941.

A demure Evangeline Cote Dahlinger (1893–1979) in old-fashioned costume, circa 1920.

mer house on Lake Huron near a Ford home. It was complete with main house, guest house, carriage house, beach house, bath house, and seaplane docking ramp. Sometime later, Ford presented the Dahlingers with a 300-acre farm near Romeo, Michigan. On it was an old farmhouse, a new house, a lake, several barns, and 300 head of cattle.

Starting in 1930, a Tudor mansion was built on 130 acres of land approximately a mile up the Rouge River from Fair Lane. This became known as the Dahlinger estate, with a gatehouse, a main house with nine fireplaces and eight bathrooms, and an attached four-car garage. Other buildings included a Kentucky show barn, a stall barn with corral, a blacksmith shop, and a six-car repair garage. According to Ford's architect, Edward J. Cutler, Ford specified the show barn to be equipped with living quarters for Raymond Dahlinger. Next to the show barn was a half-mile race track, a small lake, and a skating house. A very respectable middle-sized guest house was dubbed the carpenter's shanty. Ford is said to have paid for the many servants at the Dahlinger estate.

Evangeline on horseback.

Evangeline Dahlinger no doubt impressed Ford. She might have been described as the antithesis of his wife, Clara. She was slim, petite, and athletic, some thirty years younger than Ford, who also prided himself on being slim and athletic. Evangeline Dahlinger became the first woman in Michigan to receive a pilot's license. Ford then presented her with her personal seaplane but never flew with her. The seaplane was a Curtiss Flying Boat equipped with a Hispano-Suiza engine. The Dahlinger estate could not accommodate a seaplane, so it was docked at Grosse Ile on the Detroit River.

Evangeline Dahlinger was an accomplished equestrian, so Ford presented horses to the Dahlingers, although he himself didn't like horses, let alone ride them. She became the tristate women's harness champion. It should be mentioned that her husband was also a pilot and horseman, but she was the kind who had to win. The Dahlinger boat

94

was the *Evangeline,* a thirty-six-foot Hacker speedboat powered by a twelve-cylinder Liberty engine—the type of engine built by the Ford Motor Company for aircraft use during World War I. Her speedboat was usually docked at the Rouge plant. She was also a good shot with a handgun or rifle, as were her husband, Ford, and Harry Bennett. There was a target range for each at their homes or offices. Each, at times, carried a gun for protection; hers was a small revolver in her purse.

The Dahlinger's duties were equally varied but quite different. They seldom worked together. She was, however, at least for a while, treasurer of Ford Farms. She helped Clara Ford with shopping and helped entertain notables visiting the Fords, acting somewhat as a personal secretary to Clara Ford. In 1943, she was asked by Ford to christen the destroyer escort U.S.S. *Dearborn* as his representative at Superior, Wisconsin. For Clara Ford, in 1935, she took charge of home building plans at the Ford winter homesite at Ways Station, Georgia.

Evangeline Dahlinger's chief interests were Greenfield Village, its buildings, and its schools. She taught social etiquette to the students and supervised courses in horsemanship. To an extent, the buildings moved to the village were selected by her, and the furnishings in the buildings were largely of her choosing.

In 1945, Evangeline Dahlinger was presented with her thirty-five-year watch. She retired from the payroll as soon as Ford died in April 1947. The night Ford died, Clara Ford summoned Evangeline Dahlinger to his bedside. She continued to help Clara Ford without pay until Mrs. Ford's death in 1950. Evangeline Cote Dahlinger outlived her husband, Raymond, by ten years. She died in a Port Huron nursing home on November 3, 1979, at age eighty-six.

Major References

Bryan, Ford R. *Beyond the Model T: The Other Ventures of Henry Ford.* Detroit: Wayne State University Press, 1990.

Dahlinger, John C. *The Secret Life of Henry Ford.* Indianapolis and New York: Bobbs-Merrill, 1978.

Lewis, David L. "The Ten Most Important People in Henry Ford's Life." *Car Collector,* June 1978.

Nevins, Allan, and Frank Ernest Hill. *Ford: Decline and Rebirth, 1933–1962.* New York: Charles Scribner's Sons, 1963.

———. *Ford: Expansion and Challenge, 1915–1932.* New York: Charles Scribner's Sons, 1957.

Obituary. *Detroit News,* November 5, 1979.

Thomson, John W. "Biography of R. C. Dahlinger." Vertical file, Henry Ford Museum & Greenfield Village Archives.

George Ebling, 1886–1955. (Photo courtesy of George Ebling, Jr.)

George Ebling

1886–1955

"George is the best photographer in the United States."
*—Henry Ford.**

As early as 1896, Henry Ford had his own camera and was taking photographs of reasonable quality. Over the years, Ford's photographers produced hundreds of motion pictures and accumulated some half-million still photo images now on file in the archives of Henry Ford Museum & Greenfield Village. A small but very select number of these were taken by George Ebling, Ford's private photographer.

George Ebling was born March 18, 1886, in Detroit. His father, Peter Ebling, was a painter and paper hanger. His mother was Margaretha Burger Ebling, who died very soon after the birth of George, whereupon he was sent to live with his grandmother. His life with his grandmother was troublesome. They were very poor, and George, with his boyhood friends, was inclined to be mischievous. He had finished only four grades of public school before leaving to help earn a living. He had peddled newspapers since age seven and worked at a variety of odd jobs including some primitive flash photography and a printing process accomplished by exposing the paper through a negative to sunlight on a rooftop. He then decided to visit his aunt in California. His passage was via freight trains as a bum, he said. He sometimes stopped to work a day or two as a hired hand on a farm in order to get a good meal. His aunt's husband was a motion picture director, and in California he became even more intensely interested in photography.

When Ebling returned to Detroit, he boarded at 347 Charlevoix and went into partnership with the firm of Litynski-Jakubowski and Company, which specialized in photography of corpses at funerals held in private homes—pictures of "stiffs," he complained, not at all like Hollywood. The partnership with Litynski-Jakubowski lasted about two years. The men had such differences that the more sensitive Ebling suffered a nervous breakdown in 1914 and was unemployed for a time.

*From the oral reminiscences of George Ebling, recalling a statement of Henry Ford to a bystander.

97

Another more permanent partnership during this period was Ebling's marriage to Alice Clemett on August 15, 1911. She had been born in Cornwall, England. The marriage took place in Old Christ Church on East Jefferson Avenue in Detroit. The Eblings lived at 932 Canton Avenue in Detroit. Ebling is listed as an insurance salesman in Detroit's 1915–1916 directory.

Ebling obtained work at the Highland Park plant of Ford Motor Company in 1917. He was first hired as a foreman on production work in the factory, but by 1918 he had been able to transfer to the Photographic Department, where Ford was producing motion pictures, still photographs, and artwork for advertising and educational purposes. Henry Ford was convinced of the great value of movies for instructional purposes, and he employed photographers to record factory operations, farming, lumbering, mining, ship building—nearly everything related to Ford Motor Company activities. These films were available to schools for educational use. Hundreds of these Ford films are now in the files of the National Archives in Washington.

After Ford had built his new home and his tractor plant in Dearborn, his interests shifted away from Highland Park. It was then that he chose Ebling as his personal photographer. The two men had pronounced similarities. They were of similar disposition and appearance, and neither had had extensive formal education. Ford preferred to be around such people—the self-made type. He furnished elaborate equipment, including large eight-by-ten view cameras, tripods, lenses, filters, and illuminating devices. This was before the days of automatic exposure control, automatic focusing, and self-loading roll film. The only camera Ebling was known to have himself was a small Speed Graphic given to him by Eastman Kodak Company. Ebling was a meticulous operator, so the expensive instruments were used with care and deliberation. Ebling did not waste film. Ford would not have tolerated such waste.

From 1919 to 1921, Ford had built houses for his employees in Dearborn, and Ebling was offered one of them. Alice Ebling, however, did not want to move out of Detroit and into the small village of Dearborn. But when the new Engineering Laboratory with Ford's office was built in Dearborn and Ebling's headquarters were transferred there, the family was convinced. In 1922, they purchased a house at 175 Adeline Street (now 22501 Edison) for about $9,000. Although it was a relatively high price for a frame home, it was unusually well built of prime lumber from Ford's Upper Michigan mills. The family now included Donald, born May 13, 1917; George, born September 6, 1918; and Clyde, born February 23, 1920. Two other boys had died in infancy

Ford Motor Company Photographic Department in 1920. Ebling is third from left in front row. (Photo courtesy of George Ebling, Jr.)

earlier. The house on Edison Street remained the Eblings' home for many years and is now occupied by a grandson of George Ebling.

At work, Ebling's photographic subjects included Henry and Clara Ford, their grandchildren, celebrities visiting the Fords or Greenfield Village, and any other subject, animate or inanimate, appealing to Ford. Although Ebling had assistants, it was he who answered to Ford's wishes. Clara Ford's occasional requests were quite a problem for Ebling. She expected very flattering photographs, but she was not particularly photogenic herself, and her roses, with which she most often

99

posed, were not always in the best of bloom. Despite his labors, Ebling was seldom praised for his work by Clara Ford.

At times, Ebling was called to the Grosse Pointe home of Edsel Ford to show movies to the children, Henry II, Benson, Josephine and William. These same children were photographed time and time again at Fair Lane when visiting their grandparents. Not many years later, Ebling was photographing the children of Henry Ford II. The Henry Ford Hospital Christmas parties as well as the Fair Lane Christmas parties for children were photographed by Ebling. Often, Henry Ford and

Standing with his hand on movie camera is Ebling. With him are two of his assistants, circa 1935. (Photo courtesy of George Ebling, Jr.)

An Ebling photograph of Clara Ford arranging flowers at Fair Lane in May 1939.

Edward Cutler would accompany Ebling to places some distance from Dearborn to photograph buildings that were being brought to Greenfield Village for restoration.

One of Ebling's most interesting assignments was as photographer on the famous Ford-Edison-Firestone-Burroughs camping trips. These annual motor expeditions through northern Michigan and the eastern United States revealed the four men in the best of spirits. These caravans, led by passenger cars and followed by trucks carrying all sorts of amenities, tried to travel incognito. And to quite an extent, they succeeded until they were joined in 1921 by most of the wives and President Warren G. Harding.

Other exciting assignments were with the 1934 Chicago Century of

Progress Exposition and the 1939 New York World's Fair. For the Chicago exhibit, the large photomurals circling the spectacular Ford Rotunda were enlargements of Ebling's photographs. Ebling was chief Ford photographer for these events.

But working directly for Ford was stressful, and Ebling was a sensitive individual. There were many times when he knew his job was at stake and the slightest misdeed could mean his dismissal. For example, when Ford invited him to send his boys to the Greenfield Village schools, Ebling did not comply because his boys much preferred to stay for their final years in the Dearborn public high school. This negative response to Ford's offer could have meant serious trouble for Ebling.

Ebling was fifty-eight in 1944 when he had his first heart attack. After recovering, he went back to work, only to have more heart trouble. In 1946, Ebling retired with a pension of thirty dollars a month. Because of his medical expenses, Ford offered him financial help, but the Eblings could make it on their own and preferred it that way. Ford would stop in on occasion to see the Eblings while George was ill.

Following George's retirement, the Eblings led a quiet life in Dearborn. Ebling died on December 5, 1955, at age sixty-nine. His wife, Alice, died on August 22, 1981, following a lengthy period of care in a nursing home after a stroke. Both are buried in Cadillac Memorial West Cemetery.

Major References

Detroit City Directories (1902–1922) and *Dearborn City Directories* (1926–1946). Detroit: R. L. Polk.

Ebling, George , Jr., son of George Ebling. Personal communication, 1990.

"Portrayal by Photography." *Ford News,* June 1934.

Read-Miller, Cynthia, curator of Graphics, Archives, and Library, Henry Ford Museum & Greenfield Village. Personal communication, 1991.

Eugene Jeno Farkas, 1881–1963.

Eugene Jeno Farkas

1881–1963

*"You know, Gene and I are going to run this place. I wish
Gene had more boldness. He's too nice a guy to work
around here."*
—Henry Ford*

Many of the unique chassis features of the Model T automobile, the Fordson tractor, and the Model A Ford can be attributed to Eugene Farkas. Henry Ford and Farkas were engineering partners not only on those well-known vehicles but also on the mysterious X Car, which after six years of experimentation was not yet ready for mass production.

Eugene Jeno Farkas was born in Kald, Hungary, on October 26, 1881. There were ten children in the family of Karoly and Anna Farkas, and Eugene was second eldest. When he was five years old, his family moved to Janoshama and then to the larger town of Sarvas, where the father became quite successful as a wagon builder.

When Eugene had finished his compulsory six years of schooling, he was sent for four years to military school. He moved to Budapest and graduated from gymnasium, somewhat equivalent to American high school. He then attended the Royal Joseph Technical University, an engineering college, where he received the degree of certified mechanical engineer in 1904. The expense of this elaborate program of training was aided by a wealthy uncle on his mother's side of the family.

Farkas spent one year in the army. Following the army training, he took work in a motorcycle factory without pay in order to obtain experience. Work was not at all plentiful in Hungary at that time, and Farkas, with a friend, set out for the United States in the fall of 1906. Knowing, as he said, "an estimated seventeen words of English," he studied the want ads in the New York papers and found his first job with Maxwell-Briscoe in Tarrytown, New York, at fifteen dollars per week. He stayed there only six months and took English lessons during that period.

Farkas was especially interested in original automotive design rather than simply detailing or copying the designs of someone else.

*From the oral reminiscences of Eugene Farkas, recalling a statement Henry Ford made to Helen Farkas.

105

He sent letters to Packard and Ford in Detroit and received a reply from Walter Flanders of Ford, offering eighteen dollars a week. He took the Ford position in September 1907, but it turned out to be work on Model R and Model S production drawings, not the experimental drafting he was seeking. He stayed with Ford about two months, then went to Cadillac, where he was given work at forty cents an hour but was not kept long because of the panic of 1907. Another position with Morgan Engineering Company in Alliance, Ohio, was also lost because of panic conditions.

In early 1908, Farkas returned to Detroit, where his good friend Joseph Galamb hired him back at Ford Motor Company. The two men roomed together and took rides together in Galamb's Model N Ford. Farkas's work at that time was designing tools and fixtures for the upcoming Model T engine production. But because of some altercation between Farkas and a man named Haltenberger, both were fired.

Farkas next worked a few months at a time for a series of automotive plants—Packard, Olds, Oakland, Rapid Motor Vehicle Company, Carter Car Company, and Hudson—but always as a tool designer rather than an auto layout designer. When General Motors bought the Carter Car Company, Farkas became chief engineer of Carter. He was with Carter about three years but then left to work for the Cass Motor Vehicle Company which manufactured trucks. Farkas designed trucks from the ground up, but he saw little future in that particular company.

In 1911, while living in Pontiac, Farkas married Helen Louise Parshall. Their first child, Raymond Zoltan, was born October 7, 1912. Three more boys were later added to the family: Louis Eugene on September 30, 1914; Don Earl on September 23, 1917; and Robert Lawrence on May 13, 1919.

Again through the influence of Galamb, Farkas was given another opportunity to work for Ford Motor Company. This time, he was given charge of the experimental drafting room at $165 per month. This was October 1, 1913. The Farkas family moved into a flat at 79 Glendale Avenue in Detroit, and Farkas often traveled to work with Evangeline Cote (Dahlinger), who lived nearby. Detroit addresses subsequently occupied by the Farkas family were 149 Colorado, 1914–1916; 46 Edmonton, 1917; 5259 Maplewood, 1918–1928. Their more permanent home was built to their own specifications at 16516 Westmoreland in the fall of 1928.

One of Farkas's early assignments was the design of a chassis for the Edison-Ford electric car. It would have a standard cabriolet body similar to other electrics, with tiller steering, a suspension similar to the Model T, and a worm-drive axle. Batteries were to be the Edison steel submarine type operating an electric motor. The car was not a resounding success because of the weakness of the Edison batteries. When lead batteries were substituted, the vehicle became too heavy for general use. Clara Ford's Detroit Electric likewise had trouble negotiating the ten-mile distance between the Ford home in Highland Park and Ford Farm in Dearborn. Electrics were most useful for short trips on smooth city boulevards.

On October 1, 1915, Charles Sorensen was requested by Henry Ford to oversee the manufacture of a Ford tractor at Dearborn. The plant had not yet been built, and the tractor had not yet been designed. Sorensen picked Farkas as his chief engineer. The tractor engine, when designed, was built and furnished to Ford by the Hercules Motor Company. Farkas then designed a three-speed transmission distinctly different from the Model T transmission. And the new tractor rear axle was driven by a worm gear very similar to that designed by Farkas for the Edison-Ford electric vehicle.

Earlier Ford tractor experiments (1907–1915) had been done using Model T components. The early Ford tractors could hardly do the work of a team of horses, but the new tractor, later to be named the Fordson, could pull a double plow through heavy clay soil. The first of the Fordson experimental design was tested in December 1915. It was not until 1917, however, that mass production was achieved, hastened by a frantic wartime order of 5,000 Fordsons by England. The first shipment to England took place October 8, 1917.

In 1918, Farkas designed a two-cylinder engine for the U.S. Air Force to be used to power a robot aircraft bomb. This device anticipated the German V-1 rockets of World War II. He also designed a three-man, six-ton tank powered by two tractor engines. The U.S. government ordered 1,000 of these tanks at $6,000 each. However, the order was cancelled shortly after the armistice in November. The government had been concerned about Ford's hiring foreign engineers to design military weapons. Ford's response: "I don't care what they are—Hungarians, Austrians, Germans. As long as they work for me and do a good job, they're all right with me."

When tractor production was moved from the Dearborn plant to the nearby Rouge plant in 1920, Farkas was assigned responsibility for developing the "X engine," replacing Allan Horton, the former engineer in charge. This engine, as visualized by Henry Ford, would be of very radical design. It would consist of two radial banks, each with four air-cooled cylinders. It thus became an eight-cylinder engine with each bank of four pistons moving at ninety degrees to the other—a design related to radial aircraft engines. Ford envisioned this engine as the successor to the Model T engine, and it is quite certain his delay in replacing the Model T was his expectation that he would be using this new X engine in his next car.

While Edsel Ford, in 1924, was racing his "999" speedboat at Miami,

107

Florida, and winning the McAllister Hotel Sweepstakes using a World War I, twelve-cylinder Liberty aircraft engine, Henry Ford was building a speedboat equipped with a twenty-four-cylinder, twin-ignition, X engine named *Miss Dearborn*. But this monster X engine was found to be very unreliable.

There were many difficulties in using the X engine in a car. There were too many undeveloped innovations. For example, Ford wanted to use the flywheel as a supercharger although the relatively slow speed of the flywheel made the scheme impractical. The air cooling was insufficient. Dirt and oil collected on spark plugs of the bottom cylinders. Although Farkas continued experimentation, he was discouraged with the prospects. In a memorandum to Ford dated January 26, 1926, Ernest Kanzler presented the case for the need of an "intermediate car" to satisfy the public until the X engine could be fully developed. Later in 1926, Ford stated, "Now we don't want to abandon this X engine. That's something for the future. But now we've got to design a car for the market, a four-cylinder one." Engineers then went to work on the Model A.

Farkas became involved in design of the Model A chassis—clutch, transmission, axle, suspension, and braking systems. His friend Galamb was in charge of bodies. Harold Hicks, an engine engineer, by redesign of the Model T engine was able to increase horsepower from twenty-five to forty, and with Farkas he raised the speed of the Model A from forty-three miles per hour to sixty-five.

With Raymond Laird assisting, Farkas designed and developed production methods for the welded wire wheels introduced on Lincoln motorcars, made optional on the 1927 Model T and standard on Ford vehicles through 1935. The four-wheel brakes and Houdille shock absorbers on the Model A were the responsibilities of Farkas. Again with Laird, in 1936, a small sixty-horsepower V-8 engine companion to the eighty-five-horsepower engine was designed by Farkas for the 1937 models. This engine served well during the World War II years when gasoline was in short supply. In 1937, Farkas built an experimental rear-engined auto with rear axle in front and the vehicle steered by all four wheels.

Farkas had been about ready to quit Ford Motor Company in 1932. When Ford heard of this, he asked Farkas whom he preferred to work for, Sorensen or Peter Martin. Farkas immediately picked Martin and was given a large pay raise, a bonus, and a Rickenbacker to drive.

Farkas often played his flute or piccolo on the Ford public radio broadcasts from the Ford Engineering Laboratory studios. Both Farkas and his wife were excellent dancers and enjoyed the old-fashioned dancing parties arranged by the Fords in the Blue Room of the Engineering Laboratory—the dances led by Benjamin Lovett, Ford's danc-

Farkas working at drafting board in Engineering Laboratory about 1940.

ing master. Sometimes Farkas would demonstrate a Hungarian solo dance to the Fords' delight.

Although his speech was without foreign accent, Farkas was not particularly talkative, and he would be inclined to favor presenting his ideas as drawings and diagrams. Ford seemed to grasp ideas best that way.

Farkas's office was in the Engineering Laboratory, where he was given a large portion of the walnut-paneled library. The office had a fireplace, and Ford liked to come there to chat and rest, sometimes falling asleep. Ford had a shoeshine kit in a drawer of Farkas's desk and would often come in with dirty shoes, cleaning and polishing them himself. Helen Farkas once called by phone asking for her husband, who was not there at the time. Thinking the one who answered was an assistant, she demanded he immediately find her husband. Ford promptly did so.

During World War II, Farkas worked on refinements of B24 bomber components and designed a twelve-cylinder radial aircraft engine which never got into production. He designed a tank engine and an automatic five-speed transmission for the 600-horsepower tank being produced by Ford. A smaller version of the same type of transmission was to be used in cars after the war. Before his complete retirement, Farkas worked two or three days a week as consultant on transmissions and continued his previous long-term assignment of evaluating mechanical patents offered to Ford Motor Company for consideration.

Upon his full retirement in 1947, the Farkases almost immediately moved to Laguna Beach, California, where he could enjoy his favorite recreation, fishing. After many enjoyable years of retirement, Farkas died rather suddenly at 30832 Marilyn Drive in South Laguna Beach on February 24, 1963. Internment followed at Forest Lawn Cemetery in Detroit. Helen Parshall Farkas passed away on November 11, 1974.

The Fordson Tractor of which Farkas was chief engineer. Photograph July 1920.

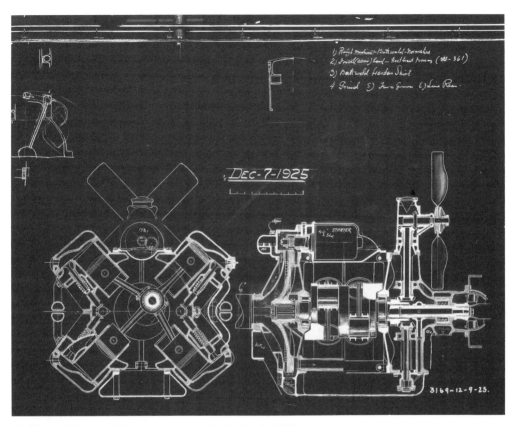

Chalkboard diagram of X engine as drawn by Farkas in 1925.

Major References

Bryan, Ford R. *Beyond the Model T: The Other Ventures of Henry Ford.* Detroit: Wayne State University Press, 1990.

Farkas, Eugene J. Reminiscences. Accession 65, Henry Ford Museum & Greenfield Village Archives.

Farkas, Robert L., son of Eugene J. Farkas. Personal communication, 1990.

"Farkas and the Fordson." *Ford Life,* May–June 1971.

"Farkas of Ford Experimental." *Ford Life,* March–April 1971.

Galamb, Joseph A. Reminiscences. Accession 65, Henry Ford Museum & Greenfield Village Archives.

Nevins, Allan, and Frank Ernest Hill. *Ford: Decline and Rebirth, 1933–1962.* New York: Charles Scribner's Sons, 1963.

———. *Ford: Expansion and Challenge, 1915–1932.* New York: Charles Scribner's Sons, 1957.

Edsel Bryant Ford, 1893–1943.

Edsel Bryant Ford

1893–1943

"Maybe I pushed the boy too hard."
—Henry Ford*

It is with some uneasiness that the writer includes Edsel Ford as merely one of Henry Ford's lieutenants. Edsel Ford was president of Ford Motor Company for nearly twenty-five years, and through some of the company's most challenging times. But during that time, Henry was reluctant to give his son the support he deserved. Henry never recognized Edsel's superior, more enlightened management capabilities. Edsel, it seems, was not as merciless a man as Henry would have preferred to run the Ford Motor Company.

Edsel Ford, born November 6, 1893, at 570 Forest Avenue, Detroit, was the only child of Henry and Clara Bryant Ford. Edsel was named after Edsel Ruddiman, a gradeschool classmate of his father. Edsel's parents had grown up on farms a few miles west of Detroit. At the time of Edsel's birth Henry was working as an engineer for the Edison Illuminating Company at the salary of about $75 per month.

As an only child, Edsel spent considerable time with adults during his early years, especially with his mother, his aunts Jane and Margaret Ford, and his grandfather William Ford. Edsel's father was attentive when not too busy with his automobile experiments. Edsel attended Detroit public schools until his father's success in the automobile business made it appropriate to place him in the Detroit University School which offered college preparatory courses.

During his teen years, Edsel lived with his parents at 66 Edison Avenue, now 140 Edison Avenue, in Detroit, and drove a Ford Model N about town. After school, he would often volunteer in the offices at the Ford Piquette Plant, addressing and stamping envelopes or some such assignment. When Henry Ford won the famous Selden patent suit in

*From "An Interview with Florence Crews Houtz: Recollection of Life at 140 Edison Avenue," by J. A. Mitchell, April 13, 1991 (a statement purportedly made by Henry Ford during his visit to 140 Edison on June 5, 1943).

113

1911, Edsel was allowed to skip school and attend the celebration of the victory in New York City.

As this was a period when teenage boys were excited about airplanes, Edsel obtained permission from his father to have an airplane built using a Model T engine. Although Edsel was not allowed to fly the plane, its moderate success satisfied Edsel's immediate curiosity and inspired a long-term interest in aviation.

After his graduation from Detroit University School in 1912, Edsel did not enter college as he would have preferred. Instead, persuaded by his father, Edsel began to accept responsibility in the Ford Motor Company at its new Highland Park plant. One of Edsel's first jobs at his father's factory was to keep inventory, fastening small numbered brass tags to new equipment. Later, Henry presented Edsel, then twenty-one, with a gift of $1 million and took him to a large Detroit bank to show him that amount in gold bullion.

In June, 1915, Edsel and two friends drove a Model T across the United States to the Panama-Pacific Exposition. Edsel, now with considerable mechanical skill, acted as mechanic as well as alternate driver.

In early 1916, the Fords moved into their new home, Fair Lane, near Dearborn. The home was equipped with swimming pool, bowling alley, and a par-three golf range. Edsel, however, had little interest in Fair Lane, enjoying instead time with his young Detroit friends. On November 1, of this same year, Edsel married Eleanor Lowthian Clay in Detroit's Central Methodist Episcopal Church. Eleanor was three years younger than Edsel, and a niece of the well known J. L. Hudson of Detroit. The Edsel Fords made their first home at 439 Iroquois Avenue. Their first child, Henry Ford II, was born September 4, 1917.

When Henry decided to build tractors as well as automobiles, he formed a new corporation, Henry Ford & Son, and in July 1917, began to produce the Fordson in a Dearborn factory. However, it seemed Edsel did not have any great interest in the tractors.

After the departure of James Couzens in 1915, it had fallen upon Edsel and the new treasurer, Frank L. Klinginsmith, to take care of the business responsibilities of Ford Motor Company. By mid-1917, there were war contracts to produce ambulances, submarine patrol boats, Liberty aircraft engines, "Flivver" tanks, and a multitude of smaller military items such as 820,000 steel helmets.

At the time of the United States's entry into World War I, Edsel was military draft age. He was not drafted, however, because of his dependents and his indispensability to a war industry. That fall of 1917, Henry ran for the United States Senate, but lost to Truman H. Newberry. It is thought that public opinion regarding Edsel's lack of conventional military service hurt Henry's popularity at the polls.

By this time, Edsel was handling major responsibilities within the Ford organization. In 1915, at age twenty-two, he had been named to the board of directors. In 1916, he had been appointed secretary of the four-member executive committee which analyzed important policy questions and reported their recommendations to the board for final enactment. These matters concerned general organization of the company including management of over thirty domestic and fourteen foreign branches.

The war was barely over when Henry, disgusted with the monetary demands of his minor stockholders, resigned as president of Ford Motor Company on December 30, 1918. On December 31, Edsel, at age twenty-five, was named president, and was to remain so for the rest of his life. Henry, by threatening to build an automobile to sell for much less than the Model T, was able, with Edsel's help, to buy out the other Ford Motor Company stockholders. Again, Henry, as major stockholder, became the "boss," although not president of the company. Edsel continued to yield to Henry in all major decisions. This reconstituted Ford Motor Company was now owned solely by Henry, Edsel, and Clara Ford, with Edsel owning about 40 percent of the stock.

With Model T profits now at their disposal, Henry, with Edsel's assistance, proceeded between 1919 and 1926 to invest $376 million on company expansion including acquisition of the Lincoln Motor Company, a railroad, a fleet of ships, iron mines, forest land, an aircraft factory, and rubber plantations in Brazil. Of all these enterprises, Edsel seems to have been most enthusiastic over the Lincoln automobile. He stated, "Father made the most popular car in the world; I would like to make the best car in the world."

As president of Ford Motor Company, Edsel took responsibility for finance and sales. Edsel was the one who came to the rescue of the company when the Model T became obsolete both in mechanism and style. Edsel had been making sketches of autos as early as 1909 when he was studying mechanical drawing at Detroit University School. He owned European sport cars before he married Eleanor in 1916. The Lincoln Motor Company was purchased to a great extent to satisfy Edsel's wishes. Edsel took charge of Lincoln design in 1922, and marketed Lincolns with customized coachwork by leading American and European designers. Edsel had developed a keen artistic sense.

When, in 1926, Henry had finally become convinced the Model T had run its course, the new Model A, introduced in late 1927, was patterned after the Lincoln. It was dubbed "The Baby Lincoln." In 1929, the Model A outsold every other car made in the United States. In 1936, the Lincoln Zephyr, a streamlined design introduced by Edsel, became a best seller in its class and a prototype for the 1937 Ford car. The

Mercury nameplate, introduced in late 1938, is credited largely to Edsel, as is the design of the 1940 Lincoln Continental, a recognized classic among automobiles.

Edsel's interest in aviation surfaced again in the 1920s. As a member and director of the Detroit Aviation Society he helped sponsor air speed races and air reliability tours. Edsel became a stockholder in the Aircraft Development Corporation and, with the support of Henry, built an airport and dirigible mooring tower in Dearborn in 1924. Edsel and William B. Mayo are credited with recommending Ford's purchase of the Stout Metal Airplane Company and the building of the famous Ford Tri-motors. Edsel was the major sponsor of Admiral Richard E. Byrd's flights over the North Pole (1926) and South Pole (1929). Byrd, in return, named an Antarctic mountain range for Edsel.

In 1919, Edsel moved his family to a larger home at 7930 East Jefferson Avenue in Detroit, and in 1927 built a luxurious mansion on Lake St. Clair beyond Grosse Pointe—a home which matched that of any other auto baron in Detroit. It was much more elegant than Fair Lane. Edsel and Eleanor now had four children: Henry II; Benson, born in 1920; Josephine, born in 1923; and William, born in 1925. Nearly every imaginable recreational facility was provided for the children in the new spacious home. In addition, there was the country estate nearby at Haven Hill, Michigan—a 2,000 acre operating farm with a variety of animals to delight the children.

In their boathouse on Lake St. Clair was the yacht *Onika,* taking them and their friends to Seal Harbor, Maine, or elsewhere for summer vacations. At their Seal Harbor "Skylands" resort, Edsel furnished several of his neighbors with his favorite "Class R" sailing sloop so they could partake in friendly competition. In Detroit, Edsel built a series of high-speed powerboats for Gold Cup racing on the Detroit River, though he did not race them himself. In winter, family vacations were spent at Hobe Sound on the Atlantic Coast of Florida where they also enjoyed boating.

The Edsel Fords were very generous with their wealth. They donated millions to such organizations as the Detroit Symphony Orchestra, Detroit Institute of Art, New York's Museum of Modern Art, Young Men's Christian Association, Detroit Community Chest, Detroit University School, American Red Cross, Shenandoah National Park, and Henry Ford Hospital. Following Edsel's death, the Edsel B. Ford Institute for Medical Research was established as a tribute to the support Edsel provided the hospital.

During the great depression, Edsel was very distressed that so many men were unemployed. Both he and Henry did all they reasonably could to keep the banks from closing, and keep as many employees

Edsel Ford with his father about the time the Ford Motor Company
presidency was turned over to Edsel.

working as possible. But the failure of Detroit's Guardian Banks, in
which Edsel was a heavy stockholder, reduced Henry's confidence not
only in bankers, but also in Edsel's financial acumen.

The depression also caused a great deal of labor unrest. Henry, as
was well known, objected strenuously to unions. Edsel believed in a
conciliatory approach, and after the Wagner Act of 1935, voiced his
strong desire for negotiations. Henry, however, ordered Harry Bennett
to fight the United Automobile Workers with every device possible, and   117

Edsel's advice was ignored. Bennett and Charles Sorensen, it seems, were driving a wedge between Edsel and his father. Though fully aware of this situation, Edsel chose not to fight.

On August 30, 1935, Congress passed the "Wealth Tax," stipulating taxes on income and estates be raised to amounts as high as 70 percent. The Fords and their legal council studied the situation and decided on a Ford Foundation, a benevolent corporation, as a way to separate money from management in order to retain family control of Ford Motor Company. The bulk (95 percent) of the Ford stock was to be "non-voting" and go to the Foundation, while a nucleus (5 percent) of "voting" stock would be retained by the family. The Foundation was established January 15, 1936. Edsel was of prime importance in this maneuver.

World War II brought new pressures to bear. Rapid conversion of

Edsel and Henry Ford take a sleigh ride together about 1930.

Henry and Edsel Ford at the Rouge plant in 1938.

factories to defense work taxed management to the limit. Henry, who despised Roosevelt, was not very cooperative in regard to Washington mandates. Edsel and Sorensen dealt with William S. Knudsen, Washington's commissioner of industrial production. Edsel was involved in essentially every major defense contract initiated at the start of the war, but unfortunately did not live to see the final returns: 8,680 Liberator bombers, 54,851 aircraft engines, 277,896 jeeps, 93,217 military trucks, 26,954 tank engines, 2,718 tanks and tank destroyers, and amphibians, armored cars, and a great variety of smaller military items.   119

The 1940 Lincoln Continental Mark I, an Edsel Ford design executed by Eugene Gregorie. (Edsel Ford's son, William Clay Ford, designed the Continental Mark II during 1952–53.)

At war's end, a total of $371 million had been spent by Ford Motor Company of which $355 million had been advanced by the government.

Edsel's health had been declining for some time. His wife and mother had been much more concerned than his father. Edsel was first diagnosed as having gastric ulcers, but finally was found to have stomach cancer aggravated by undulant fever (possibly caused by his drinking unpasteurized milk delivered from the Ford farms). At age forty-nine, Edsel Ford died on May 26, 1943, in his home at 1100 Lakeshore Drive. An enormous crowd attended the funeral services. Charles Sorensen, in tears, attended; Harry Bennett did not attend. Edsel was buried at Woodlawn Cemetery in Detroit.

Edsel's death was a shock to Detroit as well as to the nation. The future of the Ford Motor Company was known to be in great jeopardy. In spite of his advanced years, a frail and dejected Henry Ford again assumed the title of president.

Major References

Bryan, Ford R. *Beyond the Model T: The Other Ventures of Henry Ford*. Detroit: Wayne State University Press, 1990.

Office of Edsel Ford, Archives, Henry Ford Museum & Greenfield Village. Accession 6.

Gregorie, Eugene. Reminiscences. Accession 65, Henry Ford Museum & Green-field Village Archives.

Lewis, David L. *The Public Image of Henry Ford.* Detroit: Wayne State University Press, 1976.

Mitchell, J. A. "An Interview with Florence Crews Houtz: Recollections of Life at 140 Edison Avenue," April 13, 1991.

Nevins, Allan. *Ford: The Times, the Man, the Company.* New York: Charles Scribner's Sons, 1954.

Nevins, Allan, and Frank Ernest Hill. *Ford: Decline and Rebirth, 1933–1962.* New York: Charles Scribner's Sons, 1963.

———. *Ford: Expansion and Challenge, 1915–1932.* New York: Charles Scribner's Sons, 1957.

Joseph A. Galamb, 1881–1955.

Joseph A. Galamb

1881–1955

*"Joe, I've got an idea to design a new car. Fix a place for
yourself on the third floor way back."*
—Henry Ford*

For an automotive body engineer, Henry Ford depended almost entirely on Joseph Galamb. Model T bodies were designed to be both durable and inexpensive. That was the way Ford wanted them; he was not interested in style. Galamb bent the heavy sheet metal over a strong hardwood frame into a configuration to defy destruction—not to appease the stylish.

Joseph A. Galamb was born on February 3, 1881, in Mako, Hungary. After graduating from the Mako schools, he attended the Budapest Industrial Technology Engineering Course, from which he graduated in 1899. He next served the required one-year military service in the navy as an engineer. After the navy, as he stated in his reminiscences, "I went to see the world—Vienna, Dresden, Berlin, Hamburg and Bremen." He worked in Federracht at a large German shipbuilding firm for a few months, then went on to Dusseldorf for about two weeks of employment. In Frankfurt, a German automotive center, he was hired to assemble automotive engines in a process in which each engine was built completely by one man. Galamb was working there in early 1903 when the Adler Automobile Company produced their first four-cylinder engine.

Joseph Galamb came to America in October 1903, to be on hand for the St. Louis Exposition and World's Fair of 1904. He arrived in New York on October 6, with two friends and twenty-seven dollars to split three ways. His first job was in a New York paper box factory at three dollars a week, putting metal corners on the boxes. After two months in New York, he left for Pittsburgh, where he worked for Westinghouse as a toolmaker for six months at twenty-eight cents an hour.

Planning to go back to Germany in late 1904, Galamb attended the

*From the oral reminiscences of Joseph A. Galamb, recalling a statement made to him by Henry Ford in 1907 as they started work on the Model T.

123

St. Louis Exposition that summer. But instead of returning to Europe, he obtained a job as a carburetor maker with the Stearns Automobile Company in Cleveland. Then he was at Niles, Ohio, as a tool designer for the Harris Automotive Press Company. Although now he might be criticized as a job hopper, he was obtaining valuable experience.

Galamb had friends in Detroit, and while he was visiting them, he applied for work at the Silent Northern plant, the Cadillac plant, and the Ford Piquette plant. All three employers offered him work within a three-hour period. But it was C. Harold Wills of Ford Motor Company who offered Galamb the best pay—twenty dollars per week. Wills hired Galamb in November 1905. Galamb was released from his job with Harris and started work with Ford on December 11, 1905. There were about 300 men employed at the Ford Motor Company assembling the Model A from purchased parts. Ford was not manufacturing his own automobile parts yet.

Galamb was soon assigned to designing parts needed for the four-cylinder Model N. Samples of this car were to be shown at the January 1906 automobile show. During 1906, the big six-cylinder Model K was under development. Ford was pleased with the more expressive European style of draftsmanship, and for experimental projects he provided Galamb with a private drafting room with drafting board and blackboard. It was in this closely guarded cubicle adjoining Ford's experimental shop that Galamb did the design work for the Model T. Although the Model T was the result of ideas of several men, Galamb's contributions, along with those of Ford and Wills, were particularly important. Wills's contribution was primarily metallurgical. Ford spent considerable time in Galamb's private room, sketching his ideas on the blackboard. Between sketches, he sat in his rocking chair, his "thinking chair," discussing these ideas and studying the designs as Galamb drew them in detail on paper. For a period of two years, Ford and Galamb, with Eugene Farkas as one of Galamb's assistants, spent many late evenings together working out the final character of the Model T.

The Model T was revolutionary in automotive design. Whereas today there are the separate entities of styling design and engineering design, the Model T resulted solely from engineering design. It was not *styled* in the present sense of the word. Although Wills had a talent for styling, it was not appreciated by Ford. The ungainly, lightweight, but durable Ford car could hurdle ditches and wade through sand and mud and was thus tested by the majority of drivers. When complaints came in from Model T owners, it was Galamb's responsibility to design still more durable replacement parts. At that time, Ford was referring to Galamb as "Joe" and Wills labeled Galamb "the Dutchman."

One of the major deficiencies of the Model T was the lack of durability of its transmission-brake bands. These were made of cotton fabric which had to be replaced far too often. Ford admitted to Galamb, "Joe, you know that brake bands built up the Rouge plant!" insinuating that profits from the sale of brake bands had financed the Rouge. Of course, Ford was inclined to exaggerate a bit.

Ford asked Galamb to build a car that looked like a Model T, but with speed sufficient to beat the Blitzen Benz in a race. The resulting vehicle had an engine with a four-cylinder, large-bore aluminum block fitted with steel sleeves and aluminum pistons. Driven by Frank Kulick, one of Ford's race drivers, it beat the Blitzen Benz at a speed of about 125 miles per hour—so Galamb reported in his reminiscences.

Galamb is listed in the 1910 *Detroit City Directory* as a "designer" rooming at 3067 East Grand Boulevard. In 1915, he is listed as a "foreman," with his home at 1197 Cass Avenue. In 1916, he is designated "chief engineer" and had moved to 297 Longfellow. The occupations given in the directory were not official classifications. Ford did not believe in organization by title. It was not until 1919, when Edsel Ford became president of Ford Motor Company, that a formal organization chart for the company was devised.

In 1914, when Galamb was put in charge of the Engineering Department at Highland Park, he was responsible for any change in the Model T, but he could make a change only after approval of Ford. Ford's instructions: "Your job is going to be to watch it so that nobody will make a change on that car." Ford was afraid changes would increase production costs.

This was about the time closed bodies were being introduced. Ford car bodies were designed on scrap wrapping paper placed on planks across two sawhorses. Ford, Galamb said, could be very stubborn and offered some very impractical suggestions at times. On car bodies, for example, he wanted left and right doors to be identical stampings cut with square corners to avoid leaving scrap metal. Both aluminum and steel bodies were built between 1914 and 1918, until Alcoa raised prices from eighteen cents to twenty-five cents per pound, making steel much more economical.

Galamb was in his early thirties when he married Dorothy Beckham, whom he had known for some time in Toldeo, Ohio. The wedding was a grand event. Ford chartered a private train on which he and Clara Ford, the Sorensens, the Martins, the Liebolds, the Lees, and many other guests rode and dined. Although it was a tails-and-top hat affair, there is said to have been lots of fun.

During World War I, Galamb was given responsibility for building

125

submarine detectors of British design for use on the Ford Eagle boats. In addition, he designed a lightweight two-man tank driven by two Model T engines. The Army ordered 15,000 of the tanks only six weeks before the armistice. Of this order, only 15 were completed, but some of them reached France.

At the Piquette plant in 1907, Ford had said to Galamb, "Joe, we have to build a light tractor that we can use out on the farm where wheat is growing, and we need a binder. We have to build a tractor in three days." With a Model B engine, a crude frame, and binder wheels, a makeshift tractor was finished in one week. With a large water tank as a radiator, the engine overheated, and the tractor could not finish the job. But this was the first of several experimental tractors leading to the famous Fordson.

In 1915, Galamb assigned his assistant, Farkas, to the Henry Ford and Son Tractor Plant in Dearborn, while he himself divided his time between Highland Park and the tractor plant. Galamb was trouble-shooter for the Hercules engines used in the Fordson, but he did not like to work with Sorensen, superintendent of the tractor plant. Galamb thought Sorensen was "overbearing, always criticizing." After 1923, Galamb occupied an office in the new Dearborn Engineering Laboratory, where Ford engineering was centralized.

Mechanically, by 1922, the Model T had matured to say the least. Ford seemed well satisfied with the engine—his chief interest. Galamb had about 200 men with him in the Engineering Laboratory, and Ford would "jump on him" for having too many. When he sent some of his men to the Rouge to do their work, the number became less conspicuous. Their work at that time consisted primarily of body design changes that were to appear on the several models each year.

Ford's engine interests now focused largely on his experimental X engine. The X engine work was handled by Farkas, with Galamb also claiming some credit. The replacement for the Model T, in Ford's mind, was to be as revolutionary as the Model T had been in 1908. After six years of work, however, the eight-cylinder X engine was determined in 1926 to be impractical and had only served to delay introduction of the Model A, which appeared in November 1927.

Through the 1930s, Galamb had automotive body and frame design responsibility. When the Ford V-8 engine was made available in 1932, Galamb found the frame of the car too weak and had to design reinforcements. Edsel Ford had helped considerably in Model A styling and was now given considerable leeway in automotive styling by Henry Ford.

When Edsel Ford died in 1943, Henry Ford came to Galamb and

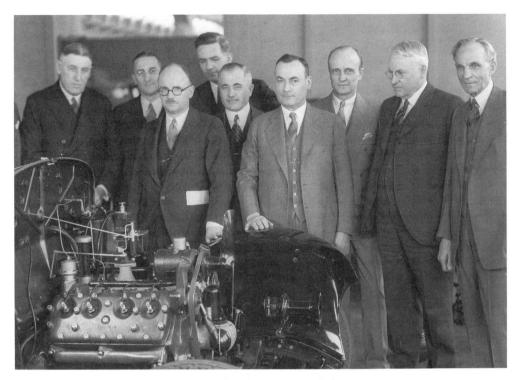

Admiring the 1932 V-8 engine, this group of Ford executives includes Galamb (center). To the right are Peter E. Martin, Eugene Farkas, Burt J. Craig, and Henry Ford.

said, "Joe, we have to go back to the old days where we were only building one model. There won't be any Lincoln or Mercury; there won't be any other model except Ford. You can put any kind of body on there as long as it is the same chassis. Don't let anybody change that idea, either."

Galamb kept Ford's instructions in mind until Henry II began to appear on the scene. Young Henry did not at all agree with the idea of only one chassis for all cars. He wanted to proceed with Edsel Ford's plans—his father's plans. This situation greatly undermined Galamb's standing in the new regime. In addition, Galamb was now working under Laurence Sheldrick of Product Engineering. Galamb's body design work did not appeal to Sheldrick,

In late 1943, at age sixty-two, Galamb was stricken by an attack of heart failure, and soon after his doctor ordered him to stop working. Galamb retired on April 10, 1944. Eugene Gregory, designer of the original classic Lincoln Continental for Edsel Ford, states in his reminiscences, "Joe was well fixed. They say he is the richest Hungarian in Detroit. Joe made $100,000 a year back in those days—equal to $500,000 today."

Galamb had spent thirty-nine years with Ford Motor Company, many of these years directly under Ford's observation. Although he said he liked working for Edsel better than working for Henry, he also stated, "I never had any trouble with Mr. Ford. I was very quiet and went ahead and did my own job without bothering anybody." Galamb lived another eleven years after retiring, dying at his home, 17325 Pontchartrain, Detroit, on December 4, 1955, at the age of seventy-four. The Galambs had two daughters, Claire and Gloria.

On February 3, 1981, a memorial plaque was placed in Mako, Hungary, to commemorate the hundredth anniversary of Galamb's birth. On the memorial: "Galamb, born in Mako, Hungary, in 1881, was a mechanical engineer who did pioneering work on the Model T Ford and the Fordson tractor."

Major References

Callahan, Joseph M. "He Helped Design Model T." *Automotive News,* December 26, 1955.

Farkas, Eugene. Reminiscences. Accession 65, Henry Ford Museum & Greenfield Village Archives.

Galamb, Joseph. Reminiscences. Accession 65, Henry Ford Museum & Greenfield Village Archives.

Nevins, Allan. *Ford: The Times, the Man, the Company.* New York: Charles Scribner's Sons, 1954.

Nevins, Allan, and Frank Ernest Hill. *Ford: Expansion and Challenge, 1915–1932.* New York: Charles Scribner's Sons, 1957.

Sweinhart, James. "Who's News Today." *Detroit News,* April 14, 1944.

Carl Edvard Johansson, 1864–1943.

Carl Edvard Johansson

1864–1943

"Perhaps Johansson, having nearly attained the absolute in flat surfaces, has released to mankind the initial secret of a whole new 'limb' on the 'tree of scientific growth.'"
—*James Sweinhart**

M odern computer-programmed, numerically controlled manufacturing machines utilize Johansson gauge blocks (Jo-Blocks) for calibration. These dimensionally accurate steel blocks are descendants of the blocks invented by Carl Johansson and sponsored by Henry Ford in the days of the Model T.

Carl Edvard Johansson was born on a farm at Frotuna in the parish of Gotlunda, province of Westmanland, Sweden, on March 15, 1864. He was the son of Johan and Carolina Rask Johansson. After finishing elementary school at Gotlunda Church, at age sixteen, he came to America, where his older brother, Arvid, had established himself in 1880 at Duluth, Minnesota. The brothers worked together in a lumber mill during summers, and both studied during winters at Gustavus Adolphus College at St. Peter, Minnesota. There they learned to speak English fairly well.

The lumber mill burned down in 1884, and the brothers returned to Eskilstuna, Sweden, where Carl went to work at the Beronius Mechanical Works and attended Eskilstuna Sunday and Evening College. He was soon working for the Carl Gustav Stad's Rifle Factory in that city. After a two-year apprenticeship at the rifle factory, he was an accomplished machine tool engineer. In his work at this Swedish arsenal, he became acutely aware of the difficulties in making precise measurements of the sizes of parts being manufactured. Johansson conceived of a set of block gauges as a means of determining the exact dimensions of objects. The exact size would be measured by comparison with his standard blocks.

When Johansson was later sent with a Swedish commission to study

*From James Sweinhart, "He Measured in Millionths," *Ford Times,* Vol. 1, 1944, pp. 18–22.

131

arms manufacture at the German Mauserwerke at Oberndorf, he saw similar blocks used as gauges to standardize the sizes of parts for their rifles. But these gauges were made exclusively for rifle parts. This successful use of gauge blocks convinced Johansson that a more elaborate series of blocks could be devised for universal use.

After returning to the rifle factory in Eskilstuna, from 1896 to 1898, Johansson took great pains to obtain a suitable crucible steel and to develop the necessary metal finishing techniques to produce a series of blocks of exact measurements which, by various combinations, would provide any length desired by a manufacturer. By 1906, his gauges provided an accuracy approaching one thousandth of a millimeter, and in 1908 the accuracy was one ten-thousandth of a millimeter.

On April 4, 1896, Johansson married Fredrika Margareta (Greta) Anderson, daughter of a local brickworks foreman. She became exceedingly helpful to her husband, helping him keep records and allowing him to convert her sewing machine into a machine for finish-polishing his blocks at home on evenings after his work at the rifle factory. The Johanssons had three children—two daughters and one son.

In 1911, Johansson left the rifle factory and in the same city went into the business of manufacturing his standardized steel gauge blocks for European industry. This was not an easy task, either technically or commercially. A gauge block accurately measured in Sweden expanded a bit when used in more southern countries. The dimension was only accurate when measured at the same temperature as in Sweden. Johansson fixed this temperature at twenty degrees centigrade. In some climates, certain types of steel tended to corrode and change the dimensions. A noncorrosive grade of steel was necessary. Ends of the blocks had to be perfectly flat and parallel to one another before exact dimensions could be assigned. Johansson's objectives, were, to say the least, difficult to attain, but industry was anxious to obtain a reliable standard system of measurement.

Perhaps Johansson's greatest achievement was to provide gauge blocks to several government laboratories for comparison of measurements on the same blocks. Sets of blocks were measured by the National Physical Laboratory in London, and the same sets were sent to the National Bureau of Standards in Washington, the Bureau International des Poids et Mesures in Paris, and later to the Physikalisch-Technische Reichsanstalt in Berlin. Calibrations from these laboratories eventually agreed within two-millionths of an inch of one another and also within two-millionths of an inch of Johansson's originally assigned values. Elaborate optical interferometric methods were used in comparing gauge block flatness and length. Differences were often measured in fractional fringes of the sodium D-line wavelength—a distance of 589 millimicrons, which could be converted to millionths of an inch.

Establishment of an agreed-upon factor to convert metric lengths to English lengths was imperative. The factor of 25.4 millimeters to the inch was finally adopted. By this cooperative effort, Johansson's gauge blocks gained wide reputation as the best commercially available. The fourteen years between 1897 and 1911 had been required for Johansson to develop his system of measurement to this unique position of assured quality.

Because of financial problems with his business in Sweden, Johansson sold most of his company stock to a Swedish bank in 1917. But in 1919, he decided to try again, this time in the United States, from which he could supply North and South American markets. Offices were set up at 245 West 55th Street in New York City and at 72 Queen Street West in Toronto, with a manufacturing plant at Poughkeepsie, New York.

Johansson's blocks, known as Jo-blocks, made it possible to manufacture items to such exact dimensions that machine parts became interchangeable although manufactured continents apart. Jo-blocks made it possible for parts of a single automotive engine, for example, to be made in widely separated locations. And who might be especially interested in such a procedure? Henry Ford, of course. Ford was not only aware of Johansson and his gauge blocks, but his business depended on them.

By 1923, however, the Johansson business in the United States was on the verge of bankruptcy. At this point, Johansson explained his predicament to Ford, and Ford was rather anxious to help. Ford had been plagued with shortages of materials necessary to build his 2 million Model T's a year. He was endeavoring to ensure the independence of Ford Motor Company from the uncertainty of outside suppliers. He was buying his own iron and coal mines, timberlands, ships, railroad—anything to ensure a steady, reliable supply of what he needed for his automobile business. These supplies included Jo-blocks.

Ford offered Johansson facilities for his business in Dearborn. Ford was building a new Engineering Laboratory, and Johansson would, by 1925, have a climate-controlled workshop for machining and inspecting blocks, together with a supply of steel melted at the Rouge plant to Johansson's personal specifications.

Ford wanted to control Johansson's operations, however, to the extent of forming the Johansson Division of Ford Motor Company. Jo-blocks were then sold by Ford Motor Company Byproducts Sales to a multitude of customers. Johansson would not give Ford the right to exclusive use of his gauge blocks. After placing Johansson under his

Johansson with an exhibit of his gauge blocks in March 1935.

wing, so to speak, Ford did not pay much attention to him. It was Edsel Ford and his assistant John Crawford who looked after Johansson's welfare.

Johansson worked at Dearborn until 1936. During this twelve-year period, he left his family at Eskilstuna and made twenty-two ocean voyages to visit them. Fredrika Johansson visited Dearborn several times, staying as long as six months. By himself, Johansson resided at times in Detroit at 5540 Cass Avenue and at other times at 246 Alexandrine in Dearborn. Johansson gauges were sold by Ford Motor Company in three grades of accuracy:

Carl Edvard Johansson

Johansson measuring differences in length in micro-inches.

Quality	Accuracy/inch	Price
B	±.000008	$285.00
A	±.000004	$340.00
AA	±.000002	$1,745.00

Standard sets, consisting of eighty-one blocks, would make 120,000 different-size gauges in steps of .0001 inch, from a minimum size of .200 inch to more than 12 inches. Smaller sets were available at less cost, and chromium-plated sets were sold at a higher price.

Johansson also manufactured gauging systems in metric measurements. Ford was especially interested in the use of metric blocks to expedite manufacture of Fordson tractors in foreign countries. He could see the advantage of metric over English units of measure. In the 1920s, Ford had proposed that American industry convert to the metric system but was told conversion would be far too expensive.

135

In July 1936, Johansson left Dearborn, returning home to Eskilstuna, where he retired with his family. He was seventy-two years old. During his tenure in Dearborn, he had received an honorary doctorate from Gustavus Adolphus College in 1932, an honorary doctorate from Wayne State University in Detroit in 1935, and many awards from technical societies both in the United States and abroad.

Production of Johansson gauge blocks at Ford Motor Company reached its peak during World War II, after Johansson had retired. Ford had built a new Tool and Die Building said to be the largest in the world. The Henry Ford Trade School had graduated nearly 8,000 students with tool and die training. In 1941, gauge block production was approximately 200 per day. Customers included nearly every branch of the military and dozens of war contract suppliers, including Ford Motor Company. Government priority ratings determined deliveries. During the week of February 22, 1943, for example, orders were received for 3,101 blocks and 213 accessory gauges. The total of blocks on order at that date was 44,437, accessories 3,328.

Johansson, living in neutral Sweden, may or may not have taken satisfaction in the fact that his unique method of measurement was of such benefit to all opponents in the war. It was during the height of World War II, on September 30, 1943, that Johansson died at his home in Eskilstuna. He had not suffered any prolonged illness. Services were held in Kloster Church in his hometown.

Major References

Accession 390, Box 65, Henry Ford Museum & Greenfield Village Archives.

Althin, Torsten. *C. E. Johansson, 1864–1943: The Master of Measurement.* Stockholm: Stockholm Nordisk Rotogravyr, 1948.

Johansson, C. E. "Measuring a Millionth." *Ford Dealer and Service Field,* January 1934.

"Johansson, Apostle of Mechanical Accuracy, in America." *Automotive Industries* 41, September 25, 1919.

Liebold, Ernest G. Reminiscences. Accession 65, Henry Ford Museum & Greenfield Village Archives.

Sweinhart, James. "He Measured in Millionths." *Ford Times,* Vol. 1, 1944.

Albert Kahn, 1869–1942. (Photo courtesy of Albert Kahn Associates, Inc.)

Albert Kahn

1869–1942

*"Kahn, thanks largely to his Ford work, is regarded as the
greatest industrial architect who ever lived."*
—David L. Lewis*

As an industrial architect, Albert Kahn consistently
pleased Henry Ford, was in Ford's employ for many
years, and thus is considered one of Henry's lieutenants. And
despite what Ford may have allowed to be said in his *Dearborn Independent* about Jews in general, Ford and Kahn
were very good friends. Now, long after Ford's death, Albert
Kahn Associates, Inc., of Detroit continues to please Ford
Motor Company with the buildings it designs.

Albert Kahn was born in Rhaunen, Westphalia, Germany, on
March 21, 1869. His father was Joseph, and his mother was Rosalie
Cohn Kahn. Albert's father was a rabbi and teacher. Albert was the eldest of six children and spent his childhood in the schools of the grand
duchy of Luxembourg.

In 1880, the father sought a better life in the United States and im-
migrated to Detroit, where the family had relatives. Both Rosalie and
Joseph worked at odd jobs to earn a living for the family, while the
children—now eight of them—attended public schools.

Kahn's first employment in Detroit was with the architectural firm
of Albert Scott. Meanwhile, a friend, Julius Melchers, found him a position in 1885 as office boy for George D. Mason of the prominent firm
of Mason and Rice. Kahn soon became a draftsman for Mason, who had
a fine reputation for designing homes for prominent Detroiters.

In 1891, at age twenty-two, Kahn was awarded a scholarship to study
abroad, traveling and sketching scenes through Europe. Following his
European experience, Kahn joined George W. Nettleton and Alexander
Trowbridge to form the Nettleton, Kahn, and Trowbridge architectural
firm. In 1896, Kahn married Ernestine Krolik, a daughter of a prosper-
ous Detroit dry goods merchant.

When Nettleton died, Kahn went back to work with Mason until
1902. During this period, he was helping his younger brother, Julius,

*From David L. Lewis,
"Ford and Kahn,"
Michigan History,
September–October
1980.

139

earn bachelor of science and civil engineering degrees from the University of Michigan. As in Kahn's case, it was not common for architects at that time to be college-trained. But he had envisioned the advantages of combining the artistic aspects of architecture with the science of engineering. In 1903, the two brothers began working together to produce architectural plans that provided both beauty and utility.

Although Kahn designed beautiful residences such as the Edsel Ford home on Lakeshore Drive in Grosse Pointe and the grand commercial edifices such as the General Motors and Fisher buildings in Detroit, his most important contribution to architecture is likely the combination of beauty and utility demonstrated in his industrial designs.

In 1900, Kahn had designed a rather conventional factory for the Boyer Machine Company in Detroit. Together, in 1903, Albert and Julius Kahn designed the University of Michigan Engineering Building. The extensive use of reinforced concrete, steel, and glass in industrial structures was first demonstrated by Kahn in a group of Detroit factory buildings for the Packard Motor Company Car Company beginning in 1905.

By this time, Henry Ford was taking note of the style of factory building exemplified by Kahn—the well-lighted, well-ventilated structure of steel, reinforced concrete, and glass with a minimum of brick. By 1907, Ford had outgrown his plant on Piquette Avenue in Detroit because of the unexpected popularity of his Model N automobile. He had now designed the new Model T, which had still better prospects. He needed to build a much larger factory.

Ford sought land for a more expansive site in Detroit's suburb of Highland Park. He had visions of a factory layout all under one roof, eliminating the cartage of various chassis components and bodies from their separate manufacturing sites to an assembly building. The manufacturing and assembly operations would be together in one huge building.

Kahn was the architect who best understood and favored Ford's concept. So it was Kahn, together with his associate Ernest Wilby, who designed Ford's Highland Park plant, the largest automotive plant of its day—the main plant of Ford Motor Company for nearly twenty years and the entire life of the Model T. Kahn worked closely with Ford engineers William B. Mayo and Edward Gray in designing a powerhouse that was the chief landmark on Detroit's main thoroughfare of Woodward Avenue. Ford's Highland Park plant became the mecca of industrialists from around the globe. This was where "Fordism" was born.

During the next few years, Kahn designed a series of Ford assembly plants across the United States and, later, many of the buildings making up the famous Rouge plant, the largest private industrial complex in the world. The majority of the buildings in the Rouge—main powerhouse, open hearth, glass plant, tire manufacturing plant, pressed steel building, auto assembly plant, foundry, cement plant, coke ovens—were Kahn-designed. All told, Kahn and his associates are estimated to have designed as many as a thousand buildings for Ford during his career—a career closely spanning that of Ford. And Kahn was not only working for Ford; he was likewise designing automotive factories and office buildings for Hudson, Packard, Chrysler, and General Motors.

During World War I, Kahn was the official architect for the Aircraft Construction Division of the U.S. Signal Corps. His firm designed the majority of army airfields and many naval bases for the U.S. government.

When in 1928 the Soviet Union announced its First Five Year Plan, Ford agreed to help the Soviets build Model A automobiles and Model AA trucks. Kahn was enlisted to design two automotive plants for the Soviets; a main production plant at Nizhni Novgorod, about 300 miles east of Moscow, and an automotive assembly plant in Moscow. Although well designed and equipped, the expected efficiency in these plants was never reached. Even so, Ford vehicles were the most commonly seen in the Soviet Union for many years. In 1929, a Soviet commission asked Kahn to build a plant to build Fordson tractors. This plant was completed in Stalingrad in 1930. Mortia Kahn, Albert's brother, spent two years in Russia instructing construction supervisors in the building of more than 500 factories.

After vacationing and sketching buildings in Italy during the summer of 1912, Kahn came back to design, with his associates, a series of buildings for the University of Michigan: Hill Auditorium in 1913, Natural Science Building in 1917, Central Library in 1919, University Hospital in 1920, Angell Hall in 1922, and the Medical Building in 1925. As special favors, he also designed a dozen or more homes for prominent Detroiters.

One of these, in 1926, was the elegant English-cottage-style mansion of the Edsel B. Fords on Lakeshore Drive in the Detroit suburb of Grosse Pointe. For Alvin T. McCauley, president of Packard Motor Company, Kahn built a Cotswold-type home in Grosse Pointe. Kahn also designed the James Couzens home in suburban Bloomfield Hills in 1928. The Kahns themselves lived at 208 Mack Avenue in Detroit, but in 1917 they built an attractive summer home on Walnut Lake in the West Bloomfield district northwest of Detroit. Kahn's Detroit office was in his own New Center Building.

The Kahn-designed buildings in Detroit are too numerous to be completely listed here. Among them, however, are: the First National Bank Building, Detroit Free Press, Detroit News, Detroit Trust Company, Harper Hospital, Herman Kiefer Hospital, Woman's Hospital, Temple Beth El, Detroit Golf Club, Country Club of Detroit, and Detroit Athletic Club. "Uptown" Detroit is dominated by the magnificent Fisher Building on Grand Boulevard, and across from the Fisher are the mammoth General Motors Building and the New Center Building, all designed by Kahn with his associates.

In 1934, Kahn designed the Ford Exposition Buildings for the Chicago World's Fair, including the well-known Ford Rotunda. And in 1939, it was Kahn who designed the New York World's Fair Ford Pavilion.

Kahn working at his desk. (Photo courtesy of Lawrence Technological University, Southfield, Michigan.)

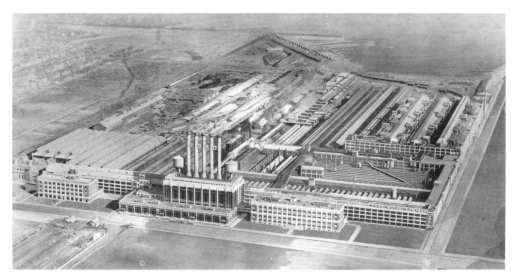

Aerial view of Ford Highland Park factory as planned by Kahn in 1910.
Photograph taken April 1923.

During World II, Albert Kahn, Inc., was employing 600 people. A sampling of their architectural projects includes plants for Curtis-Wright (St. Louis), Wright Aeronautical (Cincinnati), Dodge Aircraft (Chicago), Pratt-Whitney (Kansas City), American Locomotive Company (Auburn, N.Y.), Chrysler Tank Arsenal (Detroit), and Glenn Martin (Omaha). The 1942 Willow Run bomber plant for Ford Motor Company at Ypsilanti was one of the largest. In addition, Kahn designs were used in building naval bases in Alaska, Hawaii, Midway, and Puerto Rico, as well as at locations in the United States. It has been estimated that Kahn and associates were designing nearly 20 percent of the major industrial buildings in the United States.

Over the years, Kahn had been awarded such honors as an LLD degree from the University of Michigan (1933) and an honorary doctorate in fine arts from Syracuse University (1942); and from France, in 1937, he was awarded the Gold Medal at the Exposition of Arts and Sciences in Paris, as well as being made a chevalier of the Legion of Honor. In 1942, he was recipient of two awards from the American Institute of Architects.

Kahn was a member of the Detroit Arts Commission, the Fine Arts Society, the Arts and Crafts Society, the American Institute of Architects, and the National Building Code Committee of the U.S. Department of Commerce. He also belonged to the Bloomfield Hills Country Club, the Franklin Hills Country Club, and the Scarab Club of Detroit.   143

It is believed that the stress of war work caused Kahn's death in late

1942. He had been confined for several weeks with an illness that began as a cold and developed into a severe bronchial ailment, resulting in his death on December 8, 1942. He was seventy-three. A private funeral was conducted at his home. He was survived by his wife, Ernestine; two brothers, Louis and Felix; and four children, Lydia, Edgar, Ruth, and Rosalie.

Kahn left an architectural organization of superb reputation in very capable hands. Many additional major buildings continued to be designed for Ford Motor Company in various localities in the United States and Canada. The close partnership between Albert Kahn Associates of Detroit and Ford Motor Company of Dearborn continues until today.

Kahn's personal 3,000-volume architectural history library, together with the original bookcases, walnut paneling, and heavy doors,

The Kahn-designed home of the Edsel Fords, built in the late 1920s on Lakeshore Drive in Grosse Pointe, a Detroit suburb.

The Ford Rotunda designed by Kahn for the Chicago World's Fair in 1934.
After the fair, it was moved to Dearborn as a welcoming center for visitors to
the Rouge plant.

was donated in February 1983 to Lawrence Technological University,
where it now serves the school's architecture students and the public.

Major References

Albert Kahn Associates, Inc., Detroit.

"Albert Kahn Library Reveals Volumes about the Architect." *Detroit Free Press,*
    February 22, 1983.

Ferry, W. Hawkins. *The Legacy of Albert Kahn.* Detroit: Detroit Institute of
    Arts, 1970.

Lewis, David L. "Ford and Kahn." *Michigan History,* September–October
    1980.

————. "Kahn's Library Opened." *Car and Parts,* October 1983.

Who's Who in America. Chicago: A. N. Marquis, 1934–1935.

Ernest Carlton Kanzler, 1892–1967.

Ernest Carlton Kanzler

1892–1967

"It had always been our policy at Ford for everyone to start at the bottom. Kanzler was one of the few exceptions, and largely for that reason, I think, Mr. Ford avoided him."
—Charles E. Sorensen*

A lawyer by education, Ernest Kanzler, a relative of Edsel Ford by marriage, was invited by Henry Ford to work at the Ford tractor plant. Although of substantial benefit to Ford Motor Company, Kanzler was too closely associated with Edsel to please Henry. Henry Ford has stated, "Both Edsel and Kanzler should have been bankers."

Ernest Carlton Kanzler was born May 29, 1892, the son of Dr. Karl and Mathilde Keller Kanzler, who were natives of Bavaria and of Baden, Germany, respectively. The father came to the United States in 1878, the mother having already reached this country.

Ernest was born in Saginaw, Michigan, attended public schools in that city, and enrolled at the University of Michigan, where he received a bachelor of arts degree in 1912. He then entered Harvard Law School and won his LLB degree in 1915. His first position as lawyer was in 1916 with the firm of Carpenter, Butzel, and Backus of Detroit.

On June 19, 1917, Kanzler married Josephine Hudson Clay of Detroit. She was the sister of Eleanor Hudson Clay, whom Edsel Ford had married in November of the previous year. The Kanzlers and the Edsel Fords were to remain close friends for the rest of their lives. Their two homes were near each other on Iroquois Avenue on Detroit's east side.

Henry Ford's first contact with Kanzler was at Fair Lane when the Kanzlers were guests. Kanzler's law firm had been hired by both John Dodge and the *Chicago Tribune* in legal cases against Ford. Kanzler was doing research on these cases detrimental to Ford. Ford, it seems, was able to persuade Kanzler to abandon the practice of law to join Charles Sorensen and himself in manufacturing Fordson tractors in Dearborn.

Under Sorensen, between 1916 and 1920, Kanzler handled scheduling of materials and shipment of tractors. He was able to save mil-

*From Charles E. Sorensen, *My Forty Years with Ford* (New York: W. W. Norton, 1956), p. 307.

147

lions of dollars by synchronizing the arrival of parts with assembly and shipment to keep inventories extremely low, production rapid and orderly. This "just-in-time" delivery of materials together with precise scheduling of work made the Henry Ford & Son Tractor Plant unusually efficient.

In 1920, when tractor operations were moved to the Rouge, Kanzler was made production manager of the Highland Park plant. During the economic depression of 1920 to 1921, Kanzler assisted in lowering the price of the Model T, minimizing inventory by shipping vehicles promptly to dealers, and obtaining payment in time to pay for the materials from which the same vehicles had been made. Transactions from beginning to end were completed within 60 to 90 days. Inventory float was cut by $40 million.

While working directly with Edsel Ford at Highland Park, Kanzler carried out a program of branch plant expansion. The previous work of William Knudsen had ended when Sorensen pushed Knudsen aside. The program under Kanzler (1921 to 1925) cost $125 million and resulted in thirty-one branch factories.

In 1921, Kanzler became a director of Ford Motor Company of Canada. Following, in 1923, he became second vice president of Ford Motor Company and its subsidiaries, vice president and director of Lincoln Motor Company, and director of the Detroit, Toledo, and Ironton Railroad.

During the years 1923 to 1925, when Kanzler managed manufacturing directly under Edsel Ford, Model T vehicle production rose to more than 2 million annually, with production costs and prices at their lowest ever. Edsel Ford was handling administration while Ernest Kanzler managed production scheduling. It was not until 1955 that Ford Motor Company again produced more than 2 million vehicles.

In 1923, Edsel Ford with Kanzler organized a national advertising program whereby a fee of three dollars per car was collected from each dealer. These advertisements were widely publicized but did not name individual dealers, merely urged, "See Your Nearest Ford Dealer." Kanzler inaugurated within the Ford Motor Company the well-known ten-day reports of dealer sales and stocks in order to anticipate dealer orders and schedule production accordingly. In April 1923, Kanzler convinced Henry Ford, who was not at all in favor of installment buying, to introduce the "Ford Weekly Purchase Plan." The plan required an enrollment fee of forty-five dollars, followed by weekly five dollar installments which, when they totaled the price of an automobile in about a year, permitted delivery of the vehicle. The plan worked to an extent but was abandoned when competing plans delivered the vehicle long before full payment was made.

148

When Model T sales began dropping in late 1925, Edsel Ford and

Kanzler were particularly disturbed. It was well recognized by nearly everyone that the Model T was becoming obsolete—but not by Henry Ford. Because Henry paid little attention to Edsel's advice and was planning eventually to utilize his revolutionary but as yet undeveloped X engine in his next car, there appeared to be no change forthcoming. It was Kanzler, risking his position, who laid the facts on the line in a letter to Henry Ford, pointing out the shortcomings of the Model T. The letter was dated January 26, 1926. Ford did not respond other than to order prices of the Model T again reduced. Kanzler was no longer treated with courtesy—more often with rudeness—by Ford, thus leaving him with no alternative but to resign from Ford Motor Company. This he did on July 26, 1926.

Kanzler was only thirty-four when he left Ford Motor Company as an employee. By October 1926, he was one of the incorporators of the Guardian Detroit Bank, having been a director of the Guardian Trust Company since its organization in June 1925. No longer with Ford, Kanzler was elected executive vice president of the Guardian Detroit Bank in 1927. Edsel Ford owned considerable stock in the Guardian Detroit Bank and may have been influential in Kanzler's rapid rise in that institution.

Early in 1928, Kanzler organized the Universal Credit Corporation, of which he was president, while continuing directorships in the Guardian institutions. As president of Universal Credit Corporation, Kanzler was again meeting with Ford officials to help them finance installment buying plans for Ford vehicles. The resulting UCC finance corporation was capitalized at $11.5 million with Ford Motor Company holding 7,501 shares, Guardian Detroit Company 5,000 shares, and Kanzler 2,499 shares as trustee. It was fully organized in March 1928, just in time to help sell the "new Ford" which Henry had been so reluctant to introduce.

Kanzler again became involved with the Fords in 1932, when he was chairman of the board of the Guardian Detroit Union Group and the nation was financially paralyzed by the Great Depression. In an effort to bolster the integrity of Detroit banks, Kanzler was able to borrow $15 million from the Federal Reconstruction Finance Corporation. But that was not enough. Efforts were then made to release a portion of the $32.5 million of Ford-held funds. Edsel Ford agreed to this, but Henry did not. Henry had no sympathy for bankers and publicly scathed bankers for their misuse of private funds. Financial catastrophe was avoided by the temporary closing of all Michigan banks by the governor in February 1933. Banking recovery began to take place in Detroit after General Motors invested large amounts in the National Bank of Detroit, and the Fords purchased controlling interest in Manufacturers National Bank with branches then in Highland Park and Dearborn.

Kanzler (second from left) with Edsel and Henry Ford and an unidentified man.

At this same time, Henry Ford realized he was in the banking business himself, with his majority shares in Universal Credit Corporation, and at that very awkward time he insisted Kanzler sell those shares for cash. Kanzler was able to negotiate their sale to Commercial Investment Trust (CIT) Corporation. Universal Credit continued to serve Ford dealers and customers with Henry Ford as manufacturer but not as banker.

When Edsel Ford's health was failing at the beginning of World War II, Henry was inclined to blame Edsel's living habits. The Edsel Fords, the Kanzlers, and other wealthy Grosse Pointers were not as conservative as Henry and Clara Ford in Dearborn. Henry, therefore had never favored Edsel's closeness to Kanzler. When Edsel Ford died in May 1943, Kanzler was heartbroken but vowed to help preserve Ford Motor Company in any way he could. Kanzler was then on the War Production Board in Washington. When, on May 27, Henry again as-

sumed the presidency of Ford Motor Company, Kanzler knew Harry
Bennett would now be in control. Kanzler, as well as the Edsel Ford
family, wanted Henry Ford II, age twenty-five, to obtain the presidency.
"Uncle Ernest" became an astute and mature adviser to Henry Ford II.

The postwar challenge required complete reorganization of Ford
Motor Company. From his experience in Washington, Kanzler had
knowledge of the capabilities of several Army Air Force officers Henry
Ford II had occasion to interview in 1945. Ten of these men were hired
as a group, six of whom later became vice presidents of Ford Motor
Company, and two became presidents. In January 1946, Kanzler sug-
gested Ernest R. Breech, then president of Bendix Aviation Corpora-
tion, as possible head of Ford Motor Company. Kanzler, along with
Henry Ford II and Clifford Longley, worked out the arrangement with
Ernest Breech.

The Kanzlers lived at 2501 Iroquois in Detroit until 1935, when they
moved to 241 Lakeshore Road, Grosse Pointe Farms. There were three
children in the family: Robert Hudson, born in 1931; Ernest Carlton,
Jr., born in 1933; and Katrina, born in 1935. The Kanzlers belonged to
many of Detroit's most prestigious social and civic organizations and
were major benefactors of Harper Hospital and the Detroit Museum of
Art. They were also members of the Kebo Valley Club of Bar Harbor,
Maine, and the Bath Club of Miami, Florida. Kanzler properties in
Maine and in Florida adjoined properties of the Edsel Fords.

Kanzler's wife, Josephine, died accidentally at Hobe Sound, Florida,
in 1954. The following year, Kanzler married Rosemarie Ravelli
Weicker, a Mexican citizen who lived in Switzerland. The Kanzlers had
a home in St. Moritz, where in February 1967 Ernest suffered a heart
attack and was hospitalized for one month. Kanzler died November 12,
1967, at age seventy-five, at their Lake Shore Road home in Grosse
Pointe Farms. Services were held in Christ Church, Grosse Pointe, followed by cremation.

Major References

Burton, C. M. and M. Agnes Burton. *History of Wayne County and City of
Detroit*. Detroit: S.J. Publishing, 1930.

Case, Herbert, Ed., *Who's Who in Michigan*. Munising, Mich. 1936.

"Ernest Kanzler, Fords' Aide, Dies." *New York Times,* November 12, 1967.

"Genealogy Chart of the Hudson Family." Accession 1716, Henry Ford Museum & Greenfield Village Archives.

Nevins, Allan, and Frank Ernest Hill. *Ford: Decline and Rebirth, 1933–1962.*
New York: Charles Scribner's Sons, 1963.

———. *Ford: Expansion and Challenge, 1915–1932.* New York: Charles
Scribner's Sons, 1957.

William S. Knudsen, 1879–1948. (Photo courtesy of General Motors Public Relations.)

William S. Knudsen

1879–1948

*"I think Mr. Ford had occasion to regret losing Knudsen. I
think Knudsen was a very capable man. I liked Knudsen.
He always got along with me, and I always got along with
him. Whenever I asked him to do anything, he was right
on the trigger that quick. He had the faculty of knowing
how to handle men."*
—Ernest G. Liebold.*

Ford's loss of William S. Knudsen in 1921 was his loss to
Chevrolet in the automotive business. During Knudsen's
ten years with Ford (1911–1921), Ford's production increased from 72,000 vehicles to 1,000,948. When he moved
to General Motors from Ford Motor Company, Knudsen
raised Chevrolet production from 75,700 in 1921 to
1,001,680 in 1927, considerably more than Ford production
for that year. From that time on, Chevrolet led Ford in most
years.

Signius Wilhelm Poul Knudsen was born March 25, 1879, in Copenhagen, Denmark. His father, Knud Peter Knudsen, had operated a cooperage, and his mother, Augusta Zellner Knudsen, was the daughter of
a carriage maker. His mother was his father's second wife. Signius was
the oldest of Augusta's five children: Signius, Obeline, Louise, Anna
and Elna. Knud Peter Knudsen had lost his cooperage business in the
panic of 1873 and was working as a customs inspector at the time of
Signius's birth.

Signius started public school at the age of six, attending school in
the mornings and working as a cartage boy for a glazer in the afternoons. He completed seven years of public school and two years of government school and graduated from the Government Technical School.
At age fifteen, he was apprenticed by his father to a wholesale hardware
dealer for four years. When he left, he was earning two dollars a week.
He then worked for a Copenhagen importer of bicycle parts and earned
twenty-five dollars a month.

* The oral reminis-
cences of Ernest G.
Liebold, general secre-
tary to Henry Ford.

153

At age twenty, Knudsen was rejected for service in the Danish navy because of his six-foot, two-inch height and 150-pound weight, but he was allowed an exit permit to come to the United States, where he intended to enlist as a machinist in the U.S. Navy. After landing in New York City in 1889, he obtained his first job, and his name was abruptly Americanized to William S. Knudsen. Although he had been taught a bit of German, French, and English in Denmark, his heavy Danish accent never completely disappeared.

In the fall of 1900, Knudsen was working as a boilermaker in the shops of the Erie Railroad at Salamanca, N.Y. Here, with a rough group of workers, the somewhat pugnacious Knudsen got into frequent fist-fights and became reconciled to the nickname of "Squarehead."

Semon Knudsen, an older half-brother, dealt in bicycles in Denmark. Semon wanted to do business with the John R. Keim Mills people in Buffalo and asked William if he would act as interpreter. William did so and was very impressed by the Buffalo bicycle manufacturers. He accepted a job in 1902; the pay was much less, but his technical training would be appreciated. He became acquainted with John R. Lee, general manager, and with William H. Smith, superintendent of the plant where 200 bicycles were being manufactured daily. Knudsen was soon in charge of the pedal department and producing a record 2,000 pedals a day. He was now called "Bill" and treated with respect; he became a substantial Buffalo resident and invited his sister, Louise, to come to the United States and keep house for him.

When the bicycle business became slack, the Keim factory with its 1,500 workers looked for other work. Early in 1906, Smith and Knudsen approached Henry Ford regarding a new "forming and drawing" method of producing axle housings for autos. Ford was impressed and ordered 50,000 axle housings and crankcase covers for his Model T, then in the design stage.

Knudsen became general superintendent of the Keim plant in 1908 at age twenty-nine. They were making mufflers, gasoline tanks, fenders, and other parts for the Model T. Knudsen bought an early Model T to study it. The car was delivered to the Keim plant, where it was carefully disassembled; each part was inspected and put back together before Knudsen attempted to drive the vehicle. This experience was worthwhile because Ford was to select the Keim organization to operate his first assembly plant outside Detroit. It was Knudsen who supervised the assembly operation. Ford had so much faith in the Keim organization that in January 1911, he arranged for the purchase of the plant and hired its executives. In 1913, the plant equipment and some sixty-two key men were moved to Ford's Highland Park site.

But not Knudsen. He had been hired along with the others by Ford, but on November 1, 1911, he had married Clara Elizabeth Euler, who was not inclined to move away from her family in Buffalo. Knudsen's job with Ford, however, was to establish other assembly plants similar to the one in Buffalo. So he would not be spending much time in Detroit anyway.

Knudsen's career with Ford is legendary. In the United States, fourteen Ford assembly plants were planned and built under Knudsen's direction. Later, three more were built in Europe. With Detroit's noted architect Albert Kahn, factory construction was revolutionized. Instead of constructing a building and then planning a production layout to fit into it, the Knudsen-Kahn system first planned the most efficient layout of equipment and then constructed the building around it.

Knudsen became a U.S. citizen in 1914 and was so pleased with his progress at Ford Motor Company that he insisted his family come to Detroit, where his $1,000-a-month salary and recent $5,000 bonus bought them a modest home near the Highland Park factory. In 1915, Knudsen was given charge of all thirty or so branch assembly plants and became production manager at Highland Park, the largest Ford plant at that time. His salary became $25,000 a year, with a bonus of 15 percent. He admitted that as production boss of the highly integrated work force at Highland Park, "I learned to shout 'Hurry up' in fifteen languages." But all in all, Knudsen was highly respected as a boss, and employees worked hard for "Big Bill." Without the production genius of Knudsen, the Model T could not have reached its phenomenal position in automotive history.

As production manager at Highland Park, Knudsen supervised the manufacture of Army ambulances, trucks, and aircraft motors during World War I. In early 1918, he was also in charge of producing the "Eagle boat," a submarine chaser designed by the Navy and manufactured at a new shipbuilding plant on the Rouge River in Dearborn. The $46-million contract called for the construction of 100 of these 200-ton vessels.

Late in 1919, while Knudsen was dismantling the Eagle boat equipment at the Rouge location, he had a confrontation with Charles Sorensen, who was to move his Fordson tractor operations onto the Rouge site. Knudsen was close to fisticuffs with the overbearing Sorensen. From then on, Knudsen found that Henry Ford was countermanding orders in favor of Sorensen. Knudsen could match Sorensen in capability but had little chance with Ford backing Sorensen as production chief. Knudsen left Ford Motor Company on April 1, 1921.

But Ford's treatment of Knudsen was to haunt Ford. Knudsen naturally remained interested in the automotive business and temporarily worked as general manager of Ireland & Matthews, Detroit manufacturers of a variety of products including automotive. Soon Knudsen, through his friend Charles S. Mott, arranged an interview with Alfred P. Sloan, Jr., and Knudsen became a consultant on the General Motors staff. He started work for General Motors on February 12, 1922. Within three weeks, the president of General Motors, Pierre S. DuPont, offered Knudsen the vice-presidency of the ailing Chevrolet division at $50,000 per year. Chevrolet was at that time doing very poorly, with Ford outselling it thirteen to one.

On January 15, 1924, Knudsen was elected vice president and a director of General Motors as well as president and general manager of Chevrolet. Chevrolet production under Knudsen overtook that of Ford by 1931. In 1933, Knudsen became executive vice president of General Motors in charge of all vehicle operations in the United States and Canada. In 1937, he succeeded Sloan as president, with personal income more than $500,000 a year.

In May 1940, President Roosevelt asked Knudsen to serve on a seven-man National Defense Advisory Committee as commissioner of industrial production at one dollar per year. Knudsen, being especially anxious to serve because of the Nazi invasion of Denmark, resigned his General Motors posts in September 1940. On the Defense Advisory Committee, which controlled contracts of $500,000 or more, Knudsen was responsible for Army ordnance, aircraft, and other "hard goods."

The Defense Advisory Committee's authority, however, was gradually weakened by political indecisions, inducing Knudsen to accept, in 1942, an Army commission of lieutenant general, acting as special agent for the under secretary of war. This assignment allowed him directly to expedite production at factory sites. In 1944, he became director of the Air Technical Command with responsibility for procurement and maintenance of all Army Air Force equipment. During his service for Washington, Knudsen was again involved with Henry Ford, Edsel Ford, and Sorensen on war contract work, but all were by then on friendly terms.

For his military service, Knudsen received the Distinguished Service Medal in 1944 and the Oak Leaf Cluster in 1945. He resigned from the Army on June 1, 1945. General Motors welcomed him back as a director, and he left for Europe to assess the damage to General Motors plants. On this tour, the king of Denmark presented him with the Grand Cross of Danneborg, Denmark's highest honor. Retirement at age sixty-five was mandatory at General Motors, but Knudsen remained on the board of General Motors and also became chairman of Hupp Corporation, a Detroit auto supplier.

When Knudsen started to work for Ford, he boarded at 122 Medbury
in Detroit. When the family came to Detroit in 1915, a home was pur-

Knudsen with Henry Ford at a banquet during World War II.

chased at 137 Moss Avenue, only three blocks from the Ford Highland Park factory. This was a very modest home on a pleasant street. In 1917, the family bought ten acres on Grosse Ile, an island in the Detroit River. On the property and overlooking the river was an 1850s house known as "Water's Edge." The house was restored and used by the Knudsens as a summer home.

It was not until 1925, when Knudsen was vice president of General Motors, that the family moved into a larger home at 1501 Balmoral Drive in Detroit, a location barely a mile farther north. This was where the family was living at the time of Knudsen's death in 1948. The locations and the unpretentiousness of their homes point to a very conservative life-style.

Knudsen was devoted to his family and to the Lutheran church. He donated generously to the church, providing funds to build two fine edifices in the city. There were four children: Semon Emil, Clara Au-   157

Knudsen (with medals) following World War II, talking with Henry Ford II and Benson Ford.

gusta, Elna Louise, and Martha Ellen. The son, Semon, a graduate of the Massachusetts Institute of Technology, became well known as a General Motors executive and later as president of Ford Motor Company. Knudsen died on April 27, 1948, at age sixty-nine of a cerebral hemorrhage. Burial was in Acacia Park Cemetery in Detroit.

Major References

Beasley, Norman. *Knudsen.* New York: McGraw Book Company, 1947.
"Knudsen, William S." *Who's Who in America,* Vol. 2. Chicago: A. N. Marquis, 1950.

Nevins, Allan. *Ford: The Times, the Man, the Company.* New York: Charles Scribner's Sons, 1954.

Nevins, Allan, and Frank Ernest Hill. *Ford: Expansion and Challenge, 1915–1932.* New York: Charles Scribner's Sons, 1957.

"William S. Knudsen" (a biography). General Motors Corporation, Public Relations, Detroit, March 1951.

William S. Knudsen

Raymond Hendry Laird, 1898–1968. (Photo courtesy of Ralph Laird.)

Raymond Hendry Laird

1898–1968

*"You know, I used to thresh for his grandfather. I would
like to see him get ahead."*
—Henry Ford *

Quite a few relatives of Henry Ford obtained work at Ford
Motor Company, but it was not a result of Henry's encouragement. Henry's advice was to go into business for
themselves. This his two brothers did. Despite the good advice, several of Ford's relatives obtained common factory
work by getting a note from John N. Ford addressed to
Charles Sorensen. Raymond Laird, a son-in-law of John N.
Ford, had no trouble getting that starting job, but it took
years of night school study to work his way up to the responsible position of director of commercial engineering, the
highest position among the Ford relatives, and high enough
to be considered that of a lieutenant.

Raymond Hendry Laird was born December 1, 1898, son of James
King Laird and Margaret Hendry Laird of 476 Twelfth Street in Detroit.
His father was secretary-treasurer of the David Scott Flour Milling
Company, a position he held for forty years. His father's parents had
come from Edinburgh, Scotland. His mother was the daughter of Mr.
and Mrs. Albert Hendry, substantial farmers living six miles west of
Detroit. Raymond had one sister, Elizabeth, who died of tuberculosis at
age twenty, when Raymond was about ten years old.

Raymond spent summer vacations at his grandfather Hendry's farm,
which was in the neighborhood of several farms belonging to Ford
families. Directly across the road was the family of John N. Ford, who
had children near Raymond's age. Earl Ford, who was of the same age,
became Raymond's best friend for life. Another John N. Ford child,
Emma, eventually became Raymond's wife.

* From the oral remi-
niscences of Eugene
Farkas, recalling a
statement made to
him by Henry Ford.

161

Raymond attended public schools in Detroit, including Central High School, and came within only one semester of graduating. In 1916, at age seventeen, he obtained a summer job at the Henry Ford & Son Tractor Plant in Dearborn. He was hired by William Ford, brother of Henry Ford, to work in the tin shop at twenty-eight cents an hour, $13.44 a week—such high wages that he continued work that fall rather than return to school.

In June 1918, he obtained a leave from the tractor plant to help his uncle, Edward Hendry, on his eighty-acre farm. Hendry was not at all well, and his nephew did all the heavy work. World War I was raging in Europe, and as soon as the farm work permitted in September, Laird enlisted in the Army. He went through basic training at Raleigh, North Carolina, and was on a troop ship in New York Harbor, ready to leave for Europe, when the war ended. He was mustered out at Camp Custer in January 1919.

Laird went back to the tractor plant to work on lathes and grinders making piston rings, valves, and crankshafts. In 1919, he enrolled in night classes at the Detroit Institute of Technology. There, for twenty years as a part-time student, Laird studied engineering subjects—drafting, mathematics, physics, chemistry, metallurgy—gradually accumulating a sound background in mechanical engineering. With some knowledge of drafting, Laird left the machine shop to work in the blueprint department handling engineering drawings. Next, in 1920, he managed to transfer to Engine Engineering under Eugene Farkas.

According to the Farkas reminiscences, it wasn't long before Henry Ford asked about Laird. Farkas immediately assigned Laird to the design work on the wire wheels that would appear on the 1926 Model T.

Nearby, in the same tractor building, was Emma G. Ford, Earl Ford's sister, working on the *Dearborn Independent,* a weekly newspaper published by Henry Ford. At times, Emma and Raymond would have lunch together outside the tractor building. They had known each other for almost twenty years. On June 8, 1922, they were married. He was twenty-four, and she was twenty. Henry Ford had known Emma Ford better than Raymond Laird. After the wedding, Ford told Emma, "Tell that young man of yours to stick it out. I have plans for him."

Laird was to be assigned a great many confidential tasks. Some of these commissions involved business to which even his wife was not privy. But one assignment on which both Lairds worked together was construction of the Ford family tree. This project, begun in 1924, required collection of genealogical information concerning approximately 600 members of the Ford family. Family members in the United States and also in Ireland were questioned regarding themselves, their ancestors, and their children. Some 210 sheets of information were collected and organized into three large looseleaf notebooks. These volumes are now in the Archives of Henry Ford Museum & Greenfield Village. The Lairds nearly wore out two Model T Fords and wrote hundreds of letters in obtaining a rather complete compilation of data prior to the year 1926.

On April 29, 1924, the Lairds lost their first child, three-day-old James Edward Laird. Henry Ford visited them in their sorrow. At the Ford Cemetery, Ford asked Laird to compile a record of all the plots and graves. These records are also in the Ford Archives. Some graves were moved to keep them within cemetery boundaries. Henry Ford was then taking care of the cemetery. He wrongly assumed he owned it because he had purchased the surrounding farmland. Henry and Clara Ford are now buried in this one-acre cemetery on Joy Road near Greenfield in Detroit. This cemetery is now in the custody of the Episcopal church. The Raymond Lairds were to have two more sons: John Raymond and Ralph Ford Laird.

Laird was one of several people to whom Ford gave personal instructions almost daily. One year, Ford gave him responsibility for the Fordson tractor exhibit at the Michigan State Fair. Another time, Laird made drawings for a clock having all wooden works as a present for Edsel Ford. In December 1930, Laird, with Emil Zoerlein, was asked to build a one-tenth-scale working model of the first Ford car for the Ford grandchildren. In the Menlo Park Machine Shop in Greenfield Village, the miniature car was finished at 2:00 A.M. Christmas morning.

At the Engineering Laboratory, where he had his office, Laird testified, "If I got to work at 8:00 A.M., the watchman would say, 'The boss was here fifteen minutes ago and left.' When I came in at 7:00 A.M., he had come in earlier. I finally started at 6:30 A.M. Then I'd leave at 3:30 P.M.— The watchman's story was, 'The boss came in after you left.'" At the Fair Lane residence of the Henry Fords, where Laird sometimes worked, Ford would appear at the drafting board before breakfast expecting Laird to be already at work.

From 1928 to 1932, Laird provided drawings for Ford's first V-8 engine. Hundreds of drawings were necessary, including many design changes before production. Much of the experimental design work was done secretly in the Menlo Park Machine Shop. Later, the smaller sixty-horsepower V-8 engine was designed by Laird and Farkas. Between 1936 and 1940, Laird designed and supervised testing of the first Ford in-line six-cylinder production engine.

Emma Ford Laird and Raymond Laird, wedding photo in June 1922.
(Photo courtesy of Ralph Laird.)

The Ford Motor Company accepted several World War II defense contracts in 1940. One of these called for building several thousand Pratt-Whitney-designed, eighteen-cylinder rotary engines to be used on bombers. The hundreds of detailed drawings furnished by Pratt-Whitney needed rigid interpretation preparatory to production. Laird was assigned as liaison officer between Ford Motor Company and Pratt-Whitney, and between Ford and the government, which inspected all

Raymond Hendry
Laird

Laird (facing camera) at retirement party May 18, 1949.

Ford production. Laird made many trips to the Pratt-Whitney plant in East Hartford, Connecticut, and to Washington.

Later, Laird was called to the Willow Run bomber plant in Ypsilanti to assist superintendent Mead Bricker with manufacturing problems. Laird's contribution there was in developing spot-welding procedures to be used in place of riveting for joining aluminum panels on many of the subassemblies. These applications were saving more than 70,000 man-hours per month during a period when bombers were being built at a rate of 405 per month.

Following the war, Laird returned to the Engineering Laboratory at Dearborn, where he was appointed director of engineering for Ford commercial engines. In this position, he was responsible for the engineering of truck, tractor, bus, stationary, and marine engines. It is significant that of the numerous relatives of Henry Ford, Laird advanced to the highest position within Ford Motor Company—with the exception, of course, of Edsel Ford. Henry Ford was known to be decidedly against nepotism within the company. He usually advised his relatives to go into business for themselves.

Laird was director of commercial engineering in April 1947, when Henry Ford died. To Laird an era had ended. New and more cumbersome management procedures were making it more difficult for him to effect engineering changes within a reasonable time. Changes previously adopted within days were now requiring weeks or even months. Laird decided he would retire from Ford Motor Company on June 1, 1949.

Upon his retirement, the Lairds left Dearborn, at 5519 Maple Avenue, to live at their summer residence on Torch Lake near Elk Rapids. There, Laird was active in the Elk Rapids Masonic Lodge and served as president of the Elk Rapids Rotary Club. He was a member of the Consistory of the Knight Templars, the Shrine, and the Eastern Star. In retirement, he also found time to write poetry.

In December 1967, at age sixty-five, Emma Ford Laird died in Punta Gorda, Florida. Less than a year later, on August 29, 1968, Laird passed away at age sixty-nine. Both are buried in the Ford Cemetery on Joy Road near Greenfield Road in Detroit.

Major References

Bryan, Ford R. *The Fords of Dearborn.* Detroit: Wayne State University Press, 1987.

Farkas, Eugene. Reminiscences. Accession 65, Henry Ford Museum & Greenfield Village Archives.

Henry Ford Office. Accession 23, Boxes 27–31, Henry Ford Museum & Greenfield Village Archives.

Laird, Raymond H. "I Worked for Mr. Ford." *Dearborn Historian,* Vol. 10, no. 1, Winter 1970.

Nevins, Allan. *Ford: The Times, the Man, the Company.* New York: Charles Scribner's Sons, 1954.

Ralph Laird Papers. Accession 1635, Henry Ford Museum & Greenfield Village Archives.

Ernest Gustav Liebold, 1884–1956.

Ernest Gustav Liebold

1884–1956

*"All Mr. Ford had to say to Liebold was, 'Do this, do that,'
and he'd carry out the most ambitious projects. He had a
great deal of ability and was very thorough."
—Irving R. Bacon**

With power of attorney for both Henry and Clara Ford, Ernest G. Liebold handled practically all Ford business other than that of Ford Motor Company—and it was a tremendous amount. Without bothering Henry Ford, Liebold settled the bills, answered business inquiries, and managed personal projects large and small. Liebold's name or initials are on hundreds of documents pertaining to the great multitude of personal enterprises in which the Fords engaged.

Ernest Gustav Liebold was born in Detroit on March 16, 1884. He attended public schools through Detroit's Eastern High School before graduating from Gutchess College, where he majored in business studies including shorthand and bookkeeping. Immediately after graduating, he accepted temporary positions until he was hired by Peninsula Savings Bank in Highland Park, a suburb of Detroit. Beginning as a messenger at twenty dollars a month, Liebold progressed to bookkeeper and assistant teller. In 1910, he is listed in the *Detroit City Directory* as a teller, Peninsula Savings Bank, with residence at 49 Pasadena Avenue, Highland Park. On March 17, 1910, he married Clara Reich. He had begun by this time to prepare important legal documents for the bank, and handled a $3.4-million transaction involving W. C. Durant and the Cadillac Motor Company.

During Liebold's tenure at Peninsula Savings Bank, his capabilities had attracted the attention of James Couzens, general manager of Ford Motor Company. Couzens was planning a bank near the Highland Park manufacturing plant to handle the Ford payroll and otherwise serve employees. Couzens offered Liebold the position of cashier of the pro-

* From the oral reminiscences of Irving R. Bacon.

169

posed new bank. Liebold accepted the offer and took charge of organizing the bank. He was given ten shares of bank stock, appointed to the bank's board of directors, and made president of Highland Park State Bank.

Liebold's next assignment came from Henry Ford himself. In Dearborn was the D. P. Lapham Bank, a private bank Ford had reason to believe was insolvent. Ford wanted to save this bank in his hometown. Liebold was sent to examine the Lapham Bank in February 1911. Ford bought the Lapham Bank and had it organized by Liebold as the Dearborn State Bank. In managing the Dearborn bank, where Ford had a private account, Liebold was receiving Ford's personal bills and was expected to handle their payment. This led to his answering more and more of Ford's personal business correspondence, until by 1913 Liebold is listed in the *Detroit City Directory* as a secretary, residing at 94 Rhode Island Avenue, Highland Park. Although Liebold's office at the time was at Ford Motor Company in Highland Park, he was paid directly from Henry Ford's account in Dearborn, not by Ford Motor Company. It is quite possible Liebold made out his own paycheck. Ford had sufficient trust in Liebold's integrity to offer him the power of attorney for both himself and Clara Ford on July 13, 1918. This power was used many times in behalf of the Fords during the next twenty-six years.

Liebold regularly participated in conferences as Ford's representative. He accompanied Ford when dealing with the U.S. Shipping Board in 1917, regarding the building of ships for the Navy during World War I. Liebold is said to have convinced the board that submarine chasers would be more valuable than building additional cargo ships only to be sunk. He apparently selected the name "Eagle" for the chasers subsequently built by Ford. When Ford's World War I "Peace Ship" efforts in conjunction with the Neutral Conference for Continuous Mediation were stalled because of Ford's premature return from Norway, Ford designated Liebold as overseer of the project and its termination at the Hague.

Liebold, "with a mind like a balance sheet," became not only Ford's executive secretary and business representative but also accountant and financial manager of the multitude of personal projects conceived by Henry Ford—in fact, nearly all of Ford's business outside Ford Motor Company. A list of all these diverse activities would more than fill this page.

One project of consequence was the Henry Ford Hospital. It had been planned as Detroit General Hospital by a group of influential Detroiters with Ford as a major contributor. But the way the project was developing did not satisfy Ford, so he ceased contributing; without his support, the building program was stalled. Ford offered to pay back the other contributors and build the hospital himself, telling Liebold to go ahead with the whole thing. After previous contributors were repaid, Liebold hired architects and contractors, managed completion of the building, hired doctors, and instituted several innovative features not only in the building structure but in the hospital's operation. Built with 486 private rooms, the institution operated as a "closed hospital" with salaried doctors, charging patients low fixed fees not related to patient income. This procedure greatly disturbed the American Medical Society at that time, but it was Ford's preference.

Another business in which Liebold was involved was the *Dearborn Independent*. Henry, Edsel, and Clara Ford were officers of the Dearborn Publishing Company in 1919 when the *Independent* was first produced by Ford. Liebold was general manager with an office in Dearborn. The weekly paper reached a circulation rate of 900,000 in 1925–1926. But after the paper experienced trouble because of its anti-Semitic articles, Edsel and Clara Ford withdrew as officers of Dearborn Publishing Company. Henry Ford remained president, and Liebold became vice president and treasurer. Liebold is said to have reviewed and approved the content of the *Independent* along with William Cameron, the editor. Liebold, being German, was accused of fostering the anti-Semitic attitude of the paper, but many were convinced Ford not only condoned but encouraged the Jewish attacks. After losing a lawsuit in July 1927, the *Dearborn Independent* was discontinued with the December 1927 issue.

Many of the enterprises assumed to be those of Ford Motor Company were in reality personal projects of Henry Ford and his family. One of these was the Detroit, Toledo, and Ironton Railroad, purchased in 1920, of which Henry Ford was president and Liebold was vice president and financial manager. Ford was, of course, the boss, but he depended on others, especially Liebold, to carry out his business wishes. Liebold saw that the railroad made a profit. Although very few private projects that Ford initiated were self-supporting, those managed by Liebold nearly always were. Many of the means of making the DT&I more efficient were devised by Liebold. The road was sold in 1929, with a profit of $9 million.

Another Ford venture, organized and managed by Liebold as president, was the Dearborn Realty and Construction Company, established in the spring of 1919. The major purpose of the company was to furnish housing for employees of Henry Ford & Son Tractor Plant. Dearborn Realty and Construction Company operated until 1943 under Liebold's direction, building about 250 houses in Dearborn and tackling such varied undertakings as a huge grain elevator and mill and a deck house for one of Ford's yachts. These building ventures, under Liebold, closed with a healthy balance of $600,000.

Speaking of yachts, in 1917, Liebold handled the purchase and operating expenses of Ford's first and largest yacht, *Sialia,* instructing the master in regard to the size of crew he needed, the wages to be paid, and prices for individual supply items. Liebold was Ford's official penny pincher, and Ford apparently appreciated the service. After 1923, when Ford's new Engineering Laboratory was built in Dearborn, Liebold occupied an office very close to Ford's on "Mahogany Row."

A number of Ford's friends living in the village of Dearborn expressed an interest in having a golf course in the village. Although Ford did not play golf, he agreed that a well-designed course, open to the public, would be beneficial to the community. It would serve as a gesture of friendship for old acquaintances. The project became Liebold's responsibility. Ford donated 160 acres of land and $250,000 for a clubhouse. On recommendation of Edsel Ford, Liebold engaged Donald Ross of Pinehurst, North Carolina, to lay out the course and commissioned Albert Kahn to design the clubhouse.

With about 100 members, many of them Ford Motor Company executives, a Dearborn Country Club corporation was formed, and the course opened for play in April 1925. A board of governors handled routine operations under Liebold's directions. Ford, however, set general policies which included such rules as prohibiting smoking and drinking—impossible for Liebold to enforce strictly. But compromises were reached, and it helped that the Fords themselves did not use the club a great deal. Ford owned and Liebold managed the Dearborn Country Club until 1944, when the club was transferred to a Ford subsidiary, Seaboard Properties Company, from which the membership took steps to purchase the property in 1951.

The stressful banking situation of 1932–1933 was too much for Liebold. He disappeared from his office for several days without notice to ponder the situation. There was no suspicion of his having been guilty of any wrongdoing whatsoever, but when he returned, because of his short absence, he had lost some credibility among his associates, including Ford. The incident gave Harry Bennett and Bennett's friend Frank Campsall a chance to move closer to Ford. Bennett became an intimate adviser of sorts, and Campsall became Henry and Clara Ford's personal secretary. Together, the two took over much of Liebold's responsibility. Between 1933 and 1944, when he left Ford, Liebold played a less important role in behalf of the Ford family. It was Bennett who

Liebold family, Clara Liebold standing, Ernest Liebold holding baby. Photo
taken in 1923.

had been most envious of Liebold's position, and it was Bennett who
engineered Liebold's retirement at age sixty in 1944.

Liebold had very few intimate friends at Ford Motor Company. He
was obviously well known but was strict and impersonal in his dealings
both inside and outside the company. In answering a complaint regarding Liebold's obstinacy, Ford once replied, "When you have a watchdog,
you don't hire him to like everybody that comes to the gate." Liebold
admitted in his reminiscences that he did not encourage close friendship within the company, preferring to work for Ford as an indepen-

dent without cronies. Liebold is said to have operated like a business machine.

After retirement, with their children grown, the Liebolds moved from their large Boston Boulevard home in Detroit to one at 1050 North Oxford Road in Grosse Pointe Woods. There, Liebold died on March 4, 1956, leaving his wife and eight children, Marian, Ernest, Nelson, Russell, Kathleen, Ruth, William, and Robert. He was buried in the Lutheran cemetery.

Major References

Bryan, Ford R. *Beyond the Model T: The Other Ventures of Henry Ford.* Detroit: Wayne State University Press, 1990.

Lewis, David L. *The Public Image of Henry Ford.* Detroit: Wayne State University Press, 1976.

Liebold, Ernest G. Reminiscences. Accession 65, Henry Ford Museum & Greenfield Village Archives.

Nevins, Allan. *Ford: The Times, the man, the company.* New York: Charles Scribner's Sons, 1954.

Nevins, Allan, and Frank Ernest Hill. *Ford: Decline and Rebirth, 1933–1962.* New York: Charles Scribner's Sons, 1963.

———. *Ford: Expansion and Challenge, 1915–1932.* New York: Charles Scribner's Sons, 1957.

Clifford Boles Longley, 1888–1954.

Clifford Boles Longley

1888–1954

*"Edsel Ford thought that if his father were to die, most of
the Ford fortune would pass to the government. He wanted
to follow Longley's advice to have Mr. Ford's will changed
with most of the property put in escrow."*
—Harry Bennett*

Clifford B. Longley worked as attorney on the majority of important legal cases involving Henry Ford and
the Ford Motor Company. First as a company employee
and later with his own legal firm, he represented both the
Henry Ford and Edsel Ford families. The law establishment
founded by Longley is today a prominent Michigan legal
institution.

Clifford Boles Longley was born in Chicago on November 25, 1888.
He was the son of William Hey Longley and Isabelle Maud Smoot Longley. The father was an executive of the American Playing Card Company. There were nine children in the family, of which all graduated
from college—seven with degrees in engineering or law.

Clifford attended public schools in Chicago, followed by graduation
from Lewis Institute in 1907. In 1913, he received the LLB degree from
the University of Michigan and was admitted to the Michigan Bar.

Longley's first legal position was with Choate, Robertson, and Lehman of Detroit. He roomed at 34 Davenport and worked with this firm,
located in the Dime Bank Building, for four years. He married Harriet
Lawrence of Cleveland on September 16, 1916. They moved into a
home at 1507 Second Avenue and were to have two children: James
Lawrence and Mary Frances. Between 1917 and 1919, Longley was associated with Ward N. Choate in the practice of law.

In 1919, Longley joined the legal department of Ford Motor Company and became legal counsel for the company from 1921 to 1929.
One of Longley's first assignments with Ford concerned establishing
the recapitalized Ford Motor Company as a Delaware corporation in

* From Harry Bennett,
*We Never Called Him
Henry* (New York:
Fawcett Publications,
1951), p. 87.

June 1920. This was a period of great business activity on the part of Henry Ford, who had bought out his minor stockholders and could push forward the vertical integration of his business. Longley became involved in such ventures as the purchase and operation of the DT&I Railroad, of which he was a director, the purchase of extensive lumber and iron ore properties in the Upper Peninsula of Michigan, coal-mining properties in West Virginia and Kentucky, as well as the acquisition of the Lincoln Motor Company by Ford in 1922.

Of the many legal actions settled from 1921 to 1929, the highly publicized *Aaron Sapiro* and *Herman Bernstein* cases were most prominent. These cases resulted from derogatory articles printed in the *Dearborn Independent,* a weekly newspaper published by the Dearborn Publishing Company which was owned by Henry Ford. From 1925 to 1927, Longley was secretary of the *Independent* and active in the defense of Henry Ford.

With several lawyers as assistants, Longley's everyday responsibilities included the legal aspects of contracts with dealers, the adjustment of patent or trademark infringements, personal injury cases against the company, miscellaneous property transactions for both Henry and Edsel Ford, the devising of investment programs for employees, and the interpretation of domestic and foreign government standards and regulations applying to the automotive industry.

In 1924, Longley's home office staff at Highland Park consisted, besides himself, of J. M. Cahill, E. L. Davis, G. W. Flowers, R. E. Hefelich, T. J. Hughes, E. E. Juntunen, E. J. Matz, W. R. Middleton, and A. O'Reilly. Additional lawyers worked under Longley's direction in other parts of the country as warranted on local cases. DeLancy Nicoll, head of the firm Nicoll, Anable, Fuller, and Sullivan in New York seemed to be almost constantly involved in Ford Motor Company cases in that city. Foreign lawyers were needed, for example, in the establishment of Ford Motor Company of Brazil in 1923. Longley's assistant, Wallace Middleton, in a jovial note to Longley, who was then out of town, wrote: "When do you expect to return home? We have a few more hundred thousand matters requiring someone's attention."

While on the staff of Ford Motor Company, Longley is listed in the *Detroit City Directory* between 1921 and 1927 as vice president of the Jervis B. Webb Company, living at 1624 Cedar Hill in nearby Royal Oak.

In 1929, Longley left the Ford Motor Company as an employee and went into private practice as a consultant to Ford Motor Company and to the Ford family. He also accepted the presidency of the Guardian Detroit Union Group under Ernest Kanzler as chairman. The Guardian Group consisted of a chain of financial institutions, including the

Guardian Trust Company, Guardian National Bank of Commerce, and

With Henry and Clara Ford at Fair Lane. Longley is at far right with dark suit.
(Photo courtesy of Elizabeth Longley Tice.)

Detroit Bankers Company. Edsel Ford and Ford Motor Company were major depositors in these institutions, and Edsel Ford was on the board of directors.

As the depression fell on the city of Detroit, the Guardian Group and the U.S. government expected the Fords and Ford Motor Company to come to the rescue of the Guardian Group. About $12 million of Ford holdings were subordinated as requested, but Henry Ford would go no further. As the Guardian Group collapsed in 1933, two new banks were organized in Detroit: the National Bank of Detroit under General Motors sponsorship and Manufacturers National Bank under Ford sponsorship. Longley became general counsel for Manufacturers National Bank. These are still major banking institutions in the Detroit metropolitan area. Through all this financial crisis, Longley was sufficiently 179

Longley, in center facing camera, meeting with the press following Henry Ford's death, April 7, 1947. (Photo courtesy of Elizabeth Longley Tice.)

adroit to be held in high regard by Edsel Ford in particular. Henry Ford had little love for banks or bankers either before or after the crash.

In 1931, Longley's legal firm became Longley, Bogle, and Middleton, with offices at 748 Buhl Building in Detroit. The Longleys were then living at 11 Tourraine, Grosse Pointe Park. During the depression years, Longley's law firm grew to Bodman, Longley, Bogle, Middleton, and Farley, and the Longley family made a series of domestic moves: to 440 University Place, Grosse Pointe; to 412 Grosse Pointe Boulevard; and finally to 24 Beverly Road, Grosse Pointe Farms.

As Edsel Ford's attorney, Longley played a major role in drafting wills for both Henry and Edsel Ford in February 1936. These wills provided for the formation of a Ford Foundation whereby 95 percent of the Ford stock held by the deceased would be given to the foundation without voting rights, and the remaining 5 percent of stock would be given to Ford heirs with retained voting rights. Thus, the bulk of stock dividends would be collectible by the foundation, but voting control of Ford Motor Company would remain in the Ford family. Although a seemingly drastic financial move, the alternative might have meant the family's losing control of Ford Motor Company to banking interests in order to satisfy the exorbitant inheritance taxes, likely more than $300 million. Edsel Ford served as first president of the Ford Foundation, with Longley, B. J. Craig, and Frank Campsall as members of the board of directors.

In 1946, at the time Henry Ford II was attempting to entice Ernest R. Breech to become president of Ford Motor Company, Longley, as Ford's attorney, together with Kanzler and William Gossett (associated with Bendix Corporation) worked out an agreement acceptable to both Ford and Breech.

After Henry Ford's death in 1947, Longley, as a member of Bodman, Longley, Bogle, Armstrong, and Dahling, assisted Clara Ford in legal matters. The sale of the Richmond Hill, Georgia, 70,000-acre plantation and Ford winter home was one of these items. After Clara Ford died in 1950, Longley's firm handled the case involving claims against Clara's estate by her brother Edgar LeRoy Bryant.

Longley never completely retired from legal work. He was active in the Citizen's Research Council of Michigan and in the United Foundation, and he became a leader in the formation of the Phoenix Memorial Project at the University of Michigan. The Phoenix project provided a source of basic research in the application of atomic energy to peacetime purposes.

Longley loved the state of Michigan and enjoyed traveling its length over and over. He was on an automobile tour of Michigan parks on July 15, 1954, when he was stricken by cerebral hemorrhage. He died within hours of his admission into Jennings Hospital of Detroit, an institution of which he was a trustee. Surviving were his wife, his two children, a sister, and five brothers. Burial was in Detroit's Woodlawn Cemetery.

Major References

Accession 75 (legal), Henry Ford Museum & Greenfield Village Archives.

Clifford B. Longley Papers. Accession 1740, Henry Ford Museum & Greenfield Village Archives.

Case, Herbert S., ed. *Who's Who in Michigan.* Munsing, Mich., 1936.

"Longley, Ex-Ford Aide, Dies." *Detroit News,* July 16, 1954.

Longley, James, and Elizabeth Longley Tice, son and granddaughter of Clifford B. Longley. Personal communication, 1991.

Nevins, Allan, and Frank Ernest Hill. *Ford: Decline and Rebirth, 1933–1962.* New York: Charles Scribner's Sons, 1963.

Benjamin Basil Lovett, 1876–1952.

Benjamin Basil Lovett

1876–1952

"However important Mr. Ford's role was in bringing back old-fashioned dancing, Mr. Lovett's part in the reemergence of the popularity of Early American dancing must not be underestimated."
—*Eva O'Neal Twork* *

Henry Ford enjoyed the old-fashioned dances of his youth and was convinced everyone, young and old, should likewise enjoy them. To accomplish this revival of old-fashioned dancing, Ford hired Benjamin B. Lovett to teach the calls and the steps. Ford furnished the musicians. For years in Dearborn, dancing quadrilles and cotillions at the monthly Ford parties became obligatory for anyone who expected to associate socially with Henry and Clara Ford.

Benjamin Basil Lovett was born in West Swanzey, New Hampshire, on February 2, 1876, the second eldest of nine children. His parents were Joseph L. Lovett and Florence McConlough Lovett. Soon after Benjamin was born, his parents moved to Ayer, Massachusetts, where Joseph Lovett worked in a shoe factory.

Beyond ordinary public school, Lovett was essentially self-educated. He enjoyed music, became an accomplished clarinet player, and spent his summers with a musical group at Martha's Vineyard. An incident that is said to have influenced his turn to dancing was the refusal of a pretty girl to attend a dance with him, telling him he was too clumsy on the dance floor. At that moment, he vowed he would learn to become an exceptionally fine dancer.

Lovett took dancing lessons, became an excellent dancer, and began to give lessons to others. On August 5, 1905, he married Charlotte L. Cooke, the twenty-five-year-old daughter of Charles and Adella Cooke of Alstead, New Hampshire. She was a secretary. The Lovetts would have no children.

As Lovett's dancing career flourished, his wife began to help him with his work. As a dancing team, they became well known in the Bos-

* From Eva O'Neal Twork, *Henry Ford and Benjamin B. Lovett: The Dancing Billionaire and the Dancing Master* (Detroit: Harlo Press, 1982), p. 262.

ton area and beyond. They conducted dancing schools in such Massachusetts cities as Worcester, Fitchburg, Maynard, Marlborough, and Hudson. Lovett became well enough known to become president of the International Association of Masters of Dancing. During World War I, he served in France as an entertainer with the YMCA.

In 1923, Lovett was teaching at Marlborough, Massachusetts, when Henry Ford was at nearby Sudbury visiting his Wayside Inn. Ford was restoring the inn with its large ballroom. Both Henry and Clara Ford, now middle-aged, were looking back to their youth and the old-fashioned dances they had enjoyed. They had heard of Lovett's outstanding reputation as a teacher. Ford invited Lovett to Wayside Inn to discuss the promotion of old-fashioned dancing, and Lovett was engaged by Ford to direct dances there.

The next year, Ford had induced the Lovetts to move to Dearborn, where they were to organize dancing programs for both adults and children. Ford and Lovett agreed that dancing lessons and dancing parties offered valuable social training as well as enjoyable recreation. The first dancing engagement conducted in Dearborn by Lovett was a Halloween party held in the barn of the 1860 Ford family homestead. Hosting dancing parties conducted by Lovett greatly enhanced the social life of the Fords. They had avoided modern social affairs with the attendant smoking, drinking, and sophisticated chatter. They felt old-fashioned dancing was more wholesome.

For three years, the Lovett address in Dearborn was 93 Lapham Street, until they bought a Ford-built home at 22525 Nona. Although the Lovetts were married in a New Hampshire Congregational church, in Dearborn they attended the Episcopal church to which the Fords belonged.

Lovett's office was near Ford's in the newly constructed Engineering Laboratory of Ford Motor Company. In this laboratory building, a large area was reserved as a dance floor. Here, with a small group of musicians playing such instruments as violin, dulcimer, cymbal, sousaphone, and accordion, and with Lovett as caller, friends of the Fords were invited to participate in evening dances. The Fords especially liked the quadrille, the waltz, schottische and varsovienne. Some of the men invited were Ford executives who were quite annoyed at being expected to attend. They had probably worked harder that day than Henry Ford had. With their jobs at stake, however, almost all did participate when asked.

Charles Sorensen, one of the few Ford executives who would not attend the dances, stated in his autobiography: "Lovett complained to me that Henry Ford never quite caught the rhythm of the dance music. The dance seemed mechanical to him. He had his choice of partners who could help him keep time, and when he had a partner who didn't

Benjamin and Charlotte Lovett dancing in the "Blue Room" of the
Engineering Laboratory about 1925.

dance better than he did, he soon got rid of her. It was Lovett's responsibility to rescue Ford from a clumsy dancer."

In 1925, old-fashioned dance classes were organized for Dearborn
schoolchildren. Some parents, however, considered dancing of any type
to be immoral and petitioned the school board to ban the classes. But
after Lovett demonstrated the dances to a citizens committee with a
group of talented dance couples, the classes were accepted by the board
of education. Lovett himself, of course, could not teach in all of the
Dearborn schools, but he trained gymnasium teachers who in turn
taught the children. Old-fashioned dancing became part of the school
physical education program.

Dance classes in the schools were very formal. Lovett was strict,
although at times he displayed a sense of humor. Participants in his
classes were to be well groomed and exceedingly courteous. Both Benjamin and Charlotte Lovett exemplified perfect deportment. In Dear-

185

Lovett, at left with baton, instructs a dancing class in Lovett Hall, April 1944.

born high schools, dancing became as important as football and included the same players. The dance classes were exercises in social training.

By 1928, Lovett had introduced dance classes in schools and colleges in at least ten states in the eastern United States. He traveled with the title Professor of Social Training. He was especially proud of his special classes for handicapped children—deaf, blind, or crippled. He was convinced that nearly half of the public schools in the United States with physical education programs were offering dancing classes. The public schools of Detroit had 100,000 children taking his classes. Lovett employed several assistant callers and groups of musicians to go to seventy or eighty schools a week to conduct dancing classes.

In order to standardize old-fashioned dancing in America, Lovett produced the book *Good Morning: After a Sleep of 25 Years, Old Fashioned Dancing Is Being Revived by Mr. and Mrs. Ford.* By 1929, Lovett's efforts in the revival of early dances were well recognized. This was the

186

year Henry Ford opened his Greenfield Village Schools in Dearborn and put Lovett in charge of them. Lovett headed the schools until 1937. Satellite schools at Sudbury, Massachusetts; Richmond Hill, Georgia; Belterra, Brazil; and several southeastern Michigan locations were also under Lovett's direction. It was not until the formation of the Edison Institute of Technology, with its need to be college accredited, that Lovett (who lacked recognized educational training) was replaced by Carl Hood.

As part of Ford's new education complex, a large recreation building was constructed in 1937, with the most elegant of Ford ballrooms. This was named Lovett Hall, and it still carries that name. Lovett was still head of the Department of Social Training and the Art of Dancing, and his wife was on the staff. Lovett was on Ford's personal payroll, receiving at least $10,000 a year.

After the death of his son, Edsel, in May 1943, Henry Ford had little inclination to dance. He suffered a stroke that year and at eighty was becoming quite frail. Lovett himself was sixty-seven and recognized the lack of support for his programs. The Lovetts had purchased a house at 145 Oak Street in Braintree, Massachusetts, in 1942 as a retirement place. They also had a summer cottage on Lake Millen in New Hampshire. The Lovett home in Dearborn was sold in December 1942, although the Lovetts did not formally leave Dearborn until July 1944.

Lovett, stricken by heart disease, died at South Shore Hospital in Weymouth, Massachusetts, on September 4, 1952, at age seventy-six. His ashes were buried at Forestville Cemetery at Hudson, Massachusetts, where he was living when Ford first met him. After his death, Charlotte Lovett went to live with her niece, Helen Holmes. Charlotte Lovett died April 14, 1956, also at age seventy-six.

Major References

"Ford Revives Dying Dances." *Detroit News,* August 2, 1925.

Lewis, David L. *The Public Image of Henry Ford.* Detroit: Wayne State University Press, 1976.

Lovett, Benjamin B. *Good Morning.* Dearborn, Mich.: Dearborn Publishing, 1926.

"Lovett Hall Opens with Old-Fashioned Dance Party." *Herald,* Vol. IV, no. 21, November 12, 1937.

Moreland, Faye Witt. *Green Fields and Fairer Lanes.* Tupelo, Miss.: Five Star Publishers, 1969.

Richards, William C. *The Last Billionaire.* New York: Charles Scribner's Sons, 1948.

Twork, Eva O'Neal. *Henry Ford and Benjamin B. Lovett: The Dancing Billionaire and the Dancing Master.* Detroit: Harlo Press, 1982.

Russell Hudson McCarroll, 1890–1948. (Photo courtesy of Charlotte M. Vincent.)

Russell Hudson McCarroll

1890–1948

*"The V-8 crankshaft started as a forging. Hud McCarroll
and I searched for a steel that could be cast and still meet
the physical requirements of crankshaft. Out of this came
the discovery that our cast steel was better crankshaft
material than any suitable forging bar."*
—*Charles E. Sorensen* *

Among the unsung heroes of Ford Motor Company was
R. Hudson (Hud) McCarroll. Automobiles are made
mostly of metal, and the quality of the metal largely deter-
mines the durability of the vehicle. McCarroll was nationally
recognized as an outstanding chemist and metallurgist, but
he was seldom featured in the popular press or noted on the
countless pages of Ford lore.

Russell Hudson McCarroll was born in Detroit on February 20,
1890, the son of Rev. Canon John McCarroll, M.D., and Emily Middleton Roberts. The father had graduated from McGill Medical School, but
after three years as professor of classical languages was ordained as an
Angelican clergyman.

The McCarrolls had come to Detroit in 1884 and resided on Washington Boulevard at Michigan Avenue. At the time of their son's birth
in 1890, their home was at 89 Hancock Avenue West.

Hudson, as he was called, first attended Miss Liggett's School and
later Detroit University School. He was a schoolmate of Edsel Ford at
both of these schools, and they became lifelong friends. During this
period, Henry and Clara Ford were living in Detroit, attending St.
Paul's Episcopal Church, where Dr. McCarroll was their clergyman.

McCarroll studied at the University of Michigan; in 1914, he received
the B.S. degree in chemical engineering. Right out of school, he took
a position with the Solvay Process Company on West Jefferson Avenue
in Detroit. This concern manufactured such chemicals as caustic soda,
soda ash, ammonia, coke, gas, tar, and calcium chloride. Within a few

* From Charles E.
Sorensen, *My Forty
Years with Ford* (New
York: W. W. Norton,
1956), p. 230.

189

months, Henry Ford persuaded young McCarroll to join Ford Motor Company. It was in January 1915 that McCarroll started work at the Highland Park plant. He is listed at that time in the *Detroit City Directory* as a clerk living at 691 John R Street, the same address as his father. McCarroll had one sister, Lyndon, who became assistant director of the Henry Ford Hospital Nursing School.

On September 30, 1916, McCarroll married Muriel C. Channer at Adrian, Michigan. They established their residence at 241 Elmhurst in Highland Park, where they lived until 1921, when they moved to Dearborn at 402 Nona Avenue. The Dearborn house was in a subdivision of houses that had been built by Henry Ford for his employees.

McCarroll's early tasks for Ford at Highland Park concerned problems related to car finishes, abrasives, water-soluble oils, and lubricants. He undoubtedly became acquainted with Charles E. Sorensen at that time, and later, when Sorensen took over management of the larger Rouge plant, McCarroll was asked to transfer to the Rouge to work under Sorensen. His initial chemical engineering responsibilities at the Rouge involved coke oven, blast furnace, and foundry operations. This was around 1920.

At the Rouge plant, McCarroll developed methods by which large amounts of the by-products ammonium sulphate and benzol could be produced from the coke ovens. Ford sold both of these items through his automobile dealers. Detroit area motorists not only could fill their gas tanks with "Ford Benzol," but they could buy a bag of inexpensive, nitrogen-rich "Ford Ammonium Sulphate" fertilizer for their gardens. Ford employees also could fill their basement bins with Ford coke at low prices.

In 1927, Ford had decided to try to produce rubber on a 2.5-million-acre plantation in Brazil. At one of the regular noon executive "roundtable" luncheons in Dearborn attended by McCarroll, Ford mentioned the need for one of them to go to Sumatra in the Dutch East Indies to examine methods of rubber production there. He directed the group, "Well, you think it over who should go, and after you get it all decided, if you don't pick the man I do, I'll tell you who we will send." Ford had already decided on McCarroll. McCarroll did go to Sumatra for Ford in January 1928. His wife and their two daughters, Charlotte and Marjorie, accompanied him on what became a glorious around-the-world trip. He returned with considerable useful information, presented a comprehensive written report, but said privately he hoped he would not be sent to Brazil. Because of family considerations, he never went to Brazil.

The chemistry of iron and steel became a specialty of McCarroll's.
The blast furnaces being located adjacent to the production foundry

made it possible to chemically tailor pig iron for the needs of the foundry. The chemical composition of cast iron became more controllable. McCarroll's central laboratory at Rouge Gate 4 analyzed both blast furnace and foundry specimens with speed and accuracy not before achieved. Sorensen, who wanted to cast all of the automotive parts he could, had a very helpful partner in McCarroll.

By 1925, McCarroll was known as Ford's chief chemist and found himself in charge of all Ford chemical and metallurgical research and control activities. McCarroll had responsibility for all Ford testing laboratories. In the Detroit area alone, there were at one time twenty-nine laboratories, many equipped with X-ray, metallographic, spectrochemical, and physical testing facilities as well as customary "wet" chemical analysis. With these facilities available, McCarroll and his assistants were able to develop special alloys of iron and steel. Chemical correlations between the properties of iron and steel were investigated in detail. McCarroll was becoming widely recognized as a metallurgical authority.

McCarroll was very modest and did not claim credit for himself. He was quoted as saying, "In our type of work, one must first have a plan, then a staff, and then an organization such as that in the Ford Motor Company to attain any worthwhile improvements in industrial engineering. We not only have as fine a staff as is available, but we also have an enthusiastic and cooperative manufacturing division." McCarroll, operating on that basis, had the whole Rouge plant as his experimental laboratory. Occasionally, a production manager would consider a McCarroll project a temporary hindrance to production, but any improvement produced by the experiment was readily accepted. McCarroll obtained some fifty patents, which were, of course, turned over to Ford Motor Company. In 1931, the McCarrolls built a fine new home at 205 River Lane in Dearborn.

In addition to metallurgical research, McCarroll directed work leading to improved procedures for organic products such as artificial leather. He was also deeply engaged in the utilization of farm crops in industrial products—an obsession on the part of Henry Ford. In 1935, it was McCarroll who represented Ford Motor Company as he addressed the First Dearborn Conference of the National Farm Chemurgic Conference. In his speech, McCarroll divulged the huge quantities of farm crops used in building Ford automobiles—cotton, wool, vegetable oils, and particularly soybeans. Ford Motor Company's well-known soybean paints were developed under McCarroll's direction. John Lansford McCloud became the paint expert under McCarroll.

McCarroll was well known in professional circles, especially among metallurgists. He was active in the American Society for Metals, the

McCarroll (left) with Henry Ford and Fred Black at the opening of the Ford buildings at the Chicago World's Fair in May 1934. McCarroll was in charge of chemical and metallurgical exhibits. (Photo courtesy of Charlotte M. Vincent.)

American Foundryman's Association, the Society of Automotive Engineers, the American Chemical Society, and others. And although Ford was not particularly receptive to college-trained employees, he seems to have highly respected McCaroll's capabilities. McCarroll held his position without question throughout the years, surviving the purges engendered by Sorensen and Harry Bennett. In 1937, McCarroll was granted an honorary degree of master of science by his alma mater, the University of Michigan.

Quite late in life, Ford was convinced that sugar was harmful to people because of the very sharp corners on sugar crystals. One of the first expensive electron microscopes in this country was purchased by Ford to study sugar crystals. McCarroll tried to convince Ford that the

Celebrating the 25-millionth Ford at the Rotunda in Dearborn on January 18, 1937. From left: Charles E. Sorenson, Edsel Ford, Henry Ford, Peter E. Martin, William Cameron, and McCarroll.

crystals dissolved harmlessly without damaging the digestive tract. Ford had spent millions for his Henry Ford Hospital with its excellent staff, but he did not trust his medical doctors to know everything.

At the beginning of World War II, McCarroll accompanied Edsel Ford, Sorensen, and Albert M. Wibel on their visit to East Hartford, Connecticut, to study the adaptability of the Pratt-Whitney aircraft engine to mass production. On the basis of their findings, the War Department was notified that Ford was ready to produce. Ford Motor Company received an immediate $14-million allotment for a special plant to produce the engines. A total of 57,851 of these eighteen-cylinder radial engines were made. McCarroll was responsible for all of the required laboratory tests to be conducted by Ford on military contracts during the war.

Henry Ford II, in taking over Ford Motor Company, gathered together a "temporary team," appointing McCarroll in charge of all engineering. The first of a series of General Planning Committee meetings convened on October 3, 1945, with McCarroll in attendance to discuss company problems. On July 17, 1947, McCarroll was appointed director of chemical and metallurgical engineering and research. When Harold T. Youngren, a prestigious mechanical research engineer, agreed to join Ford Motor Company on August 1, 1947, Henry Ford II reorganized engineering, reappointing McCarroll as director of chemical and metallurgical engineering.

For recreation, McCarroll favored fishing and small game hunting. On March 27, 1948, while returning from a northern Michigan fishing trip with a friend who worked for Bethlehem Steel Company, McCarroll was stricken by brain hemorrhage. He was on the road near Bay City and was taken to Bay City Mercy Hospital, where he died on March 31, 1948. Funeral services were held at Christ Episcopal Church in Dearborn, with hundreds of friends and employees in attendance. Burial was in Woodmere Cemetery, Detroit. McCarroll was survived by his widow, Muriel, his sister, Lyndon McCarroll, and his two daughters, Charlotte Vincent and Marjorie McCarroll.

Major References

Lindbergh, Charles A. *The Wartime Journals of Charles A. Lindbergh.* New York: Harcourt Brace, 1970.

"McCarroll, Ford Executive, to Be Buried Saturday." *Dearborn Independent,* April 1, 1948.

McCloud, J. L. Reminiscences. Accession 65, Henry Ford Museum & Greenfield Village Archives.

Nevins, Allan, and Frank Ernest Hill. *Ford: Decline and Rebirth, 1933–1962.* New York: Charles Scribner's Sons, 1963.

Patton, Walter G. "Assembly Line." *Iron Age,* April 15, 1948.

"Russell Hudson McCarroll—Metallurgical Engineer in the Automotive Business." *Metal Progress,* September 1947.

Roy Donaldson McClure, 1882–1951. (Photo courtesy of Henry Ford Hospital Archives.)

Roy Donaldson McClure

1882–1951

*"Dr. McClure went to Fair Lane every day to give Henry a
checkup. Much to his indignation, Mr. Ford summoned his
chiropractor, Dr. Coulter, for treatments."*
—*Charles E. Sorensen* *

The name McClure has been prominently associated with
Henry Ford Hospital for seventy-five years. Roy D. Mc-
Clure was the hospital's first chief surgeon and Henry Ford's
favorite physician. Today, his son Douglas T. McClure is
chairman of the board of trustees of Henry Ford Health System, with its thirty-three outpatient centers throughout
southeastern Michigan.

Roy Donaldson McClure was born January 17, 1882, in the little
village of Bellebrook, Ohio. His father, James Albert McClure, was a
medical doctor, as were his grandfather and great-grandfather. His
great-grandfather had practiced medicine from horseback. His mother
was Ina Hester Donaldson McClure. He graduated from North High
School in Columbus, Ohio, in 1900. In 1904, he graduated from Ohio
State University, where he was captain of the basketball team, manager
of the football team, and classmate of Charles F. Kettering, the famous
General Motors inventor. McClure next attended Johns Hopkins University in Baltimore, where he received his M.D. degree in 1908, and
he became house surgeon of New York Hospital from 1909 to 1912.
Then he returned to Johns Hopkins for three more years.

Meanwhile, in Detroit, plans were being made for a new Detroit
General Hospital. An association had been formed of which Henry Ford
was treasurer as well as a major financial donor. When progress on the
hospital began faltering in 1914, Ford reimbursed the other donors and
took over the completion of the hospital. The hospital became the
property of Henry Ford and became known as Henry Ford Hospital.

Ford had definite ideas about the operation of a hospital. He had
visited the renowned Mayo Clinic in Rochester, Minnesota, and had in

*From Charles E.
Sorensen, *My Forty
Years with Ford* (New
York: W. W. Norton,
1956), p. 266.

mind similar services for the average working man. Cost to the patient was to be uniformly moderate, and everyone should pay. The doctors would be paid an adequate salary by the hospital and would be solely responsible to the hospital and its patients and not be involved in private practice. So Henry Ford Hospital, from the start, became a "closed" hospital and still operates as such. Newspapers exaggerated, however, in stating the new hospital would have 1,000 private rooms and would charge two dollars a day for room, board, and nurse attendant.

To staff the hospital in 1915, Ford assigned Ernest Liebold as general manager. He chose a Detroit doctor, Frank N. Sladen, as chief of medicine. Sladen had once operated on Clara Ford, and the two couples were good friends. Sladen was a graduate of Johns Hopkins University and had remained on its medical staff until 1913, so Sladen and McClure had been acquaintances. In 1916, McClure was invited to become chief of surgery at Henry Ford Hospital. Dr. James E. Mead of the Highland Park Ford factory was to head the hospital dietary unit, where he would teach people how to eat properly. (Ford's statement was, "People consume three times too much food.") So under a board of trustees consisting of Henry and Clara Ford and Edsel and Eleanor Ford, the three men—Liebold, Sladen, and McClure—initially controlled Henry Ford Hospital. Liebold had other important assignments for Ford and was soon replaced by Dr. J. N. E. Brown as superintendent of the hospital.

Sladen and McClure were both highly regarded by Ford. McClure was somewhat Ford's favorite as a friend. Perhaps McClure more closely represented an old-fashioned country doctor in his mannerisms. For years, McClure had a standing luncheon appointment with Ford.

The opening of Henry Ford Hospital took place in October 1915, but it was hardly an occasion to be celebrated. The first occupants of the hospital were around one hundred derelicts, alcoholics, and drug addicts. Emergency cots, bedding, clothing, and food were hastily supplied. Detroit's city lodging houses and missions had been overtaxed. And Ford realized he was considerably responsible for the problem. He had offered such high factory wages that people were induced to come from far and wide to obtain employment. There was insufficient work for all, and many of these people were not capable of employment. This problem belonged to Ford as well as the city of Detroit. The hospital supplied medical treatment for about 600 men, and in all, some 3,685 homeless were given shelter. A few were given jobs, and some were given railroad fare home.

To prevent the spread of vermin, the men were first bathed, and their clothing was put into a large steam cabinet. The outcome nearly caused a riot when the men found their wool clothing shrunken to a ridiculously small size. Liebold, to the rescue, ordered new, relatively inexpensive clothing to be furnished to all. The purpose of the hospital was beginning to be assumed as exclusively for Ford Motor Company employees, alcoholics, and dope addicts.

During this hectic period, on March 4, 1916, McClure married Helen Keene Troxell, a Baltimore nurse. They were to have three children: Mary Keene, Roy Donald, and Douglas Templeton McClure. Their first home was at 528 St. Paul Avenue in Detroit. About five years later, they would be living in their permanent Detroit home at 3031 Iroquois in the Indian Village district.

In October 1918, the Henry Ford Hospital was turned over to the government to serve World War I veterans. McClure, along with others on the staff, became an army medical officer. As a major, he served in France as commanding officer of Evacuation Hospital No. 33 of the American Expedition Forces. Other doctors serving at the hospital in Detroit during this period included members of the Ford Motor Company Highland Park factory hospital, a group of nine working under the direction of Mead.

McClure was to spend thirty-five years as a respected surgeon and loyal supporter of Henry Ford Hospital. McClure's close friendship with Ford generated considerable financial support for many programs at the hospital. Advances included an outstanding school for nurses which incorporated a luxurious home for the students, an internship training program for house physicians, and adequate salaries for all members of the staff. Medical research and participation in medical conferences were enthusiastically encouraged. Ford was much more liberal with his physicians in this regard than he was with his engineers at Ford Motor Company.

There were many instances when Ford sent people to his hospital at his own expense. Hundreds of schoolchildren were given physical examinations and corrective treatment when necessary. McClure performed surgery on many patients sent to the hospital by Ford, from as far away as Richmond Hill, Georgia, and Michigan's Upper Peninsula. If an operation would benefit a worker or a member of a worker's family, Ford was inclined to offer assistance. These favors were commonplace in many remote communities where Ford operated manufacturing plants or farms.

Archaeology was one of McClure's hobbies. In 1930, he joined a party of Ohio State alumni on a cruise to the Galapagos Islands in the South Pacific, hosted by Kettering, McClure's 1904 classmate. Kettering's yacht, the *Olive K.*, provided accommodations. In 1932, a similar party visited Chichen Itza in the Yucatan of Mexico. Following each trip, McClure described their adventures in the *Ohio State University*

199

Monthly. McClure and Kettering also worked together on medical research projects. One of these developments was a device for measuring the oxygen content of blood, a photoelectric oxy-hemograph.

In November 1932, Ford himself, at age sixty-nine, was stricken suddenly with a pain in his right groin, and McClure went to Ford's home to diagnose the illness. The condition was a strangulated hernia which required immediate surgery. During surgery, it was found that an appendectomy was also needed.

All went well until, following the surgery, Ford would not stay in bed. The very next day, he was up, sat in a chair, and insisted on walking to the lavatory. Doctors feared for Ford's life and the likely necessity of another operation to correct the damage caused by his unorthodox behavior. But Ford was ready to go home in one week, and to everyone's amazement he remained cured. Ford's operation and his unusually rapid recovery were widely publicized.

McClure, center with ball, captain of the Ohio State basketball team in 1904. (Photo courtesy of Henry Ford Hospital Archives.)

McClure is at far right in this photograph taken in Washington, D.C., in 1923. Ford was discussing the purchase of Muscle Shoals with Secretary of War John W. Weeks (center). Far left is William B. Mayo.

During his long tenure at Henry Ford Hospital, McClure became well known and respected in medical circles. He wrote at least 112 technical papers, many in the fields of thyroid, breast, stomach, and gall bladder surgery. One of his contributions involved radioactive iodine in establishing the usefulness of iodized salt for the prevention of goiter.

He was chosen president of the Ohio State University Association in 1925 and president of the Detroit Academy of Surgery in 1929. He became a fellow and later a member of the board of governors of the American College of Surgeons. He lectured in postgraduate medicine at the University of Michigan and served on the editorial boards of the *American Journal of Surgery* and *Annals of Surgery*. McClure was a member of the International Surgical Society, often traveling to Europe. Perhaps his most satisfying position was as regional representative on admissions to Johns Hopkins University.

McClure was, of course, well known locally, as a member of the American Medical Society, the fraternal organizations of Phi Beta Kappa and Sigma Xi, the Presbyterian church, and the Republican Club

At the twenty-fifth anniversary of the Henry Ford Hospital School of Nursing and Hygiene. From left: Elizabeth S. Moran, director, School of Nursing; Benson Ford; Mrs. Frank Sladen; McClure; Clara Ford; Dr. Frank Sladen; Eleanor Ford. (Photo courtesy of Henry Ford Hospital Archives.)

of Michigan. Although he had very little spare time, he and his family were members of the Grosse Pointe Country Club, the Indian Village Club, and the Dearborn Country Club.

McClure had been plagued by coronary heart disease for many years, having experienced seven separate attacks of thrombosis. But he worked until the day of his death, which was at home on March 31, 1951. The *Detroit News,* in its front-page headline, simply stated, "Dr. McClure Dead." Readers immediately recognized the name. Funeral services were held on April 1 at the Jefferson Avenue Presbyterian Church, with burial in White Chapel Memorial Cemetery. Left were his wife, Helen, his sons, Roy and Douglas, and daughter, Mary Stearns. He was also survived by two sisters and a brother.

Major References

Case, Herbert S., ed. *Who's Who In Michigan,* Munising, Mich., 1936.

Greenleaf, William. *From These Beginnings.* Detroit: Wayne State University Press, 1964.

Lam, Conrad R. "Roy D. McClure, 1882–1951." *Transactions of the American Surgical Association* 69 (1951).

Liebold, Ernest G. *Reminiscences.* Accession 65, Henry Ford Museum & Greenfield Village Archives.

Zuidema, Dr. George D. "The Henry Ford–Johns Hopkins Connection." Speech delivered June 21, 1986, St. Regis Hotel, Detroit. Manuscript on file at Sladen Library, Henry Ford Hospital, Detroit.

Roy Donaldson
McClure

Samuel Simpson Marquis, 1866–1948. (Photo courtesy of the Cranbrook Archives.)

Samuel Simpson Marquis

1866–1948

*"Mr. Ford went into Dr. Marquis's office and said, 'Come
on, Dr. Marquis, let's go down to the hospital and lay
the cornerstone.'"*
—Ernest G. Liebold*

Although nominally an Episcopalian, Henry Ford was perhaps basically an agnostic. He apparently placed some credence in reincarnation. For respectability, he attended church and built seven edifices of an interdenominational character. The one man most closely allied with Ford in a religious capacity was the Reverend Samuel S. Marquis.

Samuel Simpson Marquis was born in Sharon, Ohio, on June 8, 1866. He was the son of John E. and Sarah P. Marquis. There had been generations of Episcopalian ministers in the Marquis family, and as Samuel himself confided, "They say that when I was born, my aunt looked at me and said to my mother, 'This is the homeliest baby I ever saw,' to which my mother replied, 'All right, then, he shall be the minister.'" After a public school education, he was sent to Allegheny College in Pennsylvania to pursue ecclesiastical studies. He was expelled twice, "during periods of intense doubt about religion," and later reinstated to graduate with a bachelor of arts degree and honors in 1890. He next attended Cambridge Theology School in Massachusetts, where he earned a bachelor of divinity degree in 1893.

Marquis married Gertrude Lee Snyder of Warren, Ohio, on August 23, 1894. After being rector of Trinity Church of Woburn, Massachusetts, from 1893 to 1897, and of Trinity Church in Bridgewater, Massachusetts, from 1897 to 1899, Marquis was transferred to Detroit as rector of St. Joseph's Church in 1901. With daughters, Dorothy, born in Woburn in 1895, and Barbara Lee, born in Bridgewater in 1897, they settled at 29 Lothrup Street in the St. Joseph area. In Detroit, a son, Rogers Israel, was born in 1901, and another daughter, Gertrude Lee,

*From the oral reminiscences of Ernest G. Liebold.

in 1907. Marquis's alma mater, Allegheny College, in 1905 awarded him a degree of doctor of divinity. On May 15, 1906, Marquis became dean of St. Paul's Cathedral in Detroit.

This was about the time Henry and Clara Ford, also Episcopalians, were to move into their new home at 66 Edison Avenue in Detroit. The Marquises called on them. Marquis was soliciting financial aid for the church. Clara Ford was particularly supportive of the Episcopal denomination. The couples became well acquainted and spent many evenings together. As a churchman, Marquis was especially interested in family economics and working conditions as well as church affairs. One of the major objectives of Marquis's ministry was a religion for the working man. This was a concept that appealed to the Fords.

As dean of the newly constructed St. Paul's, Marquis worked long and hard and was near the point of exhaustion in early 1915. When his doctor advised him to take a year's vacation, Marquis's reply was, "A change in work would be more beneficial to me than being idle." Marquis arranged to work with John R. Lee as a volunteer in the Ford Motor Company Sociological Department. Ford was elated and remarked, "I want you, Mark, to put Jesus Christ in my factory."

One of Marquis's earliest assignments was administered by Clara Ford. During late November 1915, Henry Ford had become convinced he might be able to stop World War I by joining leading pacifists and social evangelists to lead a peace mission to support the cause of "mediation." One of Ford's expressions at that time was, "Men sitting around a table, not men dying in a trench, will finally settle the differences."

Ford chartered a ship and was planning to lead the expedition to Europe, but Clara Ford and Marquis did not think Henry himself should go. Until the final hour of departure, Clara Ford and Marquis tried to convince Ford that the trip was ill advised. When Ford, insisted on going to the very last, Clara Ford appealed to Marquis to accompany and protect her husband on the trip.

Many on the ship were of questionable character. There were about eighty peace delegates, twenty-five students, thirty-five journalists, and at least two photographers. The entrances to Ford's suite on the ship were through either the cabin of Raymond Dahlinger or that of Marquis. After a trip of two weeks, the Ford peace party reached Oslo with its December temperature of twelve degrees below zero. Ford had contracted a cold and stayed in his hotel room, making no public appearances or public peace pronouncements.

Because Ford's health did not improve and the illness could easily develop into pneumonia, Marquis had little difficulty convincing him that he should return to Dearborn. Marquis devised a plan to whisk

Ford away secretly by train to Bergen, Norway, where a ship was scheduled to sail for New York. Marquis successfully spirited Ford away from
his persistent adherents, but it was no easy accomplishment.

In 1913, when Ford had instituted the Sociological Department at
his Highland Park plant to promote the welfare of his employees, he
put John R. Lee in charge of the new department. Marquis's description
of Lee: "He is a man of ideas and ideals. He has a keen sense of justice
and a sympathy with men in trouble that leads to an understanding of
their problems. He has an unbounded faith in men, particularly in the
'down and outs,' without which no man can do constructive work. Under his guidance the department put a soul into the company." Ford's
Sociological Department, where Marquis was working, became most
conspicuous in 1914 after the five-dollar-per-day wage was announced.
To be eligible for this high pay—this $10-million employee profit-
sharing plan—the employee "must show himself sober, saving, steady,
industrious and must satisfy the superintendent and staff that his
money will not be wasted in riotous living." It was the responsibility of
the Sociological Department to prove to management that each employee either did or did not meet the prescribed requirements. Marquis
was working with Lee at this time and helped organize the investigative
program. At its peak, the department was utilizing as many as 160 men,
with about half performing investigative work.

The Sociological Department was given wide authority over pay in-
creases and discharges. The rule: "No man was to be discharged until
every possible effort had been made, and every means exhausted, toward lifting him up to the requirements of the Company, and to the
equal of his fellow men." Many new Ford employees were immigrants,
speaking no English, making no attempt to budget income. Some lived
in tents. Through interpreters when necessary, employees were offered
free legal services, real estate appraisals, investment advice, and
English-language lessons when necessary. A plant hospital with X-ray
facilities, surgical operating room, and medical laboratory was established under Dr. J. E. Mead. Special attention was given to finding jobs
for deaf, blind, and crippled applicants. Paroled criminals were placed
whenever possible because Ford firmly believed in rehabilitation. At
that time, more criminals were paroled to Marquis than to any other
person in Michigan. The world-renowned Henry Ford Trade School,
which provided a practical education for thousands of boys from needy
families, was initiated by the Sociological Department.

When Lee left Ford to go with C. Harold Wills to found the city of
Marysville, Michigan, and launch the Wills Sainte Claire automobile,
Marquis had become head of the Sociological Department. The depar-
ture of such men as Wills, Lee, and Clarence W. Avery signaled Ford's

Marquis (left) with Henry Ford on deck of the S.S. *Oscar II* en route to Norway in 1915.

declining interest in Highland Park operations. He was depending more on Sorensen and Bennett at the expanding Rouge complex. Marquis found it difficult to apply the policies established at Highland Park to Rouge operations under Sorensen. Sorensen had convinced Ford the Sociological Department seriously interfered with production. Sorensen was allowed to repeatedly countermand the decisions of Marquis. After stating to his family, "I don't know how long I can take it. I think I'll get out," Marquis resigned from Ford Motor Company on January 25, 1921.

Henry Ford and Marquis together about 1918.

All in all, the Ford sociological program, from 1913 to 1921, was beneficial and generally appreciated by employees. Although working at Ford was not easy, the great majority of employees were proud to have Ford jobs. Some were proud enough to wear their Ford badges to church on Sunday. Although Marquis did not consider his investigative program as prying, he did change the terms "investigator" to "adviser" and "Sociological Department" to "Education Department." He considered Ford's concept very idealistic. Today, the same program would be considered by many to be far too paternalistic.

Marquis was surprised and not at all satisfied with Henry Ford's decision to strip the Sociological Department of its strength. He returned to St. Joseph's Church, and in 1923 published the book *Henry Ford: An Interpretation,* an in-depth analysis of Ford's character. Marquis was bitter. Gertrude Marquis had insisted that some of the most critical 209 statements be omitted from the manuscript. Even so, statements in the book were not entirely complimentary; for example, "Men of great wealth and limited education readily overestimate their judgment on questions outside their proper sphere." When the Fords read the book, they attempted to limit its circulation but failed. Clara Ford was annoyed to the point of not speaking to either of Marquises again. Henry Ford, less disturbed, is said to have later visited Marquis when he was a hospital patient.

In May 1924, Marquis received a letter from George G. Booth regarding the intention of establishing a church and school in Bloomfield Hills, Michigan. Marquis helped in founding Christ Church in Cranbrook and was its first rector. In May 1925, the Marquis family moved from Detroit to Cranbrook and occupied the gardener's house until the church and rectory were built.

As rector of Christ Church, Marquis was considered a very liberal thinker, and some went so far as to classify him as a heretic. The church school was organized in 1931, and construction of the unusually elegant Christ Church began in 1938.

Gertrude Marquis was "entered to rest" on October 26, 1940. Samuel S. Marquis died in retirement on June 21, 1948.

Major References

Marquis, Samuel S. *Henry Ford: An Interpretation*. Boston: Little, Brown, 1923.

Marquis 1914–1923. Accession 293, Henry Ford Museum & Greenfield Village Archives.

Marquis 1915–1923. Accession 63, Henry Ford Museum & Greenfield Village Archives.

Nevins, Allan. *Ford: The Times, the Man, the Company*. New York: Charles Scribner's Sons, 1954.

Nevins, Allan, and Frank Ernest Hill. *Ford: Expansion and Challenge, 1915–1932*. New York: Charles Scribner's Sons, 1957.

"One Hundred Years 1824–1924." St. Paul's Cathedral, Detroit, Detroit Saturday Night Press, 1924.

Samuel S. Marquis Papers. Cranbrook Educational Community Archives, Bloomfield Hills, Mich.

Peter Edmund Martin, 1882–1944.

Peter Edmund Martin

1882–1944

*"Ed Martin and I worked together for thirty-two years with
no real break in our relations."*
—Charles E. Sorensen *

Peter Martin and Charles Sorensen went hand in hand as
top production bosses during the early years of Ford Motor Company. Both were considered hard as nails. Both were
greatly feared by Ford workers. Of the two, however, Martin
was less severe in his actions and less anxious, it seems, to
gain notoriety as top man in the factory. Henry Ford was
very satisfied with both.

Peter Edmund Martin was the son of Adolphe Martin, a French-
Canadian carpenter, and Eleonore Marchildon Martin, who had been
married in LaFontaine, Ontario, on June 12, 1881. Peter Martin was
born April 17, 1882, in Wallaceburg, Ontario.

He was the eldest in a family of four boys and three girls. The family
moved to Detroit before he was ten years old. At the age of twelve, after
only five years of schooling, but with broad shoulders and inventive
mind, he was handling a man's job in a Detroit box factory. From there,
he went to a can factory, where he operated a stamping machine.

Martin was then hired by C. Harold Wills of the Ford Motor Company, and began work at the Mack Avenue plant on December 15, 1903.
His job was in the "Experimental Room." On April 26, 1904, Martin
married Rose Louise Giroux of Detroit, and their home was listed as
452 Mullett Street.

In 1905, when Henry Ford moved his operations to the larger Piquette plant, Martin was put in charge of the Experimental Room on
the night shift. Then, in February 1906, he was made foreman of the
Ford Manufacturing Company, a parts manufacturing shop on Bellevue
Avenue in Detroit. By July of that same year, he was put in charge of
the Assembly Department of the Piquette plant. In October 1906, Martin was made assistant to Thomas Walburn, who was in charge of all

* From Charles E.
Sorensen, *My Forty
Years with Ford* (New
York: W. W. Norton,
1956), p. 50.

213

of the manufacturing plants of the company. Sorensen became his assistant.

It is obvious that Martin was a hard worker to have risen in rank so rapidly. It is said he was able to operate any machine under his supervision, and he is credited as an accomplished machine designer as well. In 1908, Martin's salary was approximately $2,300 per year, with a bonus of $170.

In 1908, at the Piquette plant, Martin, with the help of Sorensen, was responsible for the launching of the Model T. He had to physically reorganize the entire plant to handle the prodigious production required. The increased man-hours and consumer demand led to a strict discipline of the workers, often harsh treatment accompanied by very high turnover. Martin is said to have been a reasonable man, but his superintendents and foremen often played a rough game with the workers.

His respect for a man's labor led to Martin's being the only manager later permitted to enter the Rouge plant during a bitter strike. After the infamous "Battle of the Overpass" on May 26, 1937, Walter Reuther of the United Automobile Workers allowed Martin to retrieve personal papers he had left in his desk.

In December 1913, at the much larger Highland Park plant, the moving final assembly line reduced automotive assembly time from twelve hours per vehicle to approximately two hours. Martin along with Clarence W. Avery, Sorensen, Wills, and Ford share credit for this accomplishment. Martin also applied time and motion studies to Ford production operations. By 1913, reflecting the tremendous success of the Model T, his bonus alone was $18,000. The Martin family is listed in 1917 as living at 59 Trowbridge in Detroit, with Martin's occupation given as superintendent.

On January 3, 1919, only two days after Edsel Ford had become president of Ford Motor Company, Martin was appointed general superintendent of production. Six years later, on December 24, 1924, Martin was named first vice president in charge of manufacturing. This was a period during which Ford was producing record numbers of Model T's at the Highland Park plant, where Martin was headquartered. In addition to his regular salary as vice president, Martin received compensation equivalent to dividends paid to stockholders on 1,000 shares of Ford stock.

Martin's former assistant, Sorensen, had left Ford Motor Company in October 1915 to work for Henry Ford & Son building tractors in Dearborn. At that time, the Rouge factory was intended to become a huge tractor plant, and Sorensen meant to be in charge. As Martin's star was rising in Highland Park, so also was Sorensen's in Dearborn. During the mid-1920s, when Highland Park manufacturing was being

Martin and Henry Ford considering front-end structure of a new Ford V-8 in March 1932.

shifted to the Rouge, there was a serious conflict of authority developing between Martin and Sorensen. In 1926, Martin even offered to resign his position as vice president of manufacturing, "if it would result in better coordination of executives." But neither Henry nor Edsel Ford wanted to lose Martin. His resignation was not accepted.

Martin's not being power-hungry and Sorensen's knowing that Martin was there to stay allowed the two executives to share production responsibilities reasonably well at the Rouge. The quietly stern Martin and the unpredictably outspoken Sorensen were both feared by all but Henry Ford himself. In the plant, just the sight of either man sent shivers through the average worker and was likely to be a subject for discussion at the workers' supper table that evening. At work, Martin was described as hardboiled.

Martin's influence was less spectacular than Sorensen's. Martin

Luncheon "Roundtable" in Engineering Laboratory. From left, Edsel Ford, Henry Ford, Charles E. Sorensen, Martin, and Albert M. Wibel.

shunned the limelight, and his actions led to fewer dramatic episodes. Together, these two men must be credited with many Ford Motor Company production records—not without severe strain on the workers, however.

Around the company, Martin was called "Ed" or "Pete," but on company documents it was always "P. E. Martin." He was described as the "World's Apostle of the Conveyor." At the Rouge plant, there were eighty miles of conveyors. He spent most of his working day on the factory floor rather than in his office. Although Martin, in 1914, expressed the opinion that five dollars a day was too high a wage, he later was a good friend to the United Automobile Workers.

At home, he was a devoted husband and father. A devout Catholic, he lived by the rules and required the same of his family. They lived on Trowbridge Street while the children were small but in 1923 moved to a larger home at 1488 Chicago Boulevard as the children grew and Martin's salary increased. After he became vice president, their next address was 1411 Wellesley Drive in the prestigious Palmer Woods district. The Martins were large donors to many charitable causes.

The Martins had fourteen children, ten of whom grew to adulthood. Aunt Ida Giroux helped take care of them. They had a summer cottage on Pine Lake in Oakland County as early as 1915 and later a Chris-Craft boat equipped with, of course, a Ford V-8 engine. There was also a

216

larger craft on which the family sometimes crossed Lake St. Clair to visit relatives in Wallaceburg, Ontario. All of these relatives spoke French. The Martins could understand and speak the language to some extent—sufficient to carry on a conversation with each other yet avoid comprehension by the children.

Because many weekends were spent on the water, Ford wanted to put a radio phone on the boat for Martin to use. Martin explained that this was the only way he could get away from everything to spend time with his family and politely declined the gift.

In the late 1930s, Martin suffered a light heart attack, and on July 10, 1941, he reluctantly resigned as vice president and director of Ford Motor Company because of health. His resignation was accepted July 17, 1941. Martin died at his home on Wellesley Drive on October 8, 1944, at age sixty-two. He was survived by his wife, Rose Louise, and children Edmond, Harry, Norman, Hazel, Lucille, Marvin, Peter, James, Eleanor, and Mary, and mourned by many friends and business associates.

Major References

McLaughlin, Mary, daughter of Peter E. Martin. Personal communication, 1991.

Marvin Martin Papers. Accession 1146, Henry Ford Museum & Greenfield Village Archives.

Nevins, Allan. *Ford: The Times, the Man, the Company.* New York: Charles Scribner's Sons, 1954.

Nevins, Allan, and Frank Ernest Hill. *Ford: Expansion and Challenge, 1915–1932.* New York: Charles Scribner's Sons, 1957.

Wilke, David J. "Automotive Biographies—Peter E. Martin." *Cleveland Plain Dealer,* November 4, 1940.

William Benson Mayo, 1866–1944.

William Benson Mayo

1866–1944

"Mayo, I know, would do splendidly in setting up designs for the most efficient, up-to-date—even advanced—iron smelting plant."
—Charles E. Sorensen. *

When one sighted the monstrous automotive plants at Highland Park and on the River Rouge in Dearborn, the name "Ford" was emblazoned on the tall powerhouse stacks. In touring the plants, however, the names of the plant designers, Albert Kahn and William B. Mayo, were never mentioned. One of the nine giant steam-gas power generators from Highland Park is the largest single item on display in the Henry Ford Museum, but the name of Mayo, its designer, is not mentioned. Mayo was another of the many exceptionally talented men Henry Ford used to the utmost and then cast aside.

William Benson Mayo was born in Chatham, Massachusetts on January 7, 1860, the son of Andrew Benson and Amanda Nickerson Mayo. Chatham is on the southern tip of Cape Cod. At that time, the small town was made up largely of fishing folks and retired sea captains. William's father was a carpenter who supplemented his income by fishing.

William had two brothers and one sister. They attended public elementary school at Chatham, where William displayed some artistic talent and showed an interest in mechanical devices. Without resorting to higher formal education, despite the objections of his parents, he went to Boston, where he worked as an apprentice to an outdoor sign painter and soon became a partner in the business. But since he liked machinery, and since sign painting was not a year-round job, at age twenty-two he accepted a position as office boy with the Hooven-Owens-Rentschler Company, a manufacturer of Corliss steam engines.

These engines were sometimes huge machines, often used to pump

* From Charles E. Sorensen, *My Forty Years with Ford* (New York: W. W. Norton, 1956), p. 163.

219

water for municipal water systems. The company headquarters were in Hamilton, Ohio, with sales offices in major cities throughout the United States. Mayo soon became a junior salesman and worked his way to top salesman in the Boston office. At age thirty, he was offered a sales position in the New York office with a substantial pay increase. He had married Susan Harrall Dana of nearby Chelsea on January 8, 1891, and his wife was somewhat reluctant to move from their home in Everett, outside Boston. But Mayo accepted the new position and commuted from New York to Boston on weekends. With his success on the new assignment, the couple moved to New York, where they stayed for ten years, during which time they had three children, two sons and a daughter.

In 1906, Mayo was offered the position of secretary at the main office of Hooven-Owens-Rentschler in Hamilton. Again, his wife was reluctant to move, this time to the Midwest, which was even farther from the Boston area where her family resided. But Mayo could be a very persuasive man, and they did move to Hamilton, where Mayo became general manager and later vice president of the company.

As vice president of Hooven-Owens-Rentschler, Mayo handled the largest machinery orders. In 1913, the company was approached by Ford Motor Company to make proposals on the largest steam-gas power generators Mayo had ever considered. They were for Henry Ford's Highland Park automobile plant north of Detroit. There were at least five companies competing for the massive project. Negotiations with Ford lasted for more than a year, during which Mayo and Ford became well acquainted. Ford became very trustful of Mayo and not only bought the Hooven-Owens-Rentschler equipment but hired Mayo away from his employer of twenty-five years. Mayo became Ford's chief power engineer. The two men were both middle-aged and had both risen to their positions through self-education.

Installation of the nine huge "Gasteam" units at Highland Park required almost two years. One of these monsters is now in the Henry Ford Museum, where the three-story engine is the largest exhibit on display.

The next large Ford project was at the Rouge site in Dearborn, where in 1917 Mayo was given charge of planning and construction of this world-famous industrial complex, an effort requiring several years of utmost concentration. Directly under Mayo were at least 250 assistants in departments of architectural engineering, mechanical engineering, powerhouse design, and general construction. Mayo's son, Dana, a recent graduate of the University of Michigan's College of Engineering, also worked for his father. Mayo made the choices when selecting spe-

cialized engineering firms for design of blast furnaces, coke ovens,

Evaluating property in the West Virginia coal region about 1923. From left, Wallace R. Middleton, E. G. Kingsford, native guide, Clifford B. Longley, Mayo (with shovel), native, Abner Lunsford.

coal, ore, and limestone handling equipment—even ships to carry the raw materials.

In 1916, the Dodge brothers, who were stockholders of Ford Motor Company, had tried to stop Ford from building the Rouge plant. It is said to have been Mayo who suggested the Fords buy out their minor stockholders, including the Dodge brothers. And it was through Mayo's connections with eastern banks such as Old Colony in Everett, Massachusetts, that the Fords were able to secretly obtain all the stock by July 1919. When the several purchases were completed, it was Mayo who broke the news to Ford.

Ford did not hesitate to call on Mayo for a variety of assignments where utmost confidentiality was required or where either steam or water power was involved. For example, in 1917, when Ford wanted to explore iron ore deposits in Cuba, Mayo was asked to find a yacht for the trip. Mayo enjoyed the search and found the yacht *Sialia* on which they both made the Cuban excursion and which for years remained Ford's private yacht. In 1920, Mayo was on the *Sialia* with Henry and   221

From left: Mayo, William B. Stout, Edsel Ford, and Henry Ford beside all-metal airplane in April 1925.

Edsel Ford to decide on waterpower possibilities for a large lumber mill at Iron Mountain, Michigan.

When Ford wanted to assess the feasibility of power plants on the Hudson River at Green Island, New York, or on the Mississippi at Minneapolis-St. Paul, it was Mayo he consulted. When Ford was interested in acquiring Muscle Shoals for the manufacture of fertilizers for farmers and aluminum metal for automobile bodies, it was Mayo who handled negotiations in Washington. In 1922, Mayo was one of the chief negotiators in the purchase of the bankrupt Lincoln Motor Company from the Lelands. Mayo's tact is thought to have somewhat counterbalanced Charles E. Sorensen's lack of tact in this touchy situation.

Both Mayo and Edsel Ford had been active members of the Detroit Aviation Society, so when Henry Ford became interested in dirigibles in 1919, Mayo was selected to represent him in Washington, propos-

Edsel Ford, Henry Ford, and Mayo about 1927.

ing to build zeppelins in Detroit for the U.S. government. The government was not interested, but thereafter Mayo was Ford's chief aircraft engineer.

Mayo, Edsel Ford, and William B. Stout, an aircraft designer, were stockholders in the fledgling Aircraft Development Corporation of Detroit. Mayo and Edsel Ford were instrumental in arranging for Stout to join the Fords in manufacturing an all-metal monoplane. Ford Motor Company then organized an Airplane Division, of which Mayo was head.

The Aircraft Division, eventually with 1,600 employees under Mayo, developed, built, and sold the famous Ford trimotor planes. Under Mayo's direction, several pioneering aspects of commercial aviation were initiated: a privately operated major airport open to any class of aircraft, either civilian or military; a radio beacon system; regularly scheduled mail routes; passenger and freight service; the first airport hotel; and a privately operated mooring mast to accommodate dirigibles of as much as 10 million cubic feet capacity.   223

After January 1919, when Edsel Ford was appointed president of Ford Motor Company and Henry Ford took leave of the office, Mayo became Edsel's chief consultant. They had been close friends for several years—Mayo was perhaps Edsel's most trusted employee. (It is possible that Edsel's second son, born in July 1919, was named Benson after Mayo.) Edsel Ford promoted the Aircraft Division, and aeronautics in general, much more than Henry Ford and some of his followers did. Thus, in his work as head of the Aircraft Division, Mayo was serving Edsel Ford more than Henry Ford.

The Aircraft Division flourished from 1926 until 1932; 1929 was the best year, with eighty-six planes manufactured and sold. But several factors induced Mayo to leave Ford Motor Company in August 1932. Among them was the fact that Ford Motor Company was no longer expanding, and Mayo was associated almost exclusively with the depressed aircraft business. Also, there was lack of enthusiasm on the part of Henry Ford in respect to the aircraft industry and the need to modernize design of the trimotor. And, perhaps most importantly, Mayo was now sixty-six years old, ready to give up production responsibilities.

After retiring from Ford Motor Company, Mayo remained at his home, 1457 Seminole in Detroit, and held positions as officer of various transportation companies. For example, he was vice president of the Detroit Motorbus Company; president of the Chicago, Duluth, and Georgian Bay Transit Company; and manager of the Boblo Excursion Company. For these responsibilities, he occupied an office at 2272 National Bank Building in Detroit.

Mayo died in Detroit's Henry Ford Hospital of a heart attack on February 1, 1944. He was survived by his wife, Susan, and three children, Dana H. N. Mayo, Olive D. Mayo, and William N. Mayo.

Major References

"Mayo, William B." *Who's Who in America*. Chicago: A. N. Marquis, 1929.

Mayo, William N. *Reminiscences*. Accession 65, Henry Ford Museum & Greenfield Village Archives.

Nevins, Allan, and Frank Ernest Hill. *Ford: Expansion and Challenge, 1915–1932*. New York: Charles Scribner's Sons, 1957.

Richards, William C. *The Last Billionaire*. New York: Charles Scribner's Sons, 1948.

Sorensen, Charles E. *My Forty Years with Ford*. New York: W. W. Norton, 1956.

Sir Percival Lea Dewhurst Perry, 1878–1956.

Sir Percival Lea Dewhurst Perry

1878–1956

"I know of only two members of the Ford staff who ever spent a night with the Fords. One was our English manager, the present Lord Perry. I was the other.
—Charles E. Sorensen **

Ford Motor Company worldwide growth was stimulated to a great extent by the vision and resourcefulness of Sir Percival Perry. From 1906 until 1948, with the exception of a few years, Perry operated Ford's major overseas plants. The Fords were close friends of the Perrys, Clara Ford being particularly fond of Lady Catherine.

Percival Lea Dewhurst Perry was born in Bristol, England, on March 18, 1878, the son of Alfred Thomas Perry, a clerk, and Elizabeth Wheeler Perry. Percival grew up in nearby Birmingham, where he attended King Edward's School on a scholarship. He might have gone into law if he had had sufficient funds. Instead, at seventeen, he went to London, where he found work with the bicycle dealer H. J. Lawson, who was interested in automobiles as well as bicycles.

Perry was allowed to demonstrate one of Lawson's autos in the 1897 Diamond Jubilee Parade in London. By 1898, he was driving a motor tricycle of his own and frequently drove from London to Hull, where an uncle operated a printing business. Perry worked a short time for his uncle, and it was in Hull, in 1902, that he married Catherine Meals, daughter of a local postmaster.

They returned to London, where Perry's aim was to get into the automobile business. In 1904, he joined a partnership to form the American Motor Car Company which had obtained a five-year franchise to sell Ford automobiles (Models A, B, and C) throughout Europe. The franchise itself cost only 50 pounds a year. The five partners each subscribed 500 pounds, with Perry's father-in-law helping to finance Perry in this endeavor. The name of the business was changed to Central Motor Car Company in 1905—after all, it was a British concern, not American. Perry essentially ran the business and was credited in 1906

* From Charles E. Sorensen, *My Forty Years with Ford* (New York: W. W. Norton, 1956), p. 12.

with introducing Ford Model B landaulet taxicabs in London, where authorities then insisted all taxicabs were to be painted white so pedestrians could easily see them and thus avoid being struck by one of them.

Although Perry worked hard, the Central Motor Car Company was not very profitable. In 1906, he decided to go to America and suggest that the Ford Motor Company establish a branch of its own in Britain, no doubt offering to take charge of such a branch himself. His trip to the United States included a meeting in New York with R. M. Lockwood, the Ford export manager with whom he had been dealing, and a meeting in Detroit with John S. Gray, president of Ford Motor Company. Finally, Perry and his wife were to see Henry Ford himself.

The Perrys were to stay overnight with the Fords in their sixty-dollar-per-month flat at 145 Harper Avenue. Perry's impression of Ford at that time was that "he was a proper Puck." It was on a later visit, in 1908, that Perry finalized an agreement with Ford for a branch of Ford Motor Company to be established at 55 Shaftesbury Avenue, London. Perry was appointed manager of the branch. More than sixty local dealerships were soon organized throughout Britain, and the brand new Model T Ford sold exceptionally well.

In 1911, Perry leased a much larger plant in Trafford Park on the outskirts of Manchester. At this new location, he not only sold imported complete Ford vehicles but began to assemble cars using British-built bodies and fenders on the Ford chassis. It was clear his aim was eventually to build complete Ford automobiles in England, because by 1912 an expanded Manchester plant included both assembly and body-building facilities. With the sale of nearly 10,000 cars in 1914, the Ford car was far outselling its competitors in Britain.

It is interesting that as early as 1911 at Trafford Park, Perry was concerned for the welfare of his workers. He was concerned about living conditions of employees and the low pay they were receiving in the rather lucrative automobile business. This was three years before the widely heralded five-dollar-per-day program took effect in Detroit. In 1911, workers at Manchester had been receiving only sixpence, half penny an hour for a fifty-six-hour week. Perry had raised his minimum wage to one shilling threepence per hour, resulting in better production as well as a better standard of living for his workers. Perry was convinced good pay by the hour produced better results than the more common piecework pay in most factories. Perry's success with his wage program is thought to have had significant influence on Ford Motor Company's famous Detroit labor policy of 1914. The Fords had visited the Perrys in England during the summer of 1912, and they had toured the countryside together. They are known to have discussed employee

wages during that visit. Clara Ford at that time began a lifelong friendship with Catherine Perry.

Henry Ford loved birds. When he was a boy, his foster grandfather, Patrick Ahern, had taught him many bird songs which he learned to imitate. While on his tour of England with the Perrys in 1912, Ford was convinced by Perry that English birds were especially vibrant in their singing. Perry arranged to send Ford 500 English songbirds the follow- ing spring, for which Ford provided lavish accommodations on his farm estate at Dearborn.

Long after World War I broke out, Ford remained a staunch pacifist. In November 1915, he sponsored an unsuccessful mission to Europe, hoping to stop the war. The adverse publicity associated with the ven- ture seriously affected Ford sales in Britain. Ford had refused to supply England with war materials until the United States had itself entered the war in April 1917. On that very date, Perry was attempting to in- duce Ford to build farm tractors to help England with its food produc- tion. Ford did help by furnishing 6,000 tractors in record time.

Also, in March 1917, Ford looked favorably upon a plan to set up a tractor factory in Cork, Ireland, a district from which the Fords had migrated when they came to America. Perry would have preferred Man- chester in England but nevertheless found a location in Cork, acquir- ing free of charge 136 acres of government riverfront property by promising to employ at least 2,000 workers. Production started in July 1919, with 3,626 Fordson tractors built during 1920.

Prior to the postwar expansion of 1919, when Ford was planning the giant Rouge plant at Dearborn, Perry had suggested a similar installa- tion for England at the seaport of Southampton. In fact, Perry had con- tracted for sites on the waterfront for a development where complete vehicles could be manufactured with British capital and from British materials—a site from which Ford-designed, British-built automobiles could be shipped to British colonies worldwide. Ford, however, was not particularly appreciative of Perry's plans at that time. He was having troubles at home with the Dodge brothers in building the Rouge plant at Dearborn. Ford had, in fact, resigned as president of Ford Motor Company in January 1919, leaving the presidency to his son, Edsel.

Being unsuccessful with his expansion plans, Perry resigned from Ford Motor Company in May 1919 and from Henry Ford & Son Tractor Company in October 1919. Perry had organized 1,200 dealers and had 20,000 orders for cars when he left Ford Motor Company. Perry's re- placement was Warren Franklin Anderson, who until then had been Ford's branch manager at St. Louis, Missouri. Neither Anderson nor his successor did especially well until Edsel Ford's brother-in-law, Er- nest Kanzler, took charge of foreign branches in 1924. Although in

Perry with Henry Ford on September 19, 1916.

Aerial view of Perry's Dagenham plant outside London, England.

1922 a new plant site had been purchased by Ford at Dagenham, outside London, no construction had been started.

Perry and Ford remained good friends, however, and Perry went into business importing automotive products into Britain from other suppliers. But Perry's extensive automotive plans for Ford had not been forgotten in the least. Ford executives had picked the Dagenham site with Perry's objectives in mind. A resurgence of interest in western European sales led Ford to visit England in 1928, where he arranged a conference with Perry who had retired on the Island of Herm in the Channel Islands. Ford met Perry at Southampton and hired him in May 1928 to head a new "Ford Motor Company, Ltd." Perry's domain was to include, in addition to a much enlarged manufacturing plant in England, controlling interests in sales and assembly plants in France, Germany, Belgium, Holland, Denmark, Spain, Sweden, and Finland. For good measure, Middle Eastern and northern African territories were later added, as were Portugal, Italy, and Greece. With the Cork plant   231

Perry, chairman of Ford Motor Company Ltd., is guest speaker at an occasion in 1929.

again under Perry, worldwide distribution of Fordson tractors also became Perry's responsibility.

The Dagenham plant site was on the water, as Ford had insisted. However, it compared very poorly with Southhampton, Perry's choice. The site was a London dumping ground on the Thames, downriver from London. It consisted of about 500 acres of marshy ground requiring thousands of concrete piles to support structures. Nevertheless, Perry went ahead with construction, modeled after the Rouge plant in Dearborn but on a slightly smaller scale. Even so, the Dagenham plant was for its time the largest industrial complex in England. Ford and Perry agreed they should continue to accept trash from London by initiating design of a 172,000-kilowatt power plant able to utilize waste as fuel. Construction at Dagenham began in May 1929, with automotive production beginning in 1931.

During the economically depressed period of the 1930s, Perry's considerable contribution to Britain's economy was recognized by his being elevated to the title of "Baron Perry of Stock Harvard" in 1938. During World War II, Ford Motor Company, Ltd., with its far-flung holdings, was beset by difficulties of almost every imaginable sort—shortages of materials and manpower, civil war (Spain), insurgency (France), aerial bombings, multiple occupancies by Nazi forces, and mysterious disappearance of managers—a potentially chaotic situation. However, by war's end, other than a degree of independence attained by German and French branches, Perry had not lost stature; and the English plants themselves had established exceptionally high performance records.

Following the war, Perry was looking forward to retirement in 1948. Without Perry's availability, Henry Ford II decided to bring control of all foreign operations back to Dearborn. Ford Motor Company, Ltd., then became part of a new International Division of Ford Motor Company. In 1948, the year Perry retired, Ford of Dagenham produced 102,531 automobiles. After retirement, Lord Perry remained a director of Ford Motor Company until his death in New Providence, Bahama Islands, on June 17, 1956. The Perrys had no children.

Sir Percival Lea
Dewhurst Perry

Major References

Burgess-Wise, David. "Perry, Percival Lea Dewhurst—Lord Perry of Stock Harvard." Copy in vertical file, Henry Ford Museum & Greenfield Village Archives.

Interview with Lord Perry by Allan Nevins and Frank Hill, March 28, 1952, at Nassau. Accession 834, Henry Ford Museum & Greenfield Village Archives.

Nevins, Allan. *Ford: The Times, the Man, the Company.* New York: Charles Scribner's Sons, 1954.

Nevins, Allan, and Frank Ernest Hill. *Ford: Expansion and Challenge, 1915–1932.* New York: Scribner's Sons, 1957.

Sir Percival Perry—Branch Operations, 1928–1939. Accession 282, Henry Ford Museum & Greenfield Village Archives.

Wilkins, Mira, and Frank E. Hill. *American Business Abroad—Ford on Six Continents.* Detroit: Wayne State University Press, 1964.

Frederick Edwards Searle, 1871–1972.

Frederick Edwards Searle

1871–1972

"The fine tradition you established at the Trade School continues to be reflected in the activities of Ford Motor Company through the many graduates who hold positions of influence and high responsibility in our management. We will always be grateful for that heritage."
—Henry Ford II *

The education of boys and young men for gainful employment was one of Henry Ford's primary endeavors. Of Ford's many educational ventures, the Henry Ford Trade School and related vocational schools could be considered most successful. The one who headed these institutions for thirty years was Frederick E. Searle. "Pop" Searle was like a father to many appreciative students.

Frederick Edwards Searle was born August 1, 1871, in Westfield, Massachusetts, son of Frank Prentis Searle, an insurance agent and buggy whip manufacturer, and Ellen Edwards Hatch Searle. There were four children in all: Frederick, Herbert, Clara, and Helen.

Frederick graduated from Westfield High School with honors in 1889 and enrolled in Williams College to become a teacher. He graduated from Williams with a bachelor of science degree in 1893 and for two years taught at Tarrytown, New York. In 1895, through a teacher's agency, he came to Detroit, where he accepted a teaching position at the Detroit School for Boys, a college preparatory school of sixty to seventy-five students where Searle taught science and mathematics. The school was unique because it also taught woodworking and mechanical drawing. In 1900, the Detroit School for Boys merged with the Detroit Public School System and became Detroit University School.

In 1902, the *Detroit City Directory* lists Searle as director, Home Department, Detroit University School. The Home Department took care of boarding students. Searle married Josephine Hosmer Dewey of Big Rapids, Michigan, in 1903, and in subsequent years both he and his wife lived at the school. By 1906, the school had been moved to 16-48

* From a personal letter from Henry Ford II, on the occasion of Frederick Searle's 100th birthday.

235

Elmwood Avenue, and in 1914, Frederick Searle is listed as principal and Josephine Searle as teacher in that school. The Searles did not have any children.

Edsel Ford attended Detroit University School and took courses in physics and mathematics under Searle during 1911. After graduation, Edsel Ford did not go to college but instead worked for his father at Ford Motor Company. After Samuel Marquis and the Sociological Department of Ford Motor Company had instituted the Henry Ford Trade School in late 1916, Edsel Ford and his former manual training instructor, Clarence Avery, induced Searle to become head of the Henry Ford Trade School in 1917. The Searles then took up residence at 801 Lothrop Avenue in Detroit, where they would live for the next twenty years.

The Henry Ford Trade School was an exceptional institution. It offered a practical education to boys whose families could not afford to send them to high school. The Trade School offered them shop work as well as classroom training, with scholarships equivalent to wages. Because the school was accepting some boys as young as twelve, child labor laws did not permit these people to do shop work for "wages." The use of "scholarships" avoided this illegality. The Internal Revenue Service, much later, acknowledged the operation to be a school, and therefore the payments to be gifts not subject to income taxes. Scholarships ranged from about $500 per year to as much as $1,000 as the students became more proficient in their work.

The Trade School officially opened October 5, 1916, with six boys and one instructor as a nucleus. At the time Searle arrived, there were about forty boys. Three years later, there were 400 students enrolled and 6,000 on the waiting list. Henry Ford asked, "How many boys are there?" When told, he said, "Reverse those figures. Let 400 wait." So the school expanded further, enrolling as many as 200 a month. Two full-time investigators checked circumstances of applicants' families in order to select those most needing assistance. Enrollment reached 1,000 but by then 15,000 were on the waiting list. The school never did catch up. In 1921, when student enrollment was 1,800, the Sociological Department of Ford Motor Company was discontinued and the Trade School had to stand on its own. Henry and Edsel Ford's personal interest in the school, however, kept it intact. Henry Ford had told Searle, "You know, I'm more interested in education than I am in manufacturing."

Classrooms were initially on the fourth floor of the A building at the Highland Park plant. The work consisted of one-third classroom instruction and two-thirds shop experience. There was one standardized four-year course leading to the trade of tool-and-die maker. During the 1926 school year, for example, classroom subjects included English, mechanical drawing, civics, auto mechanics, commercial geography, algebra, geometry, trigonometry, physics, chemistry, qualitative analysis, quantitative analysis, metallurgy, metallography, and shop theory. Boys who wished to attend college took history and foreign languages in some other school. Many of the boys obtained college degrees by attending night school.

The school shop was separate from the Ford Motor Company factory and covered about three acres of floor space. In the shop were hundreds of the finest machines of many types. Total equipment was valued at more than $1 million. Shop work provided experience on shapers, lathes, grinders, and finally bench work. In these shop programs, Searle emphasized safety as first in importance, neatness (a Ford obsession) as second, and accuracy as third. Beyond the machine work, the young men were also given the opportunity to obtain training in such departments as forge, foundry, sheet metal, metal plating, pattern making, and carpentry.

There was an instructor for each ten to twelve students. The instructors were specialists taken from various Ford Motor Company departments and put on the Trade School payroll. During shop time, students were engaged mainly in making and repairing small tools, the tools becoming more complex as experience was gained. Occasionally, they practiced on machines useful in making Model T parts. The total value of Trade School work per year to the Ford Motor Company has been estimated at as much as $3 million. For this work, the advanced student might receive about four dollars a day, enough to support a family. Considering cost of instruction, investment in buildings, equipment, and maintenance, the Trade School was of considerable expense to Henry Ford.

In 1928, 1,000 students had been enrolled at a new Trade School location in the B building at the Rouge plant, and there were still 2,000 enrolled at Highland Park. Searle's office remained at Highland Park until 1930, the last year for the school at that location. Searle then moved his office to the Rouge plant in Dearborn, which was to be the final location for the Trade School.

At the end of four years of training, Trade School graduates were given diplomas, but the diplomas did not admit them to college. Some graduates took additional night-school work for admission to college. Trade School graduates were in immediate demand, however, for responsible shop positions throughout the United States, Of a total of more than 10,000 graduates, Searle estimated at least 150 eventually

Trade School boys leaving the Highland Park school in May 1927. The school (fitted with awnings) was adjacent to the Ford factory buildings at right.

operated their own manufacturing plants in the vicinity of Detroit, some doing more than $1 million in business annually. One of his graduates, with permission of Henry Ford, started a Henry Ford Trade School in Manila, Philippines. One of Searle's instructors organized the Henry Ford Trade School at the Ford Dagenham plant in England, and another opened a similar school at Jamshedpur, India.

Between 1922 and 1928, Ford invited nearly 600 foreign students to receive training under Searle, paying them five dollars a day for periods of a few weeks to three years. Some countries represented were China, India, the Philippines, Czechoslovakia, and the Soviet Union.

Searle also had been given responsibility for the Ford Motor Company Apprentice Schools in 1918. Apprentice Schools were operated as a separate corporation. An apprentice was defined as a student in the tool room who was regularly attending classes under the jurisdiction of the Apprentice School. Apprentice wages were set by the school. Students attended classes primarily in mathematics and mechanical drawing on their own time, with much of the instruction accomplished in the public schools.

During World War II, apprentice training reached a peak. In late 1940, the Navy asked Ford to train machinist mates and aircraft mechanics at the Rouge facility. Ford immediately invested $2 million in

238

Searle at Henry Ford Trade School Instructor's Banquet in October 1942.

classrooms and dormitories to accommodate 2,000 Navy men adjacent to the Rouge shop areas. Before Pearl Harbor, 2,450 men had graduated. This Navy school operated throughout the war, training 23,000 sailors.

At Ford's Willow Run bomber plant in Ypsilanti, a $500,000 school building was provided in 1941 to train both Army and civilian aircraft workers. With 75 instructors, 35,000 riveters were trained, each receiving 100 hours of shop instruction and ten hours of classroom work. At the peak of this wartime training program, a teaching force exceeding 1,300 was holding classes for 18,000 students. Charles E. Sorensen, 239 superintendent of the Willow Run plant, began to complain when the Ford Motor Company training budget reached $10 million a year. In all, the Ford Trade School and Apprentice Schools trained an estimated 250,000 people under Searle.

Searle received an honorary master of arts degree from Williams College in 1936 and an honorary doctor of science degree from the University of Detroit in 1942.

Near the end of World War II, Searle organized Ford Camp Legion sites for men released from hospitals with difficulties caused by disease or other physical disability. These men had been chosen for rehabilitation by veterans' organizations. The Ford camps offered medical attention, physical therapy, garden work, recreational facilities, and classroom courses.

In 1946, at age seventy-five, Searle was ready to retire. In February, he was given the position of educational adviser and consultant to all Ford schools. On July 1, 1946, Searle retired to his home at 24145 Locust in Farmington; the Searles had moved to this suburban location four years earlier. Being a member of nearly a dozen professional organizations, a director of City Bank of Detroit, and an active member of the North Congregational Church did not prevent his taking care of a fifty-tree apple orchard and an acre of blueberries on his small estate.

In August 1952, the board of trustees of Henry Ford Trade School closed the thirty-six-year-old institution, with the bulk of its assets transferred to the Dearborn Board of Education to be merged with Henry Ford Community College. One of the buildings on the campus is the Searle Technical Building.

On August 1, 1971, the state of Michigan passed House Concurrent Resolution No. 170—"Concurrent Resolution for the Centennial of Dr. Frederick E. Searle."

At the Farmington home, Searle's sister Clara and a nephew of Josephine Searle named Michael Holmes lived with Searle. After his wife died on February 21, 1949, his sister Clara had taken care of the household. Searle lived to be 101 years old. He died August 19, 1972. Remains of Searle and his wife, Josephine, are in the mausoleum of White Chapel Memorial Park in Troy, Michigan.

Major References

Alumni Files, Henry Ford Trade School. In possession of Paul E. Charette, Dearborn, Mich.

Henry Ford Trade School. Accession 680, Henry Ford Museum & Greenfield Village Archives.

Nevins, Allan, and Frank Ernest Hill. *Ford: Expansion and Challenge, 1915–1932.* New York: Charles Scribner's Sons, 1957.

Obituary. *Dearborn Press,* August 24, 1972.

Searle, Frederick E. Reminiscences. Accession 65, Henry Ford Museum & Greenfield Village Archives.

Frederick Edwards
Searle

William Adams Simonds, 1887–1963. (Photo courtesy of Henry A. Tuttle.)

William Adams Simonds

1887–1963

"In 1936, in an effort to capture the motoring public's interest, William A. Simonds, who edited the magazine Ford News *since 1926, began carrying fewer articles on Ford products and more features on the company's activities."*
—*David L. Lewis* *

William A. Simonds was a westerner, a writer who found his way to Dearborn and a friendship with Henry Ford in a rather circuitous way with the help of Fred Black. Besides being editor of *Ford News,* he received wide acclaim for his biographies of Henry Ford and Thomas A. Edison, men who were in the public limelight at that time. Simonds's later role as first manager of Greenfield Village, with its hundreds of youthful guides to be trained, required him to become a teacher of American history as well.

William Adams Simonds was born September 19, 1887, in Central City, Nebraska. He was the second son of Henry Simonds, a schoolteacher, and Lily Goodnough Simonds. Henry Simonds had grown up on the family farm near Athol in north-central Massachusetts. Henry's father had come to the United States from England before 1700. Lily Goodnough was daughter of Ellen Saxon Goodnough and Rev. August Goodnough, who had been a missionary among the Oneidas in the Wisconsin wilderness. Her mother died at an early age, and Lily was sent back east to live with her aunt in Athol. It was there she met Henry Simonds. They courted while Henry was attending Amherst College and Lily was attending Mt. Holyhoke College.

The Simonds family moved to Stevens Point, Wisconsin, where Henry Simonds was superintendent of schools. At Stevens Point, as early as age ten, William showed a special interest in writing. In the style of reporters, he described battles of the Spanish American War. He folded his handwritten stories into a small newspaper of his own which he presented to friends. About that time, his family moved to Oshkosh, Wisconsin, where his father obtained a better position. Wil-

* From David L. Lewis, *The Public Image of Henry Ford* (Detroit: Wayne State University Press, 1976), p. 333.

243

liam finished grammar school in Oshkosh. He did not study Greek as his father had, but he did absorb six years of Latin. This scholastic endeavor was well balanced by his setting pins at a bowling alley and pumping the organ at the Methodist church.

He graduated from high school at age seventeen, as valedictorian of his class. Although he won a scholarship to Lawrence University, he instead obtained a third-grade teaching certificate and taught at the Butte des Morte school, ten miles northwest of town, for twenty-five dollars a month. Room and board were obtained for ten dollars at a nearby farmhouse.

Simonds's older brother Albert lived near Bothell, Washington, a beautiful locality in the coastal mountains overlooking Lake Washington and Seattle. Simonds's father had visited Albert and had decided he would like to move to Bothell and operate a chicken ranch. So the entire family (William now had three sisters) moved to a remote, wooded forty-acre ranch high on a hill near Bothell. Albert immediately found work for William at the Griffin Wheat Company in South Tacoma, and in 1907 a position with the Albers Brothers Milling Company. The father soon became superintendent of schools in Bothell.

In 1908, Simonds entered the University of Washington as a freshman majoring in English literature. He made quite a lasting impression on that institution, according to his own story. As a reporter on the college paper, the *Daily,* he became sufficiently popular to be appointed editor at forty dollars a month, and he changed his major to journalism. His first glimpse of Henry Ford came that summer of 1909, when a Model T won the automobile race from New York to Seattle and Henry Ford was there to meet the winning drivers.

In addition to being editor of the *Daily,* Simonds was also campus editor for the *Seattle Times.* During the summer of 1910, he obtained an additional fifteen dollars a week at the *Times,* and he felt financially substantial enough to marry Margery Muncaster of Seattle. While Simonds was still in college, their first son, William Adams Simonds, Jr., was born. After school was out in 1911, Simonds obtained a full-time position with the *Seattle Times.* Although he had been one of the best-known students on campus, he apparently did not graduate from the University of Washington because he had not attended classes regularly. (Simonds received a honorary master of arts degree from Wayne State University in Detroit in 1940.)

Work at the *Times* was hectic. In addition, Simonds was attempting free-lance writing. By 1914, however, Simonds was promoted to the city desk and soon to assistant city editor. He was next appointed to fill the vacancy of automotive editor in charge of the automotive section of the *Sunday Seattle Times.*

244

At the onset of World War I, Simonds, already a member of the National Guard Coast Artillery reserve unit, advanced to Sergeant major senior grade, highest "noncom" in the regiment.

While he was automotive editor and leading a travel party on a publicity tour to Longmire Hot Springs, he became thoroughly drenched and as a result of that exposure contracted pneumonia. His sickness was serious enough to convince him newspaper work was too strenuous. When he recovered, he accepted a position as editor-partner for the *Pacific Northwest Motorist,* a publication that eventually became the official publication of the Automobile Association of America and the State Good Roads Association. This was in November 1918.

The family now included four children: William Jr., Austin, Chandler, and one-year-old Bruce Thomas. With the war over, these were joyous times. Christmas 1918 was a happy occasion. But that same winter, the influenza epidemic hit hard, and Margery died. Simonds moved the family to his father's ranch in the mountains, and from there he set about organizing the Washington Automotive Trade Association, taking the position of secretary-treasurer.

In 1920, Simonds met Theresa Callahan, a native of New Haven, Connecticut, then working in Seattle. She had three children of her own: Patricia, Elizabeth Jane, and Ford. Despite the predictable obstacles, the two married and managed to raise a family of seven children.

Simonds next became editor of the *Northwest Motorist and Truckman,* a consolidation of automobile dealers with his previous Washington Automotive Trade Association. In this capacity, Simonds became acquainted with Ray W. Hines, manager of the Seattle Ford branch. Hines induced Simonds to become advertising manager of the Seattle branch starting March 1, 1924, at $325 a month. In this position, Simonds became known to his bosses at the home offices in Highland Park and Dearborn, Michigan.

When Fred Black, general manager of the Dearborn Publishing Company, needed someone to investigate farming cooperatives in defense of the Aaron Sapiro case, Simonds in Seattle was asked to take depositions from the hay and alfalfa growers in the Yakima Valley and the wheat growers around Spokane. This assignment expanded to the Portland wool growers and the Salem prune and hop growers, and on to bean and tomato growers near Los Angeles. By the time these assignments had been finished, the position of branch advertising manager at Seattle had been abolished, and Simonds was demoted to senior road man for the branch. In 1925, another son, Vance, had been added to the family.

But Black had appreciated Simond's West Coast work, and he offered Simonds a job in the editorial department of the Dearborn Publishing Company, starting in August 1927, at $375 a month. Working for Black, Simonds was again involved with the Sapiro case, first obtaining testimony from rice growers, cotton growers, and corn growers regarding activities of cooperatives. During the actual trial in Detroit, Simonds occupied an office in the Penobscot Building and wrote press releases in defense of the *Dearborn Independent*.

With Simonds's position seemingly secure in Detroit, Theresa Simonds packed the family into their Model T and brought them from Bothnell to Dearborn, a trip lasting thirteen days. She had sold off their livestock and the furniture, and had closed the home. On the very day she and the family arrived, July 7, 1927, the Sapiro case was settled out of court. Simonds's legal work was over. In August 1927, the Simonds family was living at 419 Berkley Drive in Dearborn. The *Dearborn Independent* was discontinued by the end of 1927, and Simonds oversaw its demise. The Model T was also on its way out. Simonds wrote the article "Laying a Wreath for Old Model T" which appeared in the January 1928 issue of *Nation's Business*.

Henry Ford with Simonds (far left), Harold Koch, Benjamin Lovett, Frank Tegge, and Robert Zhanow at entrance of Martha-Mary Chapel in Greenfield Village, circa 1942.

Simonds, Clarence Brown (director), and Spencer Tracy (actor) at the time of filming the movie *Edison the Man* in 1940.

On January 13, 1928, Simonds was transferred to Ford Motor Company Advertising and Publicity at $450 a month. By August 1930, he was an editor of the *Ford News,* another product of the Dearborn Publishing Company, at $525 a month. This same year, he and Black together published *From the Ground Up,* a boys' book about the history of aviation up to and including the Ford trimotor. During this period, Simonds was working with Henry Ford on publicity for the Edison Institute (Henry Ford Museum & Greenfield Village.) His first book, *Henry Ford, Motor Genius,* was published in 1929. Simonds was asked to entertain dignitaries who came to see the museum and village as guests of the Fords. He had to study a great deal about antiques in order to converse knowingly regarding the extensive collections. In 1931, Simonds wrote *A Boy with Edison* a biography of Francis Jehl, an early assistant of Thomas Edison.   247

Simonds at his desk at A. W. Ayer Company in Hawaii about 1950. (Photo courtesy of Henry A. Tuttle.)

When the Henry Ford Museum & Greenfield Village was opened to the public in 1933, Simonds was put in charge of public relations and given charge of training and supervision of the guides (interpreters) who conducted the public through the Museum and Village. These guides were male students of the Edison Institute Schools.

Simonds kept his position with the *Ford News* and Edison Institute throughout the depression years. He became an authority on the life of Edison and Edison family history. A three-act play, *The Man Edison*, played with great success at the Edison Institute Theatre, and *Edison: His Life, His Work, His Genius* was published by Bobbs-Merrill in 1934. Simond's fifth book, *Henry Ford and Greenfield Village*, was published in 1938. He was then lecturing on early American history at

248

Wayne State University and to numerous civic organizations in the Detroit area.

In 1939 and 1940, Simonds was loaned to Metro-Goldwyn-Mayer of Hollywood as technical adviser for the motion pictures *Edison: The Boy,* starring Mickey Rooney, and *Edison: The Man,* starring Spencer Tracy. Much of the film footage was obtained at Greenfield Village.

During World War II, the Edison Institute lost many of its students to the military and virtually closed. On January 31, 1942, Simonds transferred to the Ford Willow Run bomber plant as director of public relations. He retired in 1945 from Willow Run and took a position in advertising and public relations with N. W. Ayer and Son in Honolulu, where he handled the Dole pineapple account. While in Hawaii, he did more writing, notably *Kamaaina, A Century in Hawaii* in 1949, and *The Hawaiian Telephone Story* in 1958.

Theresa Simonds died in Hawaii on March 6, 1947, and about a year later Simonds married Theresa's widowed sister, Marie Callahan Fitts of Kansas City, Missouri. In 1960, the Simondses settled 12007 107th Avenue, Sun City, Arizona. Simonds, suffering from arthritis, was engaged in writing poetry and fiction when Marie died on October 6, 1963. Only thirteen days later, on October 19, 1963, William A. Simonds died. Services were held in Youngtown adjoining Sun City, and the body was cremated. Surviving were four sons, two daughters, and fifteen grandchildren.

Major References

Lewis, David L. *The Public Image of Henry Ford.* Detroit: Wayne State University Press, 1976.

Simonds, William A. *A Boy with Edison.* New York: Doubleday, Doran, 1931.

———. *Edison: His Life and Work.* Indianapolis: A. L. Burt, 1934.

———. *Henry Ford and Greenfield Village.* New York: Frederick A. Stokes, 1938.

———. *Henry Ford: His Life, His Work, His Genius.* Indianapolis: Bobbs-Merrill, 1943.

———. *Henry Ford, Motor Genius.* New York: Doubleday, Doran, 1929.

———. Interview with Kenneth N. Metcalf concerning early days of Henry Ford Museum & Greenfield Village, June 3, 1961. Accession 65, Henry Ford Museum and Greenfield Village Archives.

———. "The Man Across the Street—The Adventures of an Ordinary Fellow." Unpublished autobiography, Dearborn, 1939.

Simonds, William A., and Fred L. Black. *From the Ground Up,* New York: Doubleday, Doran, 1930.

Tuttle, Henry A., husband of Elizabeth Jane Simonds. Personal communication, 1990.

Howard Woodworth Simpson, 1892–1963.

Howard Woodworth Simpson

1892–1963

"Shortly after World War II, an engineer named Howard W. Simpson was told he was dying of cancer. Despite this news, the little-known automotive consultant went on to invent a major automobile component that most of the industry is now adopting."
—Joseph M. Callahan *

As one of the relatively few graduate mechanical engineers employed by Henry Ford, Howard W. Simpson worked primarily on tractors and with particular emphasis on planetary gearing. Ford also had strong interest in these two developments. The two men worked closely together—perhaps too closely, as the combined accomplishments turned out to be less than if Simpson had worked alone. It was after Simpson left Ford that he was really able to prove himself.

Howard Woodworth Simpson was born on May 8, 1892, in Kalamazoo, Michigan. He was the son of John Robert Bruce Simpson and Winona Woodworth Simpson. His father was a skilled carriage maker who had moved to Detroit and worked at making car bodies. He taught the five Fisher brothers how to make bodies and later became superintendent for Fisher Body Company, making Cadillac bodies of wood and sheet aluminum. Howard started school in Kalamazoo but moved with his family in 1902 to Detroit, where he graduated from Detroit Central High School in 1910. That year, he entered a three-year apprentice program at Cadillac Motor Car Company, receiving training in toolmaking and tool design at pay averaging about fifteen cents an hour.

Simpson next enrolled at the University of Michigan and graduated in 1917 with a bachelor of science degree in mechanical engineering. This was during World War I, and his first job after graduation was drafting work on an experimental engine for the U.S. Navy. At this point, Simpson decided he would prefer to work in industry rather than

* From Joseph M. Callahan, "Design of Dying Engineer Sweeping Auto Industry," *Automotive News*, July 6, 1964.

the alternative of teaching engineering. His next position was with the Buda Company of Chicago, where he was appointed assistant to the chief engineer. Buda manufactured truck and tractor engines.

Simpson had been rejected as a volunteer in the U.S. armed forces because of poor eyesight. So in order to support the war effort, he joined the signal corps as a civilian employee. In this capacity, he became an inspector of aircraft engines at Packard and Cadillac plants in Detroit. Immediately following the war, Simpson took a job in the tool design department of Ford Motor Company in Highland Park.

During summers, Simpson had worked on his uncle's farm. From this experience, he became interested in the design of tractors and farm implements—especially the Fordson tractor. So he applied for work at the Henry Ford & Son Tractor Plant in Dearborn; was interviewed and hired by Eugene Farkas, chief engineer; and was given the job of chief draftsman. By this time, he had married Gertrude A. Haeger of Moorepark, Michigan. After the marriage, on August 28, 1918, they immediately moved into a home on Mason near Park Street in Dearborn, but soon they purchased a Ford-built home at 488 Nona Street (now 22686 Nona). The Simpsons were to have two children: Bruce, born May 19, 1921, and Charlotte, born May 18, 1924. Bruce graduated from the University of Illinois in 1947, and Charlotte from Wayne State University in 1963.

In 1921, after Henry Ford & Son had been acquired by Ford Motor Company, Simpson became a design engineer working directly under Henry Ford on special projects, predominantly tractor and transmission designs.

The Fordson tractor at that time had a tendency to tip over backward when the plow became stuck on a boulder or tree roots. Ford Motor Company was being sued because of injuries to drivers of the tractors. During the depression of 1921, Simpson was laid off from work for three months. He invested his own money to have a novel rear-wheel fender fabricated which would prevent the tractor from rolling over backward. He patented this fender design, and when he was called back to work, he gave the experimental fenders and his patent to Henry Ford, asking for only the eighty dollars he had invested in fabricating the sample fenders. These fenders became standard equipment on future Fordson tractors. Other Fordson projects included the development of a kerosene carburetor and work with water injection and alcohol fuels.

Ford had Simpson design a miniature tractor for his four grandchildren—part of the Hy-Ben-Jo-Bill set of farm equipment used by the grandchildren and displayed at fairs. Another project involving Simpson was with Harold Hicks, Ford's chief engine engineer. This was a giant twenty-four-cylinder speedboat engine. This engine was an example of Ford's favorite X design, with four giant six-cylinder banks driving a single crankshaft. With its 4,400-cubic-inch displacement, it produced 1,000 horsepower. The boat, named *Miss Dearborn,* was driven on the Detroit River but was too powerful to qualify for standard speedboat racing. Ray Dahlinger drove the boat a few times, but it was difficult to handle and difficult to service the engine, and there were a few injuries during the testing. The boat was dismantled after a cost estimated at $125,000.

Simpson was now working directly for Henry Ford and quite independent of Farkas. He found working for Ford much more difficult; Ford too often wanted one thing done one day and quite another the next. One had to guess which direction to follow. Simpson continued to spend most of his time on Fordson tractor improvements—air cleaners, carburetors, compression ratios, manifolds, power takeoffs, suspensions, and transmissions. Some of the experimental transmissions were also tested on Ford cars, but Ford's fondness for the Model T planetary design prevented adoption of Simpson's transmissions for automotive production. In 1928, when Fordson tractor production was transferred to Cork, Ireland, Ford lost interest in improving the Fordson. At this point, Simpson was directed to work on an entirely new tractor.

Ford stopped at Simpson's desk nearly every day to discuss work. At one point, Ford told Simpson he could put the whole engineering department—a hundred or so men—to work on the new tractor. "The tractor is your meat," he would say. Simpson knew more men would not help the situation. Simpson already had twenty or so draftsmen working for him. The problem was conflicting directions from Henry himself. In December 1931, Simpson started a diary consisting of instructions received from Henry Ford. The ridiculous range of suggestions offered by Ford made reasonable progress in any one direction nearly impossible.

A sample of Ford's engineering logic at that time: When Simpson mentioned that the gears in his experimental transmission would "free wheel" in reduction speed, Ford laughed and said, "A horse doesn't free wheel. You don't even have to say 'whoa' very loud before he stops dead in his tracks." For that odd reason, Ford apparently had no use for the transmission design.

Among Ford's suggestions was a one-wheel-drive tractor. When it was built, it could pull itself along a polished varnished floor, but that was about all it could do. Ford proudly demonstrated it in the Engineering Laboratory, while Simpson was ashamed of its being seen by other engineers. Another Ford-proposed experimental tractor was

253

an asymmetrical three-wheel model which had a tendency to fall on its side.

In November 1938, Henry George (Harry) Ferguson of Ulster, Ireland, brought samples of his Ferguson tractor to Dearborn. He wanted Ford to adopt his patented hydraulic implement hitch. Ford was interested in the hitch and asked Simpson to design a tractor somewhat similar to Ferguson's but much lighter in weight. Simpson was to work with a group consisting of Ferguson and two Ferguson engineers (Eber and George Sherman), all under Charles E. Sorensen's direction. Sorensen had been involved in Ford tractor production since 1915. This array of bosses and their conflicting orders was too much for Simpson, who worked best on his own.

Simpson had been doing consulting work for Harry Pierson of the Detroit Harvester Company on weekends for several years. Pierson had asked him to come to work for him. Simpson was offered the position of chief engineer at Detroit Harvester, and he accepted. Simpson left Ford Motor Company on January 29, 1939, after more than twenty years with Ford. Ford had offered more money, but what Simpson wanted was freedom to direct his own work.

At Detroit Harvester, Simpson worked on power takeoffs for trucks and tractors, mowing machines for several makes of tractors, and especially mowers for military establishments. Simpson was with Detroit Harvester until July 1, 1943, when insufficient engineering work convinced him he should go into consulting work on his own. He was interested in planetary transmissions and decided to devote full time to research and development with the purpose of patenting the designs and selling the patents to automotive and supplier companies. His first consulting work was for Spicer Manufacturing Company of Toledo. Spicer was a supplier of drivetrain components to a variety of vehicle manufacturers.

Simpson had been badly burned in a fire at his home in the summer of 1944. This accident resulted in a condition that led to kidney trouble and eventually to cancer. The cancer was diagnosed at Henry Ford Hospital in 1947, with the prognosis that he had perhaps six months to live. For about three years, Simpson was unable to accomplish much. During that period, he and his wife spent their winters in Arizona and California.

Back in Dearborn in 1950, Simpson concentrated on his transmission gear designs, and in 1952 he submitted to Ford Motor Company a fifty-page proposal that proved his transmission superior to the then-current Fordomatic transmission. On July 1, 1953, Ford Motor Company signed a licensing agreement with Simpson, who asked for only a very modest royalty. Other vehicle manufacturers including Chrysler

Howard and Gertrude Simpson. (Photo courtesy of Charlotte Simpson Martin.)

and General Motors were likewise impressed and subsequently signed similar agreements.

The "Simpson gear train," for which Simpson was well known in engineering circles, became and still remains the dominant automatic transmission gear set design in the automotive industry. Simpson's more than forty patents covered a host of applications in trucks, buses, tractors, and military vehicles. His designs are used today over a range from ten-speed truck and tractor applications to three-speed and four-speed automatics with overdrives.

One might infer from Simpson's intense interest in things mechanical that he would be somewhat antisocial, but he was not the least bit 255

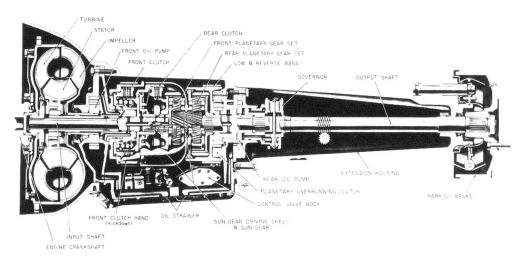

TURBINE
STATOR
IMPELLER
FRONT OIL PUMP
FRONT CLUTCH
REAR CLUTCH
FRONT PLANETARY GEAR SET
REAR PLANETARY GEAR SET
LOW & REVERSE BAND
GOVERNOR
OUTPUT SHAFT
EXTENSION HOUSING
REAR OIL PUMP
PLANETARY OVERRUNNING CLUTCH
CONTROL VALVE BODY
PARKING BRAKE
FRONT CLUTCH BAND
(Kickdown)
OIL STRAINER
SUN GEAR DRIVING SHELL
& SUN GEAR
INPUT SHAFT
ENGINE CRANKSHAFT

Drawing of a 1960 Plymouth three-speed automatic transmission as designed by Simpson. (Photo courtesy of Bruce Simpson.)

introverted. He was on his college track team, excelled in ice figure skating, and became Dearborn city champion in badminton. Simpson was an active member of Methodist, Baptist, and Presbyterian churches at one time or another. He taught Sunday school, acted as Sunday school superintendent, and helped develop the YMCA Hi-Y Program Leadership Course for young people. He was a Boy Scout troop leader for many years. During later years, Simpson helped prepare a course for young people to develop spiritual and moral values. In collaboration with Virginia Trevitt of California, this high school course, entitled "The American Heritage: Design for National Character," was offered in California schools.

The Simpson home was at 730 Crescent Drive in Dearborn when Simpson died at Henry Ford Hospital of cancer on November 4, 1963. He was buried in Woodlawn Cemetery, Detroit. Only six months before his death, he had been awarded the distinguished title of Outstanding Michigan Inventor by the Michigan Patent Law Association. He was survived by his wife, Gertrude, and his children, Bruce Simpson and Charlotte Martin, both of Dearborn.

Major References

Callahan, Joseph M. "Design of Dying Engineer Sweeping Auto Industry." *Automotive News,* July 6, 1964.

"Engineering Genius of the Modern Automatic Transmission." *Motor Trend,* October 1964.

Nevins, Allan, and Frank Ernest Hill. *Ford: Decline and Rebirth, 1933–1962.* New York: Charles Scribner's Sons, 1963.

———. *Ford: Expansion and Challenge, 1915–1932.* New York: Charles Scribner's Sons, 1957.

Simpson, Bruce H., and Charlotte L. Martin, children of Howard W. Simpson. Personal communication, 1990–1991.

Simpson, Howard W. Reminiscences. Accession 65, Henry Ford Museum & Greenfield Village Archives.

"Yes, You Can Sell an Idea to Big 3." *Detroit Free Press,* October 5, 1975.

Roscoe Martin Smith, 1894–1991. (Photo courtesy of Marion J. Falk.)

Roscoe Martin Smith

1894–1991

"You've got a dynasty all your own."
—Charles E. Sorensen*

Roscoe Smith, an electrical engineer, was best known as manager of Ford Motor Company's outlying plants, also known as Henry Ford's Village Industries. These hydroelectric manufacturing plants, numbering as many as twenty-four at one time and together generating more than 16,000 horsepower, demonstrated Ford's belief in the value of waterpower in providing industrial employment to rural areas.

Roscoe Martin Smith was born on a farm in Johnson County, Indiana, on January 22, 1894. His parents were Ernest D. and Nancy Ellen DeHart Smith. When Roscoe was about six years old, the family moved to Indianapolis, where he started school. His father worked as a cabinetmaker, and they stayed in Indianapolis about three years. Then the family moved to Cass, Indiana, a mining town where Ernest Smith bought a barber shop and became a barber. Roscoe finished seventh grade in Cass before moving with the family to Deming, New Mexico, where he finished high school in 1911. Nicknamed "Rock," he was the oldest of six children, with a brother, Earl, and sisters Mabel, Helen, Hazel, and Blanche.

Between 1911 and 1913, Smith went west as many boys his age longed to do. He stated he "did a little of everything." He worked for Cheno Copper Company, where he was a helper on a 150-man track gang; for Colorado Fuel and Iron Company, where he worked on tipple as well as underground; and for the U.S. government on Elephant Butte Dam at Engel, New Mexico.

During Smith's schooling and working experience, he was especially interested in electricity. In 1913 he enrolled in an electrical apprenticeship course at American Electric Company back in Indianapolis. With

* From the oral reminiscences of Roscoe M. Smith, recalling a statement by Charles E. Sorensen when Smith had charge of the Rouge Electrical Manufacturing Department.

259

evening study, he soon completed both the apprenticeship and the electrical engineering course from International Correspondence Schools.

On March 27, 1915, Smith married Gladys Irene Chambers, daughter of Morris and Cora Hall Chambers. The couple set up housekeeping in Indianapolis, but before long work became scarce, and the Smiths moved to Detroit, where Roscoe was employed by the Detroit Edison Company in its experimental shop. The 1916 *Detroit City Directory* lists Smith as an electrician living at 360 25th Street. The Smiths had two children: Roscoe M. Smith, Jr., born March 4, 1916, and Marion J. Smith, born April 2, 1918.

Smith obtained a job at Ford Motor Company on September 11, 1916, as an electrician maintaining overhead motors in the flywheel department. After about a year, he was transferred to electrical maintenance in the starter and generator armature department, where he stayed until January 1919. He then became foreman of a production job in charge of twelve armature winding machines. In September 1920, he was promoted to assistant general foreman. Soon after this promotion, the Smith family moved to 11611 Nardin Avenue, which was their home for the next fourteen years.

After six years of electrical manufacturing experience at Highland Park, in 1925 Smith was notified his department was being moved to the new Rouge Motor Assembly Building in Dearborn. At the Rouge, Smith worked under a building superintendent who recognized that he knew little about electrical matters himself and let Smith supervise his department with very little interference. This gave Smith opportunity to lay out new machines and inaugurate a variety of automated operations for producing starters and generators more efficiently. By 1927, his department was producing 10,000 starters and generators per day. At the Rouge, Smith was able to cut costs of manufacturing sufficiently to greatly impress Charles E. Sorensen, then top man at the Rouge.

Smith's chief competition in building starters and generators was the Electric Autolite Company. In 1927, during the changeover from Model T to Model A, Ford gave the starter-generator business to Electric Autolite, and Smith's department was temporarily abolished. At that point, Sorensen assigned Smith to the "student's course," more recently called management training. Smith was only thirty-three years old and, although possibly not aware of it, was being groomed for higher management assignments. The training program required working in departments engaged in engine, chassis, body, trim, and painting—all major aspects of building an automobile. Smith completed this training in May 1928.

Sorensen next assigned Smith to a group of engineers to troubleshoot problems at branch plants. Smith's accomplishments in this work pertained principally to the Buffalo assembly plant. In September 1929, the manufacture of starters and generators was reinaugurated at the Rouge with Smith in charge. His suggestion of a much simpler design resulted in production costs of only two dollars per unit.

Henry Ford was extremely enthusiastic regarding the industrial use of waterpower wherever it was available. One of these sites was on the Huron River southeast of Ypsilanti. At Ypsilanti, a new plant for the manufacture of electrical automotive equipment was built to utilize the 2,400-horsepower generated from the river. Smith was put in charge of moving and expanding the Rouge electrical operations at the new location. Again, new machines were designed and built in Ford shops, and the reinstallation was completed in a matter of six weeks during 1932. Smith was general foreman of the plant; he oversaw about 700 workers and again produced close to 10,000 motors and generators a day.

During this depression period, Ford Motor Company was in the business of rebuilding complete automobiles and many automotive parts. For some time at Ypsilanti, nearly 20 percent of production consisted of rebuilt starters and generators. The Ypsilanti plant was self-sufficient, with its own electricians, plumbers, millwrights, riggers, die repairmen, and so on, but it was dependent on Dearborn headquarters for purchasing, accounting, and employment.

One troublesome situation at Ypsilanti was with Harry Bennett, who was in charge of Ford employment. Smith stated that Bennett was indeed a nuisance. He assigned his friends and his friend's friends to jobs at Ypsilanti. A number of these men were sent deliberately to weaken Smith's control of the factory. Smith was a staunch disciple of Sorensen, and this was one of Bennett's ways to undermine Sorensen's standing with Ford.

In April 1937, Smith was appointed head of outlying plants. These included not only the Ypsilanti plant but a total of as many as twenty-four factories in Michigan, Ohio, and New York. These factories were all powered by water. In Michigan, they were mainly on the Huron, Rouge, Raisin, and Menominee rivers; in Ohio on the Great Miami River at Hamilton; and in New York on the Hudson River at Green Island. These outlying plants produced nearly all the automotive parts not produced at the Ford Rouge complex. By 1938, the Smiths had moved from Detroit to 6660 North Maple Road in Ann Arbor. There they eventually acquired some 800 acres of land surrounding their home.

Waterpower was of special interest to Ford, who had utilized a power dam for electricity at his farm home in Dearborn as early as 1911. His

Henry Ford talking with Emil Zoerlein, Smith (in background), and Wilbur Donaldson (at right) in 1937.

outlying manufacturing plants had been established beginning about 1920, and six more were in the planning stage in 1940 as World War II approached. Most of the outlying plants were small and, according to Smith, difficult to operate at a profit. But Ford greatly favored the concept of many small industries, each operating in a friendly rural setting.

In February 1941, Sorensen asked Smith to head a delegation of engineers to visit Consolidated Aircraft Corporation in San Diego, to determine if the four-engined B-24 bomber could possibly be built by mass-production methods. This study required approximately six months, whereupon Sorensen was advised of the definite possibility. Plans were formulated for the Willow Run bomber plant near Ypsilanti. With many of the procedures used in building Model T Fords, assembly

Smith at the Willow Run bomber plant in 1941.

lines at Willow Run, under Air Force contracts, would build the giant
B-24 Liberators at the rate of one every hour rather than the previous
rate of only one a day. Under Sorensen, Smith was put in charge of
bomber production in this immense, 3.3-million-square-foot building.

"My trouble at Willow Run was over the Frost Bite machines," stated
Smith in his reminiscences. It seems Bennett had given the lucrative
Frost Bite concession to one of his cronies, thus permitting in production areas a large number of coin machines from which employees
could buy Frost Bite ice cream bars. Not knowing of Bennett's involvement, Smith complained to Sorensen that his men were hanging
around the vending machines and not doing their work. Sorensen
agreed the machines would have to go. Bennett was enraged by the
removal of the machines and challenged Sorensen to a fistfight. When
Sorensen took evasive action, Bennett's fist landed in Smith's eye. Ben- 263

nett, as head of personnel, then removed Smith from Willow Run as punishment to Sorensen.

Smith was given back responsibility for management of outlying plants, quite likely because of intercession by Ford. This was in January 1942, and the small plants were put to work supplying needed war materials. Following the war, and after the departure of both Sorensen and Bennett, Smith was involved in the decentralization of Ford facilities under Henry Ford II and Ernest Breech. Many small operations that had been favorites of the senior Henry Ford but had been a drain on financial resources were liquidated.

In 1947, Smith was promoted to general manager of the Parts and Equipment Division, the far-flung and much enlarged counterpart of what had been termed outlying plants. Two years later, he was appointed director of quality control, manufacturing staff. It was from this position that Smith retired in September 1956, after forty years with Ford Motor Company.

Despite heavy responsibilities at Ford, Smith possessed the stamina to participate in Detroit Masonic activities, also in Rotary Club, the Elks, and the Ypsilanti businessmen's "Twenty Club." Following his retirement at age sixty-two, the Smiths built a cottage on Dickinson Island in the St. Clair Flats near Algonac. There they spent summers boating and enjoying the outdoors. Their twenty-eight-foot Chris-Craft was named *Rock*.

The Smiths moved into an Ann Arbor apartment at 1009 Woodbridge in 1970, when Roscoe was seventy-eight years old. Gladys Irene Smith passed away at that location August 5, 1988. In December of that year, Roscoe Smith moved to San Diego, where he died on April 16, 1991, at age ninety-seven. Both Roscoe and Gladys Smith were laid to rest at United Memorial Gardens in Ann Arbor.

Major References

Bishop, James T., grandson of Roscoe M. Smith. Personal communication, 1991.

Bishop, James T. "Smith, Roscoe M., Former Ford Executive" (obituary). *Ann Arbor News,* April 17, 1991.

Bryan, Ford R. *Beyond the Model T: The Other Ventures of Henry Ford.* Detroit: Wayne State University Press, 1990.

Detroit City Directory. Detroit: R. L. Polk, 1915–1940.

Falk, Marion J., daughter of Roscoe M. Smith. Personal communication, 1991.

Nevins, Allan, and Frank Ernest Hill. *Ford: Decline and Rebirth, 1933–1962.* New York: Charles Scribner's Sons, 1963.

Smith, Roscoe M. Reminiscences. Accession 65, Henry Ford Museum & Greenfield Village Archives.

Charles Emil Sorensen, 1881–1968.

Charles Emil Sorensen

1881–1968

*"In all the years I knew Sorensen, he was never a politician
in the plant. He was a cold, aloof man, and never had any
social relations with anyone in the company—
myself included."*
—Harry Bennett *

A production genius and loyal servant of Henry Ford
for thirty-nine years, Charles E. Sorensen is probably
the best known of Ford's many lieutenants. His crowning
achievement was design of the production layout of the
mammoth Willow Run plant at Ypsilanti, Michigan, where
giant B-24 bombers were produced during World War II at
the phenomenal rate of one every hour.

Charles Emil Sorensen was born in Copenhagen, Denmark, on September 7, 1881. He was brought to the United States by his parents,
Soren Sorensen and Eva Christine Abrahamson Sorensen, in 1885 and
was naturalized through his father's citizenship. Grade-school education was provided in the Buffalo, New York, public schools. At that time,
he had two sisters and one brother.

At age fourteen, young Sorensen was working summers as a surveyor's assistant, and at sixteen he was apprenticed full-time in foundry
pattern making at the Jewett Stove Works, where, by studying drafting
at night school, he quickly advanced to tool room and machine shop
positions. By 1900, the family had moved to Detroit, where he was employed for a time as a pattern maker by the Art Stove Works. While a
pattern maker for Bryant and Berry, Detroit machinists and foundrymen, in 1904, Sorensen met Henry Ford and agreed to accept a job as
experimental pattern maker at the fledgling Ford Motor Company. Earlier in the same year, on July 30, 1904, Sorensen married Helen E.
Mitchell, a bookkeeper for Sun Stove Company in Detroit. The Sorensens were to have one son, Clifford M. Sorensen.

At Ford Motor Company, Sorensen went to work in the spring of
1905 at three dollars per day as assistant to Fred Seeman, boss of the

* From Harry Bennett,
*We Never Called Him
Henry* (New York:
Fawcett Publications,
1951), p. 28.

pattern department. As an experimental pattern maker, he could provide Ford with wooden models of proposed automotive parts. The models pleased Ford much more than corresponding blueprints which he could not decipher. Sorensen found that following Ford's instructions implicitly would lead to his success. By 1907, Sorensen was head of Ford's pattern department.

During the development of the Model T in 1907, Sorensen, a conspicuously hard worker, had made sufficient impression on Ford to be made assistant superintendent of production under Peter E. Martin. With this increased authority, an almost tyrannical temperament emerged. Sorensen exhibited a very domineering, hard-driving, and explosive personality in the workplace. Ford did not mind these characteristics as long as production increased. Sorensen was particularly productive in foundry operations, where he had introduced several innovative procedures, including the casting of the one-piece, four-cylinder Model T engine block. His foundry expertise earned him the nickname "Cast Iron Charlie" throughout his forty years with Ford Motor Company.

Sorensen was instrumental in Ford's 1911 purchase of the Keim Mills factory in Buffalo—Sorensen's home at one time. With this organization came such capable men as William Knudsen, John R. Lee, and William K. Smith. With other men at Ford, such as Clarence W. Avery, Martin, William C. Klann, and Peterson, Sorensen took part in establishing the first automobile final assembly line at Highland Park in October 1913. This highly publicized event was a joint development, with Avery and Sorensen most often given major credit.

By 1915, Sorensen wielded about as much power in the factories as Martin, the production chief. When, early during World War I, the British government asked Ford to manufacture tractors in Britain, Sorensen was sent to England to plan the plant and specify the machinery necessary. In England, Sorensen established a friendly relationship with Sir Percival Perry, which would benefit both in the future. When the British found they could not furnish the workers, Sorensen was called back to Detroit to organize production of tractors in a new plant in Dearborn, very near Henry Ford's new home, Fair Lane. At that time, Sorensen also moved his family to Dearborn, building a large colonial home on the Rouge River a mile or so north of Fair Lane. At the Dearborn plant, Sorensen helped design the Fordson tractor and managed the production of thousands for both Britain and the United States before the war's end.

The Rouge plant, built in Dearborn at the close of the war, was meant to be primarily a tractor plant. Sorensen was in charge of tractor production for Ford. So when the Rouge, with its enormous steel smelting facilities, was ready for operation in 1919, Sorensen moved in with his tractor manufacturing and essentially took charge of the entire complex, leaving Highland Park men behind and choosing as his own assistants men such as Mead Bricker and Harry Bennett. William B. Mayo and Knudsen, who had planned and built the Rouge, were no longer necessary to Sorensen, who would now operate it with his own crew.

Martin eventually came to the Rouge in what Sorensen considered a secondary position, that of Rouge plant superintendent, whereas Sorensen considered himself the companywide chief of production planning and development. Ford seemed to have no formal organization plan. He believed in constant competition among his lieutenants. His maxim: "Let's you and him fight and see who comes out best."

After Ford had purchased the failing Lincoln Motor Company in 1922, he picked Sorensen and Martin to straighten out the plant's production system still managed by Henry and Wilfred Leland. The methods used by these two Ford men were sufficiently tactless to drive the Lelands completely out of the picture, much to Ford's satisfaction. By 1926, Sorensen was in charge of Ford branch operations and, along with Edsel Ford and Perry, was a board member of several foreign corporations manufacturing Ford products. About this same time, Sorensen, with Ford's approval, assigned Bennett responsibility for Ford personnel management at the Rouge plant.

Between 1929 and 1936, Ford Motor Company became involved with the Soviet government in developing a plant for the manufacture of Ford Model A vehicles. Sorensen traveled to the Soviet Union to represent Ford Motor Company in this $40-million program. And Sorensen startled the automotive industry again in 1932, this time by casting a V-8 cylinder block all in one piece, producing an engine that was to last longer than the four-cylinder Model T.

During the depression years of the 1930s, Ford dealers as well as Ford workers felt the harsh tactics of Sorensen, who was presumably carrying out Henry Ford's orders. Although Sorensen claims he was a close friend of Edsel Ford, who would have treated dealers with more consideration, Sorensen drove many small dealers out of business. During this period, at $220,000 per year, Sorensen was likely the highest-paid employee at Ford Motor Company. During the mid-1930s, he built a lavish home in Miami Beach. In 1937, Sorensen was decorated Commander of Danneborg by the King of Denmark.

Sorensen had an agreement with Henry Ford to retire in 1941 at age sixty, but because of the imminent entry of the United States into World War II, he felt the time was inappropriate, especially because of the poor health of both Edsel and Henry. In July 1941, Sorensen was asked to serve on the board of directors of Ford Motor Company as executive vice president. Sorensen found himself dealing directly with the U.S. government on Ford's war contracts. The October 1940 contract to build 4,236 of the eighteen-cylinder, air-cooled Pratt-Whitney aircraft engines, for example, became Sorensen's responsibility. By

Sorensen at his desk in the Rouge Administration Building in 1939. His secretary, Russell Gnau, stands beside him.

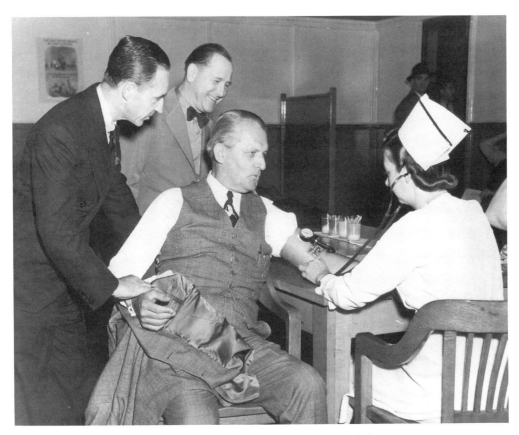

During a wartime blood drive, Sorensen gets a blood pressure reading while Edsel Ford takes Sorensen's pulse and Harry Bennett looks on amused. December 3, 1942.

1942, the order had been filled, and Ford was the largest producer of aircraft engines in the country.

The grand curtain closer for Sorensen at Ford Motor Company was the Consolidated "Liberator" B-24 bomber operation at Willow Run. Sorensen was instrumental in obtaining the prime contract for Ford to build these four-engine bombers by promising production at the rate of one per hour rather than the conventional of one per day. He was certain moving assembly lines would work for the monster bomber as well as they had for the Model T. And he proved this by using $200 million to build the country's largest manufacturing plant under one roof, where by late 1943, with a work force of 40,000, he was building 365 complete bombers per month. More than 8,000 were produced at Willow Run.

Sorensen (left) with Henry Ford and Henry Ford II at the dedication of the Edsel Ford Workshop in Greenfield Village in December 1943.

At Ford, Sorensen undoubtedly displayed great brilliance in organizing production. Being Henry Ford's chief production manager for so many years means he deserves substantial credit for the long-term financial success of the company. Sorensen has been correctly criticized, however, for his insensitive disposition, his irrational treatment of employees, and his explosive temperament.

Following Edsel Ford's death on May 26, 1943, Ford family stockholders met on June 1 and elected the senior Henry Ford president of Ford Motor Company with Charles Sorensen as vice president and Burt J. Craig as secretary and treasurer. Elected as new members of the board of directors were Eleanor Ford, Henry Ford II, Benson Ford, and Ford employees Bennett, Mead L. Bricker, and Ray Rausch. Sorensen's unique position on the board had now been weakend considerably by the presence of three of his rivals.

Henry Ford II was appointed a vice president of Ford Motor Company on December 15, 1943. It was quite clear Ford family members were intent on ridding the company of men who had been especially troublesome to their beloved son, husband, and father—Edsel Ford. This applied quite distinctly to Sorensen. Under pressure, he soon resigned from the company. This was on March 13, 1944, while Sorensen was vacationing at his winter home at 5185 North Bay Road in Miami Beach.

By June 1944, Sorensen had accepted the presidency of Willys-Overland Motors of Toledo. He also served as vice chairman of the Willys board from 1946 to 1953. The winter of 1953 found Sorensen visiting his old friend Perry at Nassau in the Bahamas. The Sorensens gave up their apartment in Detroit Towers at 8162 East Jefferson Avenue in 1955, making Miami their main residence. In March 1959, Edith Mitchell Sorensen died in Miami Beach. At that time, Charles Sorensen was president of the Miami Heart Institute.

Sorensen was a yachtsman from the time he first floated a raft as a boy on the Niagara River at Buffalo. He belonged to the Grosse Pointe Yacht Club and was commodore of the Detroit Yacht Club as well as a member of clubs in Miami Beach and the Bahamas. His *White Cloud* racing yacht was well known in southern waters. In January 1960, at age seventy-nine, he married Edith Thomson Montgomery. Their winter home was in St. Croix, Virgin Islands, with a summer home near Bethesda, Maryland. Sorensen died on August 11, 1968, at Bethesda. Services were held in the Community Church, Miami Beach.

Charles Emil Sorensen

Major References

Lewis, David L. *The Public Image of Henry Ford.* Detroit: Wayne State University Press, 1976.

Nevins, Allan. *Ford: The Times, the Man, the Company.* New York: Charles Scribner's Sons, 1954.

Nevins, Allan, and Frank Ernest Hill. *Ford: Decline and Rebirth, 1933–1962.* New York: Charles Scribner's Sons, 1963.

———. *Ford: Expansion and Challenge, 1915–1932.* New York: Charles Scribner's Sons, 1957.

Records of C. E. Sorensen, 1913–1946. Accession 38, Henry Ford Museum & Greenfield Village Archives.

Sorensen, Charles E. Reminiscences. Accession 65, Henry Ford Museum & Greenfield Village Archives.

Sorensen, Charles E., with Samuel T. Williamson. *My Forty Years with Ford.* New York: W. W. Norton, 1956.

William Bushnell Stout, 1880–1956.

William Bushnell Stout

1880–1956

"Stout stockholders invested from $1,000 to $5,000 each
with the distinct understanding that they might
lose all their money."
—Stanley Knauss *

Like Henry Ford, William B. Stout was a man with ideas considerably ahead of the times. And Stout was able to express his ideas in words, in drawings, as models, and as full-scale devices. His contributions to air, auto, and rail transportation have been truly inspiring.

William Bushnell Stout was born March 16, 1880, in Quincy, Illinois, as twin to a sister who died at six weeks of age. He was the son of James Frank Stout and Mary C. Bushnell Stout. His father was a Methodist minister who insisted the family live by Methodist rules. The father's occupation required the family to move with frequency—to Danville, Illinois, in 1881; Bloomington, Illinois, in 1884; West St. Paul, Minnesota, in 1887; southwest Minneapolis, Minnesota, in 1889; and Mankato, Minnesota. About 1897, William enrolled in the Mechanical Arts High School in St. Paul, where his father was pastor of the First Methodist Church. Although his father and mother moved on to Red Wing, Minnesota, he stayed in St. Paul, where he worked afternoons in an office copying patent papers and finished high school in 1899. He attended Hamline University for two years and taught in a country school for a year before entering the University of Minnesota.

At the university, he supported himself by writing a column for the *Minneapolis Times,* each article describing some novel device he had designed. Because of eye trouble, he left the university in 1904 and went on a solo motorcycle trip through Europe, supporting himself by writing stories describing his trip for the *Minneapolis Times.* Back from Europe, he became acquainted with Alma E. Raymond of Napanee, Ontario. They were married in Winnipeg on June 16, 1906. The Stouts were to have one daughter, Wilma Frances.

Stout was an entertaining as well as informative speaker, and in 1907, he was called upon to speak before the Minneapolis-St. Paul En-

* From the oral reminiscences of Stanley Knauss, assistant to William Stout.

gineering Society as a substitute for the famous aviator Octave Chanute. Stout was then well known locally by his pen name "Jack Kneiff," with a column for the *Minneapolis Times* for which he was paid eighty-five dollars per month. Along with his column and his technical drawing, he also sang in a church choir and amused gatherings with his Swedish-dialect stories.

In the summer of 1908, Stout and his wife explored Europe on a motorcycle; again, he sent stories back to the *Times* in return for expense money. While living in Minneapolis, Stout had been designing motorcycles and building model airplanes which he flew very successfully at local events.

By 1912, Stout's reputation as a technical writer had led him to Chicago and the position of technical and aviation editor of the *Chicago Tribune*. There he founded *Aerial Age* magazine and formed the Illinois Model Airplane Club. In 1914, he was appointed chief engineer of the Scripps-Booth Company in Detroit. He also became advertising manager and sales manager for the Scripps-Booth automobile, which tried to compete with the Model T but failed. His *Boy's Book of Mechanical Models* was published in 1916 while he was in Detroit.

In 1917, Stout became chief engineer of the Aircraft Division of Packard Motor Car Company of Detroit, but he left soon for Washington to serve as adviser to the U.S. Aircraft Board. It was then that he designed and supervised the building of the S-X plywood cantilever airplane.

In September 1917, Stout moved back to Detroit, with residence at 55 Seward Avenue, to work for Motor Products Company. Two years later, he formed the Stout Engineering Laboratory, where the Batwing plane was built for the Navy and flown on December 23, 1921, and three all-metal torpedo planes were built during 1922. In late 1922, Stout organized the Stout Metal Airplane Company, with 128 prominent Detroiters each investing $1,000. Offices were in the General Motors Building, and the Stout family residence was 250 Hague in Detroit. This organization designed and built the Air Sedan in 1923, and in 1924 the 2-AT, the first successful all-metal commercial airplane in the United States.

Among directors of the Stout Metal Airplane Company were Edsel Ford and William B. Mayo of the Ford Motor Company. Stout was anxious to have an airplane factory with its own airport in order to test and service his planes. Henry Ford agreed to build an airport with a factory adjoining it, providing Stout could convince the 128 stockholders of his company to sell out to Ford. Stout managed the sellout, and Stout Metal Airplane Company became a division of Ford Motor Company on July 1, 1925, with Edsel Ford as president, Burt J. Craig as

Nameplate used on planes built by Stout and Ford.

secretary-treasurer, Mayo as operating head, and Stout as consultant. The airport and factory had been provided, but Stout had largely lost control of his company.

Stout's influence, nevertheless, led to major innovations in commercial air service. His office at Ford Airport was in the new passenger terminal, the first of its kind. Across the street from the terminal, the Dearborn Inn would be built—the first airport hotel. In August 1925, Stout inaugurated Stout Air Services, which operated the first regularly scheduled passenger airline in the United States. Stout built Liberty-powered all-metal monoplanes to initiate this service, first flying between Dearborn and Grand Rapids. Later, from 1928 to 1932, the Stout-designed Ford Trimotors flew passengers and Ford cargo between Dearborn, Chicago, and Cleveland.

Ford-Stout Trimotors were for these few years the preferred aircraft of the fledgling airlines of the United States. Charles Lindbergh came to Ford Airport in 1927, and in a Trimotor he gave Henry Ford his very first airplane ride. In 1929, Stout sold Stout Air Services to United Aircraft and Transportation Company, now United Airlines. The Great Depression reduced sales of the Trimotor planes after 1929, and Stout left Ford in 1930. During the five years Stout worked for Ford, the Stout family lived at 146 Lawrence Avenue in Detroit.

277

Edsel Ford, Richard E. Byrd, and Stout. Edsel Ford sponsored Admiral Byrd's flights over the North Pole in 1926 and over the South Pole in 1929.

Although no longer with Ford, Stout continued to operate his Stout Engineering Laboratory at 1425 South Telegraph Road in Dearborn. At his laboratory, Stout conducted research and development on such experimental devices as the "Sky Car," the "Railplane," the "Scarab Car," and the "House Trailer." These vehicles were ultra-modern in design, incorporating many features new in both appearance and function, features not yet commonplace in vehicle design. The Stout Motor Car Company was organized in April 1934, the Skycraft Corporation in June 1940. The Pullman Corporation of Chicago sponsored the Railplane, and Palace Coach and Trailer Company of Flint was licensed to build the House Trailer.

Stout sold his research and engineering laboratory in Dearborn to Consolidated Aircraft Corporation of San Diego and became director of its research division during World War II.

About 1941, with his new son-in-law, John F. Fisher, Stout formed the Stout Homes Corporation, which manufactured and sold prefabricated panels made of aircraft materials to provide temporary housing for both civilian and military use. These panels could be shipped in Consolidated B-24 planes and erected at remote bases within a matter of hours.

In 1943, the *Dearborn City Directory* lists Research Division Consolidated Vultee Aircraft Corporation, with William B. Stout as director and John F. Fisher as division manager. Also listed is Stout Engineering Laboratories, Inc., with William B. Stout as president, Wilma F. Fisher as vice president, and John F. Fisher as secretary and treasurer. The Stouts still lived at 149 Lawrence in Detroit, the Fishers in Pontiac.

Stout was an innovator—an "Imagineer," as he said. He was exceptionally well respected in both aviation and automotive circles, and in 1935 was elected national president of the Society of Automotive Engineers. Although Stout did not personally test his experimental planes, he and his family traveled extensively in his Scarab automobile—250,000 miles around the United States.

Stout's mind never retired. In 1951, the year he wrote his autobiography, he visualized the skies filled with aircraft designed as orthopters, birds with flapping wings. He foresaw machines that could reproduce themselves.

Stout was at his home, 2211 19th Avenue, Phoenix, Arizona, when he died of a heart ailment on March 20, 1956.

William Bushnell Stout

Major References

Ingalls, Douglas. *Tin Goose.* Fallbrook, Calif.: Aero Publishers, 1968.

Knauss, Stanley. Reminiscences. Accession 65, Henry Ford Museum & Greenfield Village Archives.

Obituary. *Dearborn Independent,* March 23, 1956.

Stout, William B. Reminiscences. Accession 65, Henry Ford Museum & Greenfield Village Archives.

——. *So Away I Went.* Indianapolis and New York: Bobbs-Merrill, 1951.

Stout Metal Aircraft Company. Accession 18, Henry Ford Museum & Greenfield Village Archives.

Albert M. Wibel, 1886–1965. (Photo courtesy of Burton Historical Collection, Detroit Public Library.)

Albert M. Wibel

1886–1965

*"Edsel told Bennett to keep his nose out of purchasing and
stick to personnel and union negotiations."*
—Charles E. Sorensen *

How one could manage the purchase of all the materials
and necessary equipment to build 2 million vehicles a
year, with each vehicle containing perhaps 100,000 parts, is
beyond comprehension. Yet Albert M. Wibel did just that.
And it is said that Wibel was dismissed because he refused to
permit a shady deal cooked up by Harry Bennett.

Albert M. Wibel was born in 1886 on his father's farm about four
miles east of the town of Peru, Indiana. This was a relatively small but
rich-soiled farm of Wabash river bottom close to the little town of Rich
Valley. When he was three or four years old, his family moved into the
city of Peru, where he attended the very early grades of school. When
he was about eleven or twelve years old, the family moved farther north
into Wells County near Bufften, Indiana. There he received his later
grade school and high school education.

Wibel went directly into teaching after high school. He made
enough money to attend Indiana University at Bloomington during
spring and summer terms. He finished his university work in the
spring of 1912. He did not fully intend to quit teaching, but a friend at
college had just purchased a new Model T Ford, which was indeed an
intriguing contraption, and Wibel was curious to see how it was made.
That meant going to Detroit.

Wibel arrived in Detroit on May 2, 1912, and went to visit the Ford
Motor Company that same day. He was introduced to John R. Lee of
the Sociological Department, who asked Wibel where he came from
and what he wanted to do. Lee then brought in Oscar Bornholdt, who
was in charge of the Engineering Procurement Office. Wibel emphasized his university work and his special interest in mathematics, including calculus. Bornholdt's response was, "College education ought
to be worth something."

* From Charles E.
Sorensen, *My Forty
Years with Ford* (New
York: W. W. Norton,
1956), p. 71.

281

Wibel started work the next day, a Saturday morning. He was to receive seventy-five dollars per month and was surprised to receive a full day's pay for that morning. He worked under Bornholdt on the procurement of machine tools, needing to know where machines were needed, when they needed to be delivered, and what they would cost. With Model T production schedules being increased dramatically from 400 per day to 700, to 1,000, to 1,500, keeping up with machine requirements was a colossal task. Wibel's decisions had to dovetail with plans of machine designers, building layout superintendents, and supplier capabilities. Some algebra may have been quite useful.

Ford Motor Company stressed the design and use of highly specialized machines for very specific purposes. Ford executives wanted, for example, not a lathe that would do ten different operations but rather a lathe that would do one operation ten times as fast.

In 1913, Wibel decided to enter law school. With his previous credits, he would be able to receive a degree in three years. The evening course required his attendance five nights a week, considerably more time than he had expected to spend. But he managed both his night courses and his daily work at Ford by keeping very busy. Wibel received his bachelor of laws degree from the Detroit College of Law and was admitted to the bar in 1916.

In the *Detroit City Directory,* Wibel is listed as a clerk boarding at 121 Highland Street in 1914, but following his graduation from law school, he is listed as a lawyer living with his wife, Ada, at 103 Charlotte Avenue. Next they lived at 142 Collingwood, and in 1921 they were residing at the better address of 1747 Longfellow, where Wibel, listed as a machinist, lived with his family until 1930. The Wibels had four children, two girls and two boys.

At work, Wibel became assistant to Fred Diehl, who was in charge of all purchasing for Ford Motor Company. With the expansion of the Rouge plant, Wibel's activities soon grew to involvement in many transactions beyond machinery buying. His office correspondence reveals that he was called upon to negotiate the purchase of a variety of raw materials such as iron ore, coal, limestone, and sand for glass—items ranging from 12,000-ton ore-carrying ships to the kitchen utensils used in the galley. Large amounts of cotton and wool, for example, were used for automotive upholstery. A single order of "picker cotton," "cotton linters," and "cotton ply" amounted to 4,225,000 pounds at a cost of $262,000.

In August 1923, when Ford Motor Company was approaching its peak of Model T production, Wibel was concerned with some very large numbers. According to his office records, the company plans were to increase production from 6,000 cars in twenty-four hours to 10,000 cars in twenty-four hours, with an alternative schedule of 8,000 cars in sixteen hours. This latter plan would produce 500 Model T's an hour companywide. At this time, when Highland Park was the major Ford plant, Wibel summed up his situation as follows:

Men at work: Highland Park, 60,000
               Rouge, 34,000
Horsepower: Highland Park, 40,000
               Rouge, 23,000, plus
                      1st turbine, 66,000 h.p., delivery 9/15/23
                      2nd turbine, 66,000 h.p., delivery 12/15/23
Machinery account: Highland Park, $22,600,000
               Rouge, $11,000,000
Estimated replacement value: Highland Park, $35,000,000
               Rouge, $18,000,000
Floor space: Highland Park, 3,000,000 square feet
               Rouge, 900,000 square feet

Most of the expansion, of course, came about at the new Dearborn Rouge location, which was soon to replace Highland Park as Ford's main plant. During this period of the mid-1920s, Wibel became involved in the purchase of not only the powerplant equipment but also blast furnaces, steel mills, cement and glass manufacturing equipment, and railroad rolling stock.

Ford employee commissaries required fourteen buyers and accountants. Under Wibel, these company stores were at several locations in addition to those in Highland Park and Dearborn. Commissaries served coal miners in West Virginia and Kentucky, lumbermen in northern Michigan, and rubber plantation workers in Brazil. Food, drug, and clothing items added up to annual sales of more than $10 million a year. In contrast to carload purchases of canned peas for employee families, Wibel's men purchased 199 ocean ships from the U.S. Shipping Board for $1,697,470 in 1926. The ships were scrapped at the Rouge plant and the salvage put to use in various Ford operations.

In 1927, Wibel assumed responsibility for the entire purchasing department, with a force of 500 buyers operating not only in Dearborn but throughout the world—including Sir Percival Perry's domain in Europe. Yearly purchases by Wibel's office totaled from $400 million to $700 million. Wibel became a regular member of Ford's private luncheon table at Dearborn.

During the 1927 changeover from the Model T to the Model A, complete tooling for the Model A was needed for the Rouge plant in record time. Never before had such a tremendous machinery procurement

Edsel Ford, Charles Sorensen, Henry Ford, and Wibel at Rouge powerhouse after installation of a 110,000-kilowatt turbine generator in July 1931.

problem been encountered. At the time of changeover, the Rouge plant possessed some 45,000 specialized machines valued at about $45 million. Half of those existing tools were rebuilt, and about a quarter were scrapped. The cost of new machinery and overhaul of old totaled $18 million. When one views the impressive buildings of a manufacturing plant, one seldom realizes that the machinery within the building is likely to be many times more valuable than the building itself.

284   About 1930, the Wibels moved to Bloomfield Township, where they

Wibel, Edsel Ford, Henry Ford, Charles Sorensen, and Burt J. Craig on Henry Ford's seventy-ninth birthday, July 30, 1942.

lived at 3825 Oakland Drive and belonged to the neighboring Oakland Hills Golf Club, where Wibel and other members of his family were active in golf, riding, bowling, and tennis. Wibel kept himself in excellent physical trim. He also belonged to the Detroit Athletic Club, the Bloomfield Hills Country Club, and the Indian Creek Club in Miami. Wibel was a member of the Economic Club of Detroit and a director of the Detroit Board of Commerce and the National Defense Committee of the Automotive Manufacturers Association.

Wibel contributed greatly to Ford Motor Company's excellent reputation with the U.S. government in respect to war contracts. He was promoted to vice president in charge of purchasing on July 17, 1941. His experience in determining costs of manufacturing large quantities of military equipment was nationally recognized. His cost estimates were valued highly in the negotiation of contracts for building aircraft 285 engines, bombers, tanks, and assorted automotive vehicles. Dealings with the government were handled largely by Edsel Ford, Wibel and Charles E. Sorensen. Henry Ford played no major role.

As Henry Ford became more mentally as well as physically feeble, Harry Bennett was gaining more of his confidence. In an attempt to control Ford Motor Company, Bennett found it advantageous to deride anyone close to either Henry or Edsel. Bennett did not join the luncheon group at Henry Ford's table in fair discussion but preferred to undermine each of these men in a manner considered underhanded. Wibel, Ernest Liebold, Sorensen, and Ernest Kanzler were dismissed by Bennett, presumably with Henry Ford's approval. Bennett went so far as to fire Edsel Ford's private secretary, John Crawford, during Edsel's final illness in early 1943. Wibel was not a friend of Bennett; in April 1943, he was dismissed from Ford Motor Company as a result of Bennett's influence on Henry Ford. Wibel is said to have been fired because he refused to fill a contract Bennett had awarded to one of his cronies.

During his 31-year career with Ford, Wibel took exceptional pride in his personal encouragement of outside suppliers by giving them a reasonable profit margin so they would have the means to provide reliable and high-quality materials and parts for Ford.

The dismissal of Ford executives did not go unnoticed by other automotive concerns. It was only a matter of days before Wibel was invited to a meeting with George W. Mason, president of Nash-Kelvinator. By June 5, 1943, Wibel was vice president in charge of purchasing for Nash-Kelvinator (later American Motors). Others who left Ford and joined Nash-Kelvinator at that time were Henry C. Doss (sales) and Fred L. Black (public relations).

Wibel retired as vice president in charge of procurement at American Motors in 1956, but he was retained for several years as a consultant. Wibel died on April 11, 1965, at Henry Ford Hospital in Detroit, at age seventy-nine after a long illness. Services were held in Christ Church, Cranbrook, and burial was in Acacia Park Cemetery. Ada Wibel died March 9, 1977. The surviving children were Mary, Betty Jane, and William. The youngest son, Richard, had died September 22, 1973, at age forty-five.

Major References

"A. M. Wibel." Burton Historical Collection, Detroit Public Library.

"Close-Ups of Key Men." *Ford Digest,* November 7, 1936.

Nevins, Allan. *Ford: The Times, the Man, the Company.* New York: Charles Scribner's Sons, 1954.

Nevins, Allan, and Frank Ernest Hill. *Ford: Decline and Rebirth, 1933–1962.* New York: Charles Scribner's Sons, 1963.

———. *Ford: Expansion and Challenge, 1915–1932.* New York: Charles Scribner's Sons, 1957.

Obituary. *Birmingham* (Michigan) *Eccentric,* May 13, 1965.

"Office Files of A. M. Wibel." Accession 390, Henry Ford Museum & Greenfield Village Archives.

Wibel, Albert M. Reminiscences. Accession 65, Henry Ford Museum & Greenfield Village Archives.

Albert M. Wibel

Childe Harold Wills, 1878–1940.

Childe Harold Wills

1878–1940

"Two partnerships were to shape the history of the Ford Motor Company in its first dazzling rise: the partnership of Ford and Couzens, and the partnership of Ford and Wills. The first was a union of opposites, attended by no real liking; the second was a union of men of generally congenial tastes and ambitions who instinctively understood each other."
—*Allan Nevins* *

C. Harold Wills was working for Henry Ford before the Ford Motor Company was organized. A brilliant draftsman and designer, Wills was indispensable to Ford, who could barely read a blueprint, let alone draw one. Wills was able to decipher Ford's crude pencil sketches, produce a well-designed mechanical drawing, and direct the method of fabrication whether it be a cotter pin or chassis.

Childe Harold Wills was born on June 1, 1878, at Fort Wayne, Indiana, the third and youngest child of John Carnegie Wills and Angelina Swindell Wills. Two older children, Mary E. and John C. Wills, Jr., had died in 1875. Grandfather Wills had migrated from Scotland to Canada in 1832. John C. Wills, the father, was a master mechanic, and his wife, Angelina, must have had an appreciation of Byron's poetry to have named her son "Childe Harold." By 1885, the Wills family had moved to Detroit and was living at 220 Twelfth Street.

From his father, Wills received a very early perception of the mechanical arts. The boy's early interests seem to have been divided between commercial art, such as cartooning, and mechanical engineering. In the *Detroit City Directory* for 1895, young Wills, at age seventeen, is listed as an artist boarding at home, 1993 Trumbull Street. The previous year, he had been listed merely as a student. The need to make a living, however, drove him toward training as a machinist. After public schooling in Detroit, Wills worked for four years, from 1896 to 1899, for the Detroit Lubricator Company (where his fa-

* From Allan Nevins, *Ford: The Times, the Man, the Company* (New York: Charles Scribner's Sons, 1954), p. 227.

ther also worked), as an apprentice toolmaker receiving seven dollars and fifty cents per week until he became a finished toolmaker with pay raised to ten dollars. During this period, Wills studied chemistry and metallurgy at night school.

Wills next got a job in the engineering department of the Boyer Machine Company (forerunner of Burroughs Adding Machine Company) at eighteen dollars a week; within a few months, he became superintendent at fifty dollars. However, Wills was strongly attracted to automobiles, and especially to Henry Ford's endeavors at 81 Park Place in Detroit. In 1899, Wills approached Ford to work as his assistant on a part-time basis, sharing Ford's $125-per-month salary. Wills worked with Ford early mornings and late evenings in the small, unheated shop where they are said to have donned boxing gloves to spar every few minutes to keep warm. In 1900, the *Detroit City Directory* lists Wills as a draftsman for the Detroit Automobile Company, of which Ford was superintendent.

In 1901, the Detroit Automobile Company was reorganized as the Henry Ford Company, with Ford as chief engineer to capitalize on his racing prowess. Wills helped Ford build the famous "999" and "Arrow" racers from which Ford gained considerable prestige in racing circles. By August 1902, Wills had obtained a written contract to work for Ford, presumably full-time. By then, Ford was obtaining considerable financial aid from Alexander Malcolmson, a prominent coal dealer in Detroit.

Ford operations moved to the much larger Mack Avenue plant in April 1903, and on June 16, the Ford Motor Company was incorporated. Wills was perhaps too poor to become a stockholder, but Ford offered to share some of his own dividends, about 10 percent in the early years. It was Wills, the artist, who designed the 1906 Ford script that has adorned the many millions of Ford cars throughout the world.

Within Ford Motor Company, Wills functioned as chief designer and engineer as well as metallurgist. Ford and Wills worked so closely together that their contributions are said to have been indistinguishable. Wills was perhaps as responsible as Ford for the building of models A, C, F, and B during the first few years of the company. Ford, of course, was undoubtedly the boss, exercising close supervision of Wills.

In 1905, the Ford Manufacturing Company was formed to produce auto parts. Stockholders in this organization included Wills as secretary of the new corporation, along with Ford as president. With production of the additional models K, R, S, and the very popular Model N, Ford was eying a more expansive plant site at Highland Park in 1907.

For the Model T, which would be introduced in 1908, Ford, Wills, and a very talented assistant to Wills, Joseph Galamb, would share the major credits. The Model T was glowingly advertised as being built with the very new and tough vanadium steel. Both Wills and Ford took credit for its use in the Model T, although the alloy was overused to the extent of causing mechanical failures in some applications. Wills was conducting metallurgical research on several alloys of steel, particularly those containing molybdenum. Wills introduced molybdenum steels to the automotive industry, and he is said to have had financial interests in several steel producers supplying steel to Ford Motor Company.

In his private life, upon leaving his parents' home in 1904, Wills resided at the Plaza Hotel, until 1907, when he moved to 39 Bethune Avenue. On January 3, 1914, Wills married Mary Coyne of New York and took up residence at 1760 Jefferson Avenue in Detroit, where two children were born: John Harold Wills and Childe Harold Wills, Jr.

In 1912, while working for Ford at Highland Park, Wills and his associates built a more stylish design of the Model T to impress Ford on the Ford family's return from a European trip. Ford was so upset by the different style that he is said to have pounded the car to pieces. Ford was not interested in an improved style. During World War I, Wills was given charge of Ford's most important military contract, the production of the famous twelve-cylinder, 400-horsepower Liberty engine. Some 3,940 of these monster aircraft engines were built for France and Britain during 1918.

All during World War I, Henry Ford was planning tremendous expansion of Ford Motor Company into steel and tractor operations. The Dodge brothers were objecting and had taken Ford to court. Wills was called upon to testify in behalf of Ford. Ford lost to the Dodges and was beside himself at the outcome. In January 1919, Ford resigned as president of Ford Motor Company, leaving Edsel Ford in charge.

Henry Ford threatened to organize a new company without stockholders to build automobiles, while at the same time he was secretly buying out Ford Motor Company stockholders one by one. This upheaval within the company could have been the reason Wills, together with his close associate John R. Lee, resigned that spring of 1919. Closely following his leaving (March 15, 1919), Wills was granted $1,592,128.39 by the court in a final settlement with Ford Motor Company.

In June 1919, when Henry Ford was frightening his minor stockholders into selling their shares, a rather believable rumor arose insisting that Ford had sold his shares to Col. Du Pont of General Motors. Ford was receiving as much as $150 million for his stock, and small Cadillac cars designed by Wills would be built in the Highland Park plant. These cars would be named the "WillsLee." It seems quite possible that Henry, himself, may have planted the rumor.

Henry Ford and Wills in May 1915.

Upon leaving Ford, Wills and John R. Lee formed the Marysville Land Company and purchased 4,400 acres of land on the St. Clair River about forty-five miles from Detroit. There they founded the city of Marysville—named after Wills's wife, Mary. Both men were pursuing goals unattainable at Ford Motor Company. Wills had for years wanted to build an automobile to his own standards. He had seen the Dodge brothers succeed with their car in 1913. Wills became head of the C. H. Wills Company, built a plant in Marysville, and from 1921 until 1927 built the Wills Sainte Claire, an automobile of pleasing design and meticulous workmanship, called "the Gray Goose" or "the Molybdenum Car."

Lee, the former sociological specialist for Ford, planned the incorporation of Marysville, a real estate development of 2,881 lots for homes of workers. Together, Wills and Lee invested $3,500,000 in streets, utilities, housing, parks, playgrounds, and municipal buildings.

Neither automotive nor real estate pursuits survived the Great Depression of the 1930s. The C. H. Wills Company, in receivership in 1923, was reorganized as Wills Sainte Claire, Inc., which was liquidated September 24, 1936. Real estate interests were handled as late as 1938 by the Marysville Improvement Company.

The Wills family lived at 128-9 River Road in Marysville, spending

The Ford script designed by Wills in 1906. Here it is shown on a 1908
Model T radiator.

part of their time at 8344 Jefferson Avenue in Detroit. Their powerboat,
the *Wills Sainte Claire,* could take them speedily back and forth by
water if they preferred that form of transportation. For more leisurely
excursions, the sumptuous yacht *Marold* was at their service.

Wills received considerable royalties from his metallurgical patents,
and from 1933 until his death, he was retained as consultant by Chrysler Corporation which had purchased his factory in Marysville. Wills
was living at 930 Lakeshore Drive, Grosse Pointe Farms, when he suf- 293

The Town Car

—a special custom-built model
built only on order

The Wills Sainte Claire Town Car, as advertised in 1926.

fered a stroke and died at Henry Ford Hospital in Detroit on December 30, 1940. He is buried in Detroit's Woodlawn Cemetery.

Major References

Burton, Clarence M. *History of Detroit.* Detroit: Sid Clarke Publishing Co., 1922.

C. Harold Wills Papers: 1899–1939. Accession 418, Henry Ford Museum & Greenfield Village Archives.

"Childe Harold Wills: A Career in Cars." *Automobile Quarterly,* Vol. 5, no. 2, 1966.

Clever, Fred J. "C. Harold Wills—On His Way to Build His Perfect Motor Car." *Torque,* January–February 1980.

Nevins, Allan. *Ford: The Times, the Man, the Company.* New York: Charles Scribner's Sons, 1954.

Nevins, Allan, and Frank Ernest Hill. *Ford: Expansion and Challenge, 1915–1932.* New York: Charles Scribner's Sons, 1957.

"Wills, Motor Pioneer, Dies." *Detroit News,* December 30, 1940.

Appendix I:

Henry's Sub-lieutenants

The following people were also highly beneficial to Henry Ford and the Ford Motor Company. An expanded volume of biographies certainly would include many of these personalities.

Anderson, John Wendell. One of the original stockholders of Ford Motor Company, an attorney with fifty shares.

Anderson, Warren C. European sales representative for Ford.

Bennett, Charles H. One of the original stockholders of Ford Motor Company, with fifty shares.

Berghoff, Bredo W. Worked for Ford in Russia to assess tractor manufacturing in that country.

Bishop, James W. A Detroit Edison superintendent who helped Ford build his quadricycle in 1896 and later became collector of electrical power equipment for Henry Ford Museum.

Bonner, D. H. Manager of Ford assembly plants under William Knudsen.

Bricker, Mead L. Hired in 1915 at tractor plant. Became production superintendent under Charles E. Sorensen at Willow Run.

Briggs, L. E. Joined Ford in 1914. Treasurer of Ford Motor Company 1929–1945.

Brown, B. R. Construction superintendent. Helped build Rouge plant and overseas plants under William Knudsen.

Brown, L. V. Joined Ford in 1912 as shipping clerk. Shipping manager 1916–1949.

Brownell, Charles A. Advertising specialist for Ford Motor Company.

Burns, Charles J. Joined Ford in 1910. Controlled traffic and transportation costs. With Ford forty years.

Cordell, Harold. Secretary to Henry Ford 1921–1929.

Cowling, William C. Director of transportation in 1919. Manager of Ford sales during depression years of the 1930s.

Crowther, Samuel. Journalist, ghost writer for Henry Ford. Author of the books *My Life and Work, Today and Tomorrow,* and *Moving Forward.*

Davis, Clem. Watchmaker, supervisor of Ford Motor timeclocks, in charge of all instrument repair at Rouge plant.

Davis, J. R. Succeeded William Cowling as sales manager. Confidant of Edsel Ford.

Degener, August (Gus). Joined Ford in 1905. Specialized in heat treatment of metals. Head of inspection department in 1919.

Diehl, Fred. Purchasing agent under James Couzens. Left Ford in 1927.

Dodge, Horace. One of original stockholders of Ford Motor Company, with fifty shares. Partner in Dodge Brothers Manufacturing Company.

Dodge, John. One of original stockholders of Ford Motor Company, with fifty shares. Partner in Dodge Brothers Manufacturing Company.

Donaldson, B. R. Joined Ford Motor Company in 1919, director of advertising and sales promotion.

Doss, Henry Clay. Sales manager of Ford Motor Company for many years.

Dulmage, Roland W. Joined Ford in 1920. Responsible for operation of Rouge power plant. Power consultant for Ford until 1949.

Emde, Carl. Tool designer during early days of Ford Motor Company.

Esper, A. L. Joined Ford in 1917. Engineer and test driver associated with motor boats, aircraft, and automobiles.

Findlater, John. In charge of Rouge steel operations under Charles Sorensen.

Flanders, Walter E. Supervisor of production scheduling and material acquisition for Ford Motor Company 1906–1908.

Flint, Dutee Wilcox. In charge of Ford branch sales office and megadealer in Providence. The Flints were close friends of the Fords.

Ford, William D. Brother of Henry Ford. Employed in Fordson tractor plant. Later distributor of Fordson tractors.

Fry, Vernon C. One of the original stockholders of Ford Motor Company, with fifty shares. Cousin of Alexander Malcolmson.

Gassett, William. Radio expert in charge of radio telegraphy and radio broadcasting for Henry Ford.

Gehle, Theodore F. Manufacturing assistant to Charles Sorensen.

Gilpin, A. L. In charge of Ford branch sales office in Houston.

Gnau, Russell. Secretary to Charles Sorensen.

Gregorie, Eugene T. (Bob). Designer of Lincoln Continental under Edsel Ford.

Gregory, Fred E. Land agent for Henry Ford. Arranged purchases of properties in southeastern Michigan.

Gregory, John (Jack). Manager of Ford's Richmond Hill plantation in Georgia.

Grace, Edward. Manager of Ford Motor Company in Cork, Ireland.

Gray, John S. President of Ford Motor Company from 1903 until his death in 1906. Owner of 105 shares of Ford stock. Uncle of Alexander Malcolmson.

Hadas, Frank. Assistant to William Knudsen. In charge of Eagle boat construction during World War I.

Hagland, Phillip E. In charge of steel furnace operations at Rouge plant.

Hanson, Harry B. Assistant to Charles Sorensen. Layout engineer for steel operations.

Hartner, Charles. In charge of machine operations at Highland Park under Peter Martin.

Hawkins, Norval A. In charge of Ford sales under James Couzens.

Hicks, Harold. Joined Ford in 1919. Mechanical engineer responsible for Ford Model A and aircraft engines.

Hogue, W. S. General traffic manager at Highland Park in 1919.

Holton, C. F. Physician at Ford's Richmond Hill clinic in Georgia.

Hood, Carl Edward. Succeeded Benjamin Lovett as head of Greenfield Village and related schools.

Huff, Edward C. (Spider). Helped Henry Ford build his first auto in 1896. Co-driver of 1907 Transcontinental Race in Model T.

Johnson, Archie. Manager of the Ford rubber plantations in Brazil.

Kalmbach, C. M. Highland Park production superintendent under Peter Martin.

Kellogg, Howard C. Joined Ford in 1918. Supervisor of machinery and tool purchases.

Kiskadden, D. S. Attorney in Legal Department of Ford Motor Company prior to Clifford Longley.

Klann, William C. Assistant to Clarence Avery at Highland Park.

Klingensmith, Frank L. Successor to James Couzens as treasurer and director of Ford Motor Company for a short time.

Knauss, Stanley E. Assistant to William B. Stout in Trimotor airplane work.

Kroll, Richard. With Ford from 1905 to 1949. Mechanic in Experimental Department, in charge of inspection and later quality control.

Kulick, Frank. Test and race driver for Henry Ford.

Lee, John R. Head of Sociological Department preceding Samuel Marquis.

Leland, Henry Martyn. Owner of Lincoln Motor Company when sold to Henry Ford in 1922.

Leland, Wilfred C. Son of Henry Martyn Leland. Also associated with Lincoln Motor Company.

Loskowske, Fred W. Assistant to Raymond Dahlinger on Ford Farms.

Lucking, Alfred. Counsel for Henry Ford during Dodge suit, 1916–1917.

Lumsden, Alex. Supervisor of steel operations in Rouge under Charles Sorensen.

McCloud, J. L. Chemical engineer working closely with Russell McCarroll.

Mack, Harry. Head of Dearborn and later Southwest Regional sales branches. Friend of Harry Bennett.

McRae, E. J. Joined Ford in 1910. Chief patent attorney for Ford Motor Company after 1925.

Malcolmson, Alex Y. An original stockholder of Ford Motor Company, with 255 shares, equal to the number held by Henry Ford.

Mead, J. E. Head of Medical Department at Highland Park plant.

Miller, Logan. Joined Ford in 1914. Superintendent of Motor Building at Rouge plant, later superintendent at Willow Run bomber plant.

Minnock, P. F. In charge of Ford branch sales office in Kansas City, Missouri.

Nelson, Walter. Superintendent of Ford's Upper Peninsula operations at Iron Mountain.

Newkirk, D. L. Superintendent of blast furnaces at the Rouge plant.

Newman, Raymond. Successor to John (Jack) Gregory at Richmond Hill plantation in Georgia.

Oldfield, Barney. Race driver for Henry Ford. Raced the "999" to victory on October 25, 1902.

Oxholm, Einer. Captain of the Ford ship *Lake Ormac*. First manager of Ford settlement "Fordlandia" in Brazil.

Patterson, Charles H. Expert on tools and dies. Production superintendent at Willow Run plant.

Perini, Victor. Manager of Iron Mountain plant. Also successor to Einer Oxholm at Fordlandia.

Peters, William H. Director of manufacturing at Highland Park. Manager of Ford plants in Flat Rock, Michigan; Green Island, New York; and Hamilton, Ohio.

Pioch, William F. Joined Ford in 1912. Chief tool designer, chief engineer at Willow Run, later Chicago engine plant.

Pipp, Edwin G. First editor of Henry Ford's *Dearborn Independent* in 1919.

Plantiff, Gaston. Manager of Ford's New York sales office. The Plantiffs were close friends of the Fords.

Rackham, Horace H. One of the original stockholders of Ford Motor Company, with fifty shares.

Riecks, Frank C. Assistant power plant engineer under William Mayo.

Roberge, Russell I. Ford foreign operations manager.

Rockelman, Fred. Early vehicle tester. Later vice president and operations manager of DT&I Railroad.

Ruddiman, Edsel. Schoolmate of Henry Ford. Employed as research chemist on Ford's chemurgy projects.

Ruddiman, Stanley. Son of Edsel Ruddiman. Chief engineer and later president of DT&I Railroad.

Ryan, William A. Sales manager for Ford Motor Company 1919–1928.

Schulte, Carl. Worked closely with Henry Ford on development of Model A and V-8 engines.

Schwimmer, Rosika. Leader in proposing 1915 "Peace Ship" expedition to end war in Europe.

Sheeler, Charles. Nationally known painter and photographer who recorded scenes depicting the Rouge plant on commission of Edsel Ford.

Sheldrick, Laurence. Successor to Joseph Galamb in body design engineering.

Sladen, Frank. Chief of staff at Henry Ford Hospital. Personal physician to the Ford family.

Smith, C. J. (Jimmy). Mechanic and test driver for Ford 1906–1947. Drove Model T in 1909 transcontinental race.

Smith, William H. Head of Ford's early research laboratory. At one time supervisor of Joseph Galamb and Eugene Farkas.

Stellwagon, S. A. In charge of Ford branch sales office in Minneapolis.

Stromquist, Eric. In charge of purchase and sale of Michigan Upper Peninsula properties 1920–1951.

Tallberg, V. Y. Chief engineer for Ford of Germany prior to World War II, wartime body engineering design chief.

Ternes, Charles. Responsible for power and maintenance in Village Industries. Assistant at Rouge power plant.

Thomas, Charles. In charge of radio research and development for both interplant communication and vehicle use.

Thompson, John W. Public relations man for Henry Ford.

Thompson, L. J. Cashier in Henry Ford's Dearborn office. Manager of accounts associated with the Ford estate.

Thomson, Fred A. Joined Ford in 1918. Assistant secretary of Ford Motor Company, secretary after 1941.

Ukkleberg, H. G. Agricultural scientist for both Thomas Edison and Henry Ford. In charge of agricultural research at Richmond Hill, Georgia.

Unruh, Carl. In charge of tank building for Army during World War I. Later purchasing agent for Ford Division.

Vivian, Frank. In charge of Ford branch sales office in San Francisco.

Voorhess, Charles. Electrical engineer at Ford residence and on Ford personal projects.

Walker, R. T. Executive assistant to William Mayo during the building of the Rouge plant.

Wandersee, John F. Joined Ford in 1902 as sweeper. Helped build Ford racing cars. Became metallurgist for Ford Motor Company.

Weir, James R. Plant pathologist who provided technical guidance at Ford's rubber plantations in Brazil.

Weismyer, M. L. Joined Ford in 1918. Became manufacturing equipment manager and factory layout expert.

Willemse, Jan. A Henry Ford chef specializing in soybean recipes.

Wollering, Max. In 1906, superintendent of the Bellevue Avenue plant of the Ford Manufacturing Company, where engines and transmissions were built for Model N Fords.

Woodall, Charles J. One of the original stockholders of Ford Motor Company, with ten shares. A friend of Alex Malcolmson.

Zahnow, Charles. Secretary to Ernest Liebold.

Appendix II:

Recollections

The individuals listed here were interviewed during the early 1950s, after the deaths of Henry and Clara Ford. They were asked to provide oral reminiscences of their experiences with Henry and Clara Ford and the Ford Motor Company. The reminiscences were gathered as part of a program conducted under the auspices of the Ford Motor Company. These tape-recorded oral histories have been transcribed and are now on file as Accession 65 in the Archives of Henry Ford Museum & Greenfield Village.

About 250 of the reminiscences are hard-bound copies of typed sheets; the balance are typed but not bound. As noted in the listings, the lengths of the histories vary greatly, from a very few pages to as many as 1,536 in a single history.

Ablewhite, H. A member of the Ford Motor Company Sociological Department in 1930; remained with that department until its dissolution in 1948. He was later associated with the Henry Ford Museum. 96 pages.

Ahrens, Norman J. Describes operation of the tractor plant 1918–1925; purchasing of iron ore, coal, limestone, and other commodities 1925–1946. He was manager of the Marine Department from 1926 to retirement in 1954. 81 pages.

Alexander, P. A. A mine clerk at the Imperial Mine near Michigamme and later at the Blueberry Mine near Negaunee. 18 pages.

Alexander, Dr. W. H. Worked for Dr. Roy McClure at Henry Ford Hospital beginning in 1923, transferred to the Ford Iron Mountain plant as physician in 1925. He tells of traveling with Henry Ford and company officials on Upper Michigan trips. 28 pages.

Allen, R. T. Worked as a draftsman and tool designer at the Iron Mountain plant, 1921–1952. 16 pages.

Anderson, Joseph. An employee of Ford Motor Company at Pequaming 1923–1937 and L'Anse 1937–1951, in lumbering and sawmill operations. 49 pages.

Apple, Floyd F. Spent twenty-five years working in the powerhouse at Fair Lane after being employed by Ford Motor Company from 1922 to 1925. He tells of powerhouse operations, upkeep of grounds around Fair Lane, and the personalities of the Fords. 42 pages.

Archbald, R. S. Worked for Ford as a geologist and mining engineer, carried out exploration for iron ore in Michigan and Minnesota. 12 pages.

Avery, Leland. Worked at the Dearborn tractor plant 1916–1924, on the Ford Farms 1924–1926, as watchman at Henry Ford birthplace 1926–1928, and as gateman at Fair Lane 1928–1952. 17 pages.

Backus, A. A. Became secretary to Edsel Ford in 1923, continuing for twenty-seven years. He speaks of the relationship between Henry and Edsel Ford, between Edsel and various Ford executives, Henry Bennett's success in protecting Edsel's children, trips with the Edsel Fords, parties at the residence, and Edsel Ford's fatal illness. 20 pages.

Bacon, Irving R. Photographer for Ford Motor Company and artist for Henry Ford. 260 pages. (See biography in this work.)

Barthel, Oliver E. An automotive pioneer as engineer with Charles B. King in 1885. He met Ford shortly after and relates how Ford and King worked together on automotive problems, each producing his own car. 86 pages.

Baxter, William P. Joined the Employment Department of Ford Motor Company at Highland Park in 1913, was transferred to the Medical Department in 1916, and back to Employment in 1921. He was in Labor Relations from 1930 to 1952. 56 pages.

Beebe, Faye I. A next-door neighbor and friend of the Ford family. She describes social activities of the two families. 12 pages.

Beebe, Howard D. In tractor production 1917–1918. He was associated with the opening of the Cork, Ireland, plant in 1926 and the manufacture of engines at the Rouge 1929–1945. He tells of the reorganization of the company in 1945. 60 pages.

Beesley, Wallace G. Employed in various capacities by Ford Motor Company in Upper Michigan, describes camping trips with Henry and Clara Ford, Harvey Firestone, and Thomas Edison. 28 pages.

Beh, Joseph C. Sr. Employed first as a timekeeper at Ford Motor Company in 1915 and later as an electrical buyer. He describes Henry Ford's pacifism and provides a character sketch of Ford. 28 pages.

Bell, David M. A carriage blacksmith employed at the Edison Illuminating Company under Henry Ford in 1896. He assisted Ford in building his first car. Although later offered a job with Ford, he declined and stayed with Edison until retirement in 1929. 26 pages.

Bell, John. A native of Georgia employed as foreman of the Richmond Hill plantation sawmill and carpenter shop. 30 pages.

Bennett, Charles H. An original stockholder of the Ford Motor Company, recalls his first meeting with Henry Ford and the conversations leading to his participation in the formation of the company. 55 pages.

Bennett, Frank. Joined Ford in 1904 at the Mack Avenue plant; left and returned in 1913. He describes assembly, testing, and shipping 1904–1909; operation of the Detroit branch 1913–1917; body production 1917–1921; operations of Ford distributors in Japan, Korea, and China 1924–1930; construction of automotive factories in USSR 1930–1931. 149 pages.

Bennett, Fred. An early employee of Ford Motor Company at Iron Mountain, recalls the acquistion of land and the logging and mining operations initiated by the company. 19 pages.

Benson, Norman. Longtime Ford employee at Iron Mountain, relates his observations of operations including wood salvage methods, production of auto body parts, and military gliders. 21 pages.

Berghoff, Bredo. Joined Ford Motor Company in 1907 as draftsman. He later joined Sorensen at the tractor plant and assisted in the application of Fordsons in England (1917). Best known for his descriptions of Russian tractor factory operations in 1926. 218 pages.

Bernhardt, C. M. First employed at Highland Park in 1909. He tells of his work in the mail room, the minority stock purchases, building of the Ford fleet, salvage of 199 ships, and operation of the Airplane Division of Ford Motor Company 1925–1932. 21 pages.

Blood, Howard. Describes pioneer days of the automotive industry 1905–1909; the Cornelian car; aviation research; work with Norge Corporation, Detroit Gear and Machine Co., and Borg Warner Corp., where he developed an automatic transmission for the Ford car. 37 pages.

Boivin, Mr. and Mrs. Alexander, and Elaine Snyder. Describe their family life in Pequaming, L'Anse, and Alberta, where Alexander Boivin was employed by Ford Motor Company. 22 pages.

Bondie, A. G. Employed by Ford Motor Company in the Employment Office at Highland Park in 1910. He tells of factory working conditions, problems with employees, and work of the Sociological Department. 45 pages.

Bossardet, J. E. Describes the early days at the tractor plant and building of the Eagle boats. In 1919, he transferred to the Payroll Department, where he was involved in employee services and labor relations 1919–1952. He participated in Ford fund-raising for civic purposes and government bond sales. 55 pages.

Boyer, Georgia E. Worked in the Service Department of Ford Motor Company from 1907 until 1925. She was related to William E. Boyer, first draftsman for Henry Ford. She provides anecdotal accounts of Henry Ford. 34 pages.

Brand, Mary Louise. Daughter of Fred Gregory, who purchased Dearborn land for Henry Ford. She describes the history of the Fair Lane area, the building of Fair Lane residence, and land purchases for the Rouge plant. The importance of the Fords to Dearborn is stressed. 33 pages.

Brennan, Leo. Circuit Court judge of L'Anse, Michigan, gives a brief account of his association with Ford Motor Company on legal matters pertaining to Upper Peninsula properties. 9 pages.

Brewer, W. H. A landscape engineer employed by Henry and Clara Ford to recondition the grounds at Fair Lane in 1937. He describes the personal characteristics of the Fords and the trials of the Ferguson tractor and hydraulic system. 40 pages.

Brewton, Benjamin J. Office manager at Ford's Richmond Hill plantation in Georgia. He describes the low-cost housing projects and Ford's contribution to education at Richmond Hill. 12 pages.

Briggs, L. E. Joined Ford Motor Company in 1914 and became treasurer. He describes accounting, auditing, and financial operations of the company, including the organization and administration of European branches. 68 pages.

Brockington, William H. Was with the Iron Mountain plant from 1920 until 1952. He describes the Fordlandia program initiated at that plant, and his own general feelings toward Ford Motor Company. 28 pages.

Brown, B. R., Sr. Was employed in the Highland Park expansion 1911–1915;

in the Power and Construction Department 1916–1919; on plans for the new English plant and the Cork, Ireland, tractor plant; and during 1919–1922 provided plans for assembly plants in Argentina, Brazil, and Uruguay. Later he designed other plants, including one in Yokohama, Japan. 35 pages.

Brown, George. Joined the Ford Motor Company at the Piquette plant as an accountant. His long and detailed story covers various aspects of a half-century of Ford Motor Company history. 186 pages.

Buhler, Rosa, and J. D. Thompson. Buhler, lady's maid from 1933 to 1950, and Thompson, head butler from 1936 to 1950, have combined their memories to provide a colorful and intimate story of the Henry Ford family at home. 77 pages.

Bullwinkel, Clarence. Employed at branch operations in San Francisco, 1912–1926; Portland Oregon, 1926–1931; Richmond, California, 1931–1940. He describes Ford Motor Company dealer relations from 1912 to 1952. 39 pages.

Caesar, Irving. Relates events of the Ford Peace Ship and the Neutral Conference for Continuous Mediation. He describes Henry and Clara Ford at Fair Lane, aspects of the *Dearborn Independent,* and Ford's thoughts about the *Protocols of the Wire. Men of Zion.* 49 pages.

Clark, Constance. Public health nurse at Ways Station and Richmond Hill, Georgia. She tells how Henry Ford carried on a medical program to improve general health in the region and stamp out epidemics of malaria and hookworm. 26 pages.

Conn, A. E. Describes purchasing policies at Ford Motor Company, 1918–1955. He discusses labor and the supplier, the light car program 1945–1946, and company reorganization in 1945. 116 pages.

Cooper, H. G. Principal of the George Washington Carver School for Negroes built by Henry Ford at Richmond Hill, Georgia. He describes the school's origins and curriculum, and gives examples of graduates who were especially successful. 21 pages.

Cooper, R. L. Purchased the antebellum Georgia plantations along the Ogeechee River for Henry Ford. He describes Ford's early plans for developing the Richmond Hill area. 14 pages.

Cordell, Harold M. Assistant secretary in the Henry Ford office from 1921 to 1929. He was close to Ford and tells of the origins of Henry Ford Museum & Greenfield Village. 113 pages.

Culver, Chester M. Involved with the Employers Association and its activities, 1904–1953. He tells of the five-dollar day, labor unions, Henry Ford, and Henry M. Leland of the Lincoln Motor Co. 75 pages.

Cuson, Lee A. Tells of the early days of the automobile industry—Henry Ford, Alexander Winton, the 999, the 1909 Transcontinental Race, and the K-R-I-T car. 24 pages.

Cutler, Edward J. An artist, draftsman, and architect responsible for the design and reconstruction of historical buildings erected in Greenfield Village. 194 pages. (See biography in this book.)

Davis, Mr. and Mrs. Clarence. Close friends of Henry Ford, they describe the Ford family as they first settled in the Dearborn area. They discuss Ford's boyhood and personal recollections of the Fords in their leisure moments. Ford's ideas on food, diet, health, war, and other facets of his complex personality are discussed. 90 pages.

Davis, Clem. Watchmaker and Ford Motor Company dealer who has combined narrative and anecdote to tell of his association with Henry Ford and the company. Their common interest in antiques is described. 48 pages.

De Caluwe, Alfons. Gardener for the Ford family at Fair Lane from 1921 to 1954, tells of his experiences with the Fords. 63 pages.

Delorge, Albert. Employed from 1936 to 1951 at the Richmond Hill plantation. His reminiscences are largely concerned with labor conditions and housing facilities before and after Henry Ford's efforts to raise the economic level of that region. 40 pages.

Derrick, Robert O. Architect who designed the Henry Ford Museum, as a replica of Independence Hall, and the adjoining Education Building known as Lovett Hall. He tells of details in the building process and the manner in which Henry Ford dealt with architectural problems. 29 pages.

Dickert, George. Joined Ford Manufacturing Company in 1906, transferred to Ford Motor Company of Canada the same year. He was involved in design engineering and describes the relationship between Ford of Canada and the American company through World War II. 35 pages.

Doehler, Walter. Tells of his association with construction of the powerhouse at Iron Mountain in 1923 and its operation until his retirement as chief engineer in 1951. 49 pages.

Doell, William R. With the Mining Department of Ford Motor Company at Michigamme and Negaunee between 1923 and 1932. 21 pages.

Dolan, Hugh P. Joined the Power Department of Ford Motor Company at Highland Park in 1913. He describes Henry Ford's interest in power-generating equipment, reconditioning the Lincoln powerhouse, the Henry Ford Hospital power plant, and power installations at the Ford-owned coal mines in Kentucky. 63 pages.

Doss, H. C. Began work for the Ford Motor Company Sociological Department of the Oklahoma City branch in 1916. His responsibilities included sales policies, dealer development, and vehicle financing, 1916–1925. He left Ford, returned in 1932 as assistant sales manager, and became general sales manager in 1939. 134 pages.

Doyle, Leo. Describes his experiences while employed by the Ford Motor Company in L'Anse and Pequaming sawmills from 1923 to 1951. 21 pages.

Eagel, John H., Sr. Tells of the pioneer days of an automobile agency as employee of Haynes, Studebaker, and Oldsmobile. He was owner of a Fordson agency in Stockton, California, in 1919, and the following year he was owner of a Ford car agency. 63 pages.

Edwards, Robert. Employed by Ford Motor Company in logging operations at L'Anse, Alberta, and Big Bay, Michigan. 29 pages.

Eidson, W. E. Tells of his experiences as supervisor of the Richmond Hill sawmill from 1935 to 1951. 40 pages.

Erickson, Gust. Employed at the Ford Iron Mountain plant. He describes lumbering operations, mining methods, and administrative policy at Iron Mountain. 26 pages.

Esper, Al. Had a varied career with Ford Motor Company beginning in 1917. He was associated with motorboat racing, airplane development, and automotive testing. At retirement, he was in charge of all Ford automotive testing facilities. 112 pages.

Farkas, E. J. Worked as tool designer for various automotive companies including Ford from 1906 to 1913. He was in charge of engineering and design of the Fordson tractor 1914–1928; worked on the X engine and car 1920–1926 and Model A chassis design 1927–1931; and was close to Henry and Edsel Ford in engineering administration until 1946. 370 pages. (See biography in this book.)

Farnsworth, George E. Worked in a sales capacity for General Motors, Garford Truck, Willys-Overland, Jewett Company, Ford Motor Company, and Chrysler Corporation. He provided financial planning and supervisory assistance for Ford dealers 1919–1928. 37 pages.

Farnsworth, Capt. Grover. Describes early automobile races and the development of internal combustion engines; Henry Ford and his power-to-weight formula; the 999 and Model N; aviation progress 1903–1917; American aviation in World War I; and collaboration with William B. Stout. 55 pages.

Ferghete, George. Had several jobs with Henry Ford from 1919 to 1951. He describes the reaction of employees to the five-dollar day, and gives a rather idealistic picture of Henry Ford as seen from his views as a carpenter, gardener, and watchman at the Rouge Administration Building in Dearborn. 30 pages.

Finzel, William. A friend of the family of Clara Bryant Ford. His recollections deal with the Henry Ford and Bryant families, old-time dancing, old-time music, and fiddler contests. 12 pages.

Fleury, Archie. A resident of Big Bay, Michigan, and the owner of the public telephone used by Henry Ford to make business calls. The two often carried on lengthy conversations. 18 pages.

Ford, Clyde M. A cousin of Henry Ford, Dearborn's first Ford dealer, and later first mayor of Dearborn. He writes of the history of Dearborn Township, the Fords in Dearborn, and the accomplishments of Henry Ford. 60 pages.

Foster, Ernest. A woodworker trained in England, he did repair and remodeling work for Ford. He worked on antiques and buildings and supervised work at Henry Ford Museum & Greenfield Village. 16 pages.

Francois, Joseph. Joined Ford Motor Company in Iron Mountain, where he was placed in charge of sawmills in northern Michigan. He describes logging and sawmill operations, the school system at Pequaming and Alberta, and the Fords on their northern trips. 32 pages.

Fries, William H. Associated with the Detroit University School for many years.

His wife was a close associate of Clara Ford. He describes the personal nature of Henry and Clara Ford. 5 pages.

Galvin, Donald T. Has written a brief account of his experiences with Henry Ford and his first cars. 3 pages.

Gehle, Theodore F. Describes materials control in the automotive industry 1906–1930; the Ford tractor plant and its suppliers 1917–1920; building of the Rouge plant; reorganization of the Ford British plant; purchasing problems in France and Germany; paint purchasing and manufacture; Ford family relationships. 158 pages.

Getsinger, R. C. Worked for Chalmers Motor Company and Saxon Motor Car Corporation before becoming sales manager for Lincoln Motor Company. He describes in detail the Leland-Ford negotiations of 1922. 52 pages.

Gill, Mrs. Harry. A resident of Ways Station, Georgia, from 1920, describes in 1951 the transformation of the Richmond Hill region brought about by Henry Ford's attention to the problems of health, education, and employment. 16 pages.

Gleason, Fred. Son of Jim Gleason, who owned the steam engine Henry Ford operated as a young man. Fred tells of his sister Christine, who refused Henry Ford's marriage proposal. 30 pages.

Gray, Allen and Chester. Tell of their work on Ford's first car, the financial support given to Ford by Mayor William Maybury of Detroit, and Ford's first car company. 7 pages.

Griffith, Walter G. An automotive machinist who dated his activities from 1895, when he assisted Alexander Winton with his first car. He also worked for other automotive companies before working for Ford from 1920 to 1950. 33 pages.

Grimshaw, W. Ernest. Joined Ford Motor Company as an office boy in 1906 and studied tool making at night school. He tells of Edsel Ford as a young man, the evolution of die making 1911–1957, labor relations, and the union. 46 pages.

Hagland, P. E. Describes the origin, expansion, and operation of the electric furnaces, open hearths, and steel mill at the Rouge plant 1915–1953. Henry Ford's interest in foundry and steel mill operations is discussed. Effects of the union movement following the 1941 strike are reviewed. 108 pages.

Hakes, Willis J. A Ford dealer in Fostoria, Ohio, in 1909, tells of his association with Ford Motor Company and of his year-by-year progress in the auto business. He presents a brief history of the automotive industry from 1909 to 1955. 37 pages.

Harff, Anthony. As secretary in the superintendent's office in Highland Park and later for M. L. Bricker, he had an excellent opportunity to examine administrative methods and executive personnel from 1920 to the mid-1950s. 84 pages.

Hayes, Clarence B. An early manufacturer of automotive wheels, dating back to 1889. His memoirs outline the development of the wheel industry and the origin of the Society of Automotive Engineers. 19 pages.

Hedman, Emil. One of the inhabitants of the town of Pequaming when Ford Motor Company purchased the town in 1923. 23 pages.

Henry, Inez. A student and later staff member of the Berry Schools at Mount Berry, Georgia. She discusses the Fords on their frequent trips to the school, and their reactions to the philosophy of education practiced at Berry Schools. 47 pages.

Hicks, Harold. A graduate mechanical engineer, he joined Ford in 1919, working directly under Henry Ford on the design of engines for boats, aircraft, and automobiles. He describes each of his projects and provides anecdotes about Henry and Edsel Ford. 215 pages.

Holmes, George H. Describes the Dearborn area in the 1880s and 1890s, the birth of Henry Ford in 1863, the courtship of Henry and Clara Ford, Ford as a young mechanic, the local reaction to Ford's first car, and Ford's interest in Greenfield Village. 13 pages.

Holton, Dr. C. F. The physician at Ways Station Clinic in Georgia when it was established by Henry Ford. He describes his work in the campaign to eradicate disease and the crusade for public health carried on by the clinic in cooperation with Ford. 32 pages.

Hoppin, Glenn H. A boyhood acquaintance of William B. Stout from 1904, joined Stout Engineering Laboratories in Detroit in 1920. He describes the history of aviation in Detroit and the activities of the Stout industries in particular. 201 pages.

Horngren, Ernest A. Worked at the Iron Mountain plant from 1923 to 1951. He emphasizes plant engineering and industrial relations during that period. 8 pages.

Housenick, C. C. A pioneer auto dealer with a Ford dealership in 1906. He discusses the social and economic changes brought about by the Model T, discounts, finance plans, dealer supervision, and the Ford Dealer Council 1906–1953. 27 pages.

Hughson, W. E. Met Henry Ford in 1902 at the Chicago Automobile Show and in 1903 became the first Ford dealer with the West Coast and Hawaii as his territory. He describes Ford at the Panama-Pacific Exposition, Ford expansion in the West, and Ford dealer policy 1903–1952. 63 pages.

Hulbert, Prescott. A patent lawyer, he describes Henry Ford's automotive inventions 1897–1906, the Detroit Automobile Company, organization of the Ford Motor Company, and the Selden patent suit. 19 pages.

Husen, O. H. Describes Ford cost accounting systems 1914–1920, business methods of the Lincoln Motor Company 1920–1922, purchase and reorganization of Lincoln, government contracts in World War II, profit centers, and financial reorganization, 1945–1954. 104 pages.

Hutchins, Daniel J. Started as bookkeeper at Ford Motor Company in 1913. He gives details of Highland Park operations—procedures, personalities, material follow-up. He describes Ford methods of dealing with vendors, details of by-products sales, and truck sales. He left Ford in 1938 to join Firestone. 138 pages.

Ide, Judge O. Z. On the legal staff of Ford Motor Company handling damage cases relative to the Fordson tractor and the DT&I Railroad. He negotiated land concessions at Fordlandia, Brazil; organized the Universal Credit Company; and aided in the formation of Detroit bus lines. 70 pages.

Johnson, Alfred. Employed at L'Anse, Pequaming, and Big Bay plants of Ford Motor Company from 1927 to 1951. He speaks of these operations and their effects on living standards. 14 pages.

Kenney, J. M. Employed as a plant protection man by the Ford Motor Company at the L'Anse plant. He gives a short sketch of Henry Ford's attitude and activities while vacationing there. 11 pages.

Keown, M. Gordon. A graduate of Berry Schools in 1904 and director 1942–1944. His memoir provides a history of Berry Schools and an account of the relationship between the Fords and Martha Berry. 59 pages.

Kinietz, Louis J. One of the first employees of Ford Motor Company in 1903, he describes the Mack Avenue plant, its operations and officials, car and engineering tests 1904–1905, and his experiences as a Ford dealer 1907–1922. 13 pages.

Klann, W. C. Assistant to Charles W. Avery 1907–1928. He describes the origin, development, and utilization of moving assembly lines for magnetos, motors, and final car assembly; the development of material handling methods at Ford Motor Company; five-dollar-a-day working conditions; Liberty engine production; the manufacture of starters, generators, glass, cloth, batteries, tires, and wire; and discontent with the Model T. He comments on Henry Ford, Edsel Ford, Avery, Peter E. Martin, and Charles E. Sorensen. 375 pages.

Kroll, Richard. Joined Ford Motor Company in 1906 as experimental designer, joined Henry Ford and Son in 1915, and became head of the Inspection Department of Ford Motor Company in 1923. He describes the Ford airplane of 1909, quality of auto production, the first V-8, the Johansson gauges, and World War II production. 65 pages.

Krueger, Charles C. Worked at Keim Mills before Ford bought them out in 1911. He tells of production methods used for the Model T and his work at the Ireland and Mathews Manufacturing Company and Ternstedt Manufacturing Company. He was a close friend of William S. Knudsen. 132 pages.

Larson, Art. As traffic manager of the Iron Mountain plant, he describes his work with Ford Motor Company 1922–1952, with emphasis on glider production during World War II. 28 pages.

Larson, Charles A. An employee of Ford Motor Company at the L'Anse plant. He speaks of his special assignment as cook for the Ford family during their trips to northern Michigan. 28 pages.

LaRue, Carl D. A botanist at the University of Michigan who explored for the Ford Motor Company in 1926 the area of Brazil where Ford later established the rubber plantations of Fordlandia and Belterra. He tells of the world rubber situation, 1917–1940. 35 pages.

Lawry, Joseph. Joined Ford Motor Company in 1912 at Highland Park Tool Repair Department. He moved to the Rouge in 1921, and describes machining operations at both locations in detail. 86 pages.

Lee, Amber. Became hostess at the Richmond Hill Community House in 1943, where she worked with schoolchildren of that area. She describes old-time dances, social life at Richmond Hill, and the results of Henry Ford's theories of education. 18 pages.

Lepine, A. J. As secretary to Edsel Ford, was able to observe the inner workings of the administration of the Ford Motor Company and the business routine adopted by Edsel Ford in carrying out his duties as president of the company. 96 pages.

Lewis, Eugene W. Organized the Timken-Detroit Axle Company in 1919. He describes the early years of the automobile industry and the personality traits of Henry Ford. 16 pages.

Liebold, Ernest G. Trained as a banker, became cashier of Henry Ford's Highland Park State Bank, and in turn became Ford's general secretary with responsibility for essentially all of Ford's business activities outside Ford Motor Company. 1,536 pages. (See biography in this book.)

Litogot, Artemas L. A maternal first cousin of Henry Ford. He speaks of the Ford family and his work for Ford Motor Company as supervisor of auto repairing at the Detroit branch and at the Dearborn Engineering Laboratory. 32 pages.

Litogot, Edward B. A nephew of Henry Ford's mother, Mary Litogot, he worked at the printing trade in Detroit until 1930, when he was employed by Ford as printer for Greenfield Village. He discusses Ford's interest in printing, his interest in Greenfield Village, and relatives of Ford. 36 pages.

Loskowske, Fred W. General foreman of Ford Farms under Raymond Dahlinger. He relates his experiences during the construction of Ford Airport, Greenfield Village, and various village industries. His accounts of Ford's camping trips with Harvey Firestone, Thomas Edison, and John Burroughs are sometimes humorous. He was with Ford Farms from 1914 until 1950. 123 pages.

Lumsden, Alex. Joined Ford Motor Company in 1915 at Highland Park, where he was soon in charge of drop forge, heat treat, and spring departments. In 1925, he was transferred to the Rouge plant as head of the open hearth until 1929. He describes steel operations and the climate of employment at the Rouge. 62 pages.

McCloud, John Lanse. Provides a long and interesting discussion of Ford Motor Company and Henry Ford from his position as both friend and chemist in charge of the Chemical and Metallurgical Laboratory. He describes his business and social experiences from 1914 until 1949, when he retired as manager of the Manufacturing Research Department. 423 pages.

McDonnell, Leslie. Submitted this manuscript, with the title "Life with Uncle Henry" by Orry Barrule, to the office of Henry Ford II. The manuscript describes conditions within Ford Motor Company from 1913 until 1945. 68 pages.

McIntyre, John. Powerhouse engineer at the Ford family residence. He has recorded his impressions of the Ford family and their interests. He gives an account of the last days of Henry Ford and the power failure at the time of his death. 34 pages.

Mahaffey, Bascom. Joined the Jacksonville, Florida, branch of Ford Motor Company in 1924. In 1928, he transferred to Richmond Hill, where he assumed responsibility for all mechanical equipment at the Ford plantation until 1951. He describes Henry Ford's Southern interests and activities. 33 pages.

Martin, Aimar. As bookkeeper of the Richmond Hill plantation, he describes its financial organization and the administrative changes during his employment from 1939 to 1951. He also tells of assistance given his disabled child by Henry Ford. 33 pages.

Martineau, Omar. An employee of the Iron Mountain plant of Ford Motor Company from 1924 to 1951. He tells of company efforts to alleviate effects of the depression and the changing industrial relations during his employment. 14 pages.

Mayo, William N. Son of William B. Mayo, he tells the story of his father in connection with the Highland Park powerhouse, purchase of the *Sialia,* the minority stock purchases, birth of the Rouge plant, Muscle Shoals, the Ford Trimotor, and relationships with Henry and Edsel Ford. 45 pages.

Menge, Conrad, Sr. An old Florida river and Gulf boat captain when he met Henry Ford in 1925. He was commissioned to salvage the steamer *Suwanee* for use in Greenfield Village. He illustrates Ford's sense of humor by several anecdotes. 31 pages.

Mielke, William. An electrician who joined Henry Ford and Son in 1916. He describes operations at that location and at the Ford Dairy Farm, events at Fair Lane, and X engine developments at the Engineering Laboratory, along with many amusing incidents. 163 pages.

Miller, Carl G. As a lifetime resident of Iron Mountain and a personal friend of E. G. Kingsford, he had opportunities to meet Henry Ford in more informal moments. 12 pages.

Miller, Logan. Joined Ford Motor Company as lathe hand at Highland Park in 1914, advanced to assistant superintendent of the Rouge plant in 1935, superintendent of the Rouge in 1946, and a vice president of Ford Motor Company in 1950. He tells of production methods, labor problems, executive conflicts, and reorganization of Ford Motor Company in 1945. 87 pages.

Milner, C. G. Employed at the Ford Motor Company branch in Atlanta, Georgia, until he resigned to accept a dealership in 1924. While a Ford dealer, he met Henry Ford. They had a mutual interest in antiques, and Milner led a search for a cotton gin to be placed in Greenfield Village. He tells of the trials and tribulations of the automobile dealer. 27 pages.

Mitchum, E. D. Employed by Richmond Hill plantation in 1929 to take charge of work crews. Mitchum describes the Ford plantation, the schools, and Ford's efforts to improve living conditions in the community. 59 pages.

Moekle, Herman L. Joined the Pittsburgh branch of Ford Motor Company in 1913 and held various branch positions before being transferred to the Auditing Department at Highland Park in 1918. In 1928, he became head of the Auditing Department, a position in which he was aware of details of operations in Europe, Latin America, and the Far East. He recounts many of the problems of the company from 1918 to 1947. 216 pages.

Monnier, Edward F. Describes school days with Clara Bryant, the courtship of Clara and Henry Ford, and Henry Ford's early interest in mechanics. 16 pages.

Morse, Elba. Director of the Bay Cliff Health Camp for physically handicapped children located near Huron Mountain Club. She describes the visits to the camp by the Fords and the assistance given to the townspeople by Henry Ford. 20 pages.

Muck, E. G. Owner of a general store in Michigamme, Michigan, and one of the town's most enthusiastic boosters. He recounts the effects of Henry Ford's interest in northern Michigan. 24 pages.

Mulrooney, Matt. With Irish humor, he tells of his sawmill at the Fordlandia rubber plantation in Brazil and the problems with jungle growth and native labor. He describes housing, living conditions, and the difficulties of rubber tree cultivation. 23 pages.

Needham, H. C. Worked as a machinist for Henry Ford in Ford's shop on Cass Avenue in 1900. He tells of the first Ford car and the Winton Race in 1901. 11 pages.

Nelson, Walter G. Joined Ford Motor Company at Iron Mountain in 1924 as an hourly employee and was promoted, eventually becoming manager of the entire northern Michigan operations. He describes his personal associations with the Fords and gives an overall picture of policy and administration at Iron Mountain. 120 pages.

Newman, Ray. Describes the administration and work of the Detroit-area Ford Farms 1930–1945, and the changes he made in farming at the Richmond Hill plantation in Georgia after his appointment as superintendent in 1945. 47 pages.

Noppe, Henry. Employed as a tool and die maker by Henry Ford in 1920, worked on antiques—jewelry, guns, clocks—and special hobbies for Ford. He retired in 1953. 35 pages.

O'Connor, James. Describes methods of assembly in use by the Ford Motor Company from 1907 until 1952, including the first moving final assembly line at Highland Park. He discusses the five-dollar day, the Sociological Department, the conflict between the Rouge and Highland Park plants, labor unrest in the 1930s and 1940s, and the coming of the union. 82 pages.

O'Donnell, Dr. David. Practiced medicine in Detroit and had the Henry Ford family as patients during the last decade of the nineteenth century and the early years of the twentieth century. He tells of the birth of Edsel Ford. 6 pages.

Olsen, Oscar G. Joined the Ford Motor Company operations at Pequaming in 1923. There, in addition to his regular job, he was chosen to instruct the schoolchildren of the area in the courtesies and techniques of old-fashioned dancing. He tells of his experiences in Pequaming and sad effects of the shutdown of the mill. 39 pages.

Olson, Albert. In charge of Ford Motor Company lumbering camps Ford bought from Hebard in Pequaming, Michigan. He describes Ford efficiency and the revitalization of lumbering by Ford. 16 pages.

Orberg, Kristian. From Denmark, joined Ford Motor Company in 1915 at the

Buenos Aires branch as a bookkeeper and soon became office manager. He tells of Ford in Argentina and Brazil, where he developed sales and services. He also describes the Ford rubber plantations in Brazil. 38 pages.

Parr, Fred D. Submits his own biography, a description of his West Coast shipping enterprises and his influence on Ford Motor Company's locating a plant at Richmond, California. 61 pages.

Perini, Mrs. Victor J. Wife of Victor Perini, a toolmaker hired by Ford Motor Company in 1910 in Highland Park. She tells of her life during her husband's employment as manager of Liberty engine production during World War I and as manager of Green Island, Iron Mountain, and Manchester, England, plants. She also describes their life at the Ford rubber plantation in Brazil. 19 pages.

Phillips, Thomas. A resident of the Richmond Hill area, he speaks of the changes effected by Henry Ford in economic and social conditions in Bryan County, Georgia. 24 pages.

Picardat, John. A longtime employee of the Ford Motor Company at L'Anse and Pequaming, he briefly relates his observations of Henry Ford during visits, describes plant operations and the construction by the company of a hotel at Big Bay. 14 pages.

Pinkson, Leon J. Automotive editor of the *San Francisco Chronicle*. He speaks of his early days on the *Chronicle* and his meetings with Henry Ford during the Panama-Pacific Exposition of 1915. 12 pages.

Pioch, William F. Joined Ford as a tool designer in 1912 at Highland Park, becoming head of the department in 1926. During World War II, he was executive chief engineer of the Willow Run bomber plant. He mentions his patents, the machines developed for Henry Ford Hospital, and a five-year plan for tractor manufacture in China. He retired from Ford Motor Company in 1953. 112 pages.

Prindle, Charlotte M. A descendant of a pioneer Detroit family, she describes the city at the turn of the century, Henry Ford's first car, and Henry and Clara Ford as friendly neighbors. 12 pages.

Pring, William Walter. Joined Henry Ford in his first two unsuccessful automobile companies 1899–1902. He describes the Detroit Automobile Company, Henry Ford, Henry M. Leland, the Henry Ford Company, and Cadillac Motor Car Company 1902–1905. He worked for several other auto companies and describes changing methods until 1925. 68 pages.

Rankin, Robert. He became Clara Ford's chauffeur in 1938, and from 1945 drove for both Henry and Clara Ford. His recollections are rich in anecdotal material. 75 pages.

Rasmussen, Edward, Carol Rasmussen, and Kathryn Brady. Employees of the Huron Mountain Club where Henry and Clara Ford spent their summer vacations. They describe the Fords and their friends enjoying leisure and recreation at the club. 19 pages.

Reinhold, Herman M. In 1910, he joined the Pattern Department of Ford Motor Company at the Piquette plant. He describes the projects he worked on 1910–1949—the Fordson tractor, gas turbine, X car, and special projects for Henry Ford. He also tells of the Sociological Department and labor relations. 85 pages.

Remshardt, William. Had an auto business in Red Wing, Minnesota, near the Twin Cities Assembly Plant, in 1908. He tells about early dealerships and dealer problems between 1908 and 1956. 15 pages.

Renner, Arthur A. Specialized in tools and machines at Highland Park 1911–1925. He describes manufacturing, scheduling and cost systems, the conflict between Highland Park and the Rouge, Andrew Mellon and Henry Ford, working conditions, and union organization. He was working at the time of his interview in the 1950s. 54 pages.

Richards, Alvin E., Mrs. Alvin Richards, and Eileen Murphy. Tell about the homes, schools, and living conditions at the mining town of Michigamme during the years Alvin Richards was employed by the Ford Motor Company as superintendent of the Imperial Mine. 53 pages.

Riecks, Frank C. Started as draftsman in the Power and Construction Department of Ford Motor Company in 1916, was involved in the construction of the Rouge plant, the Dagenham plant in England, and assembly plants in France, China, and Japan. The World War II construction program is also described. Riecks was with Plant Engineering at the time of his interview in the 1950s. 117 pages.

Rinehart, William O. Describes operation of the tool room at Highland Park 1913–1921, the Machine Shop at Dearborn, the X-8 engine, Edsel Ford and motorboat racing, and Henry Ford's interest in antiques. From 1931 to retirement, he worked at the Edison Institute on special projects for Henry Ford until 1951. 47 pages.

Ring, Robert. The last superintendent of production at Iron Mountain. He describes production of wooden parts and station wagon bodies, and also describes public attitude toward Ford Motor Company in the Upper Peninsula. 23 pages.

Roberts, Albert O. Started with Ford Motor Company in 1928 as draftsman on machine development, forerunner of automation. He also tells of working directly with Henry Ford on steam engines, sawmills, a rear-engined car, automatic transmissions, and the Ferguson tractor. 36 pages.

Roeder, Dale. A graduate automotive engineer who joined Ford Motor Company in 1925, he tells of engineering problems on the Model T, the Model A, and V-8 Fords. As chief engineer, he describes truck and military vehicle engineering. 171 pages.

Rogge, John R. Worked for the Ford plantation at Fordlandia, Brazil, for about five years beginning in 1928. He describes a rubber tree seed-gathering expedition in the Amazon basin. 31 pages.

Rogge, T. A. As manager of the L'Anse plant, he describes Ford logging methods and sawmill operations, along with industrial relations, accounting procedures, and general administrative control at all Ford operations in northern Michigan. 27 pages.

Rosenfield, John. Touches briefly on his work with the Ford Farms 1917–1925 and his observations of Clara and Henry Ford during the years he was gateman at Fair Lane estate 1925–1950. 10 pages.

Ruddiman, Dr. Edsel. A lifelong friend of Henry Ford, he speaks of their school-days at the Scotch Settlement School and their later work together on the dietary qualities of soybeans. 9 pages.

Ruddiman, Margaret Ford. Has published her reminiscences in the article "Memories of My Brother Henry Ford," *Michigan History,* Michigan Historical Commission, Lansing, September 1953. 94 pages.

Ruddiman, Mrs. Stanley. A close friend of both Henry and Clara Ford from 1915 until their deaths, she presents the viewpoints of the Fords on world peace, religion, politics, and finance. She recounts the revival of old-fashioned dancing, the founding of the Edison Institute, and the home life and personal tastes of the Fords. 149 pages.

Ruddiman, Stanley. General manager and later president of the Ford-owned Detroit, Toledo, and Ironton Railroad. He first joined Ford Motor in 1915 and continued with the company until 1929, when the railroad was sold by Ford. He gives his personal impressions of Henry and Edsel Ford. 33 pages.

Rugg, Leo. Employed to work on Eagle boats, he worked on DT&I engines before being transferred to Greenfield Village. He tells of Ford's antique collection, Ford men and methods. 43 pages.

Sack, Israel. An antique dealer, he tells of antique dealers in Boston, furnishing the Wayside Inn for Henry Ford, and his cooperation with Ford in establishing the Henry Ford Museum. 44 pages.

Sammis, Arnold F. A New York tire dealer 1903–1906, he became a Ford dealer in 1906. He tells of selling the Model N Ford, the introduction and sale of the Model T, and his experiences as a dealer from 1906 to 1952. 12 pages.

Schumann, Roy. Recalls his experience with the Dearborn Realty and Construction Company formed by Henry Ford to build mass-produced homes, his work under Ford's personal supervision in collecting and refurbishing antique steam engines, the building and furnishing of the Henry Ford Museum & Greenfield Village, and many other tasks carried out for Ford. 148 pages.

Searle, Frederick. Tells of Edsel Ford at the Detroit University School and the origin, philosophy, students, faculty, curriculum, and results of the Henry Ford Trade School. 41 pages. (See biography in this book.)

Seeman, Fred W. With Ford from 1903 to 1906 and again from 1922 to 1926 as pattern maker. He describes experimental design at the Mack Avenue plant, Henry Ford and the company pioneers, production at Mack and Piquette plants, and Henry Ford Trade School. 65 pages.

Sharpe, Marvin. Became assistant superintendent of Richmond Hill plantation in 1931. He describes the plantation, the Ford residence, community house, schools, sawmill, cash crops at Richmond Hill, and the improved living standards. 37 pages.

Shaw, Robert A. Joined Ford Motor Company in 1913 and two years later was placed in charge of all safety engineering, a position he held until his resignation in 1927. He describes the Ford safety and hygiene program 1915–1927, the Sociological Department, the Ford English School, and safety in industry in general. 92 pages.

Sheldrick, L. S. Joined the Lincoln Motor Company in 1922 after it was purchased by Ford. First a layout draftsman, he worked on Lincoln designs, the X-8 engine, and later tank and aircraft engines. He provides a detailed account of engineering projects and personalities at Ford Motor Company from 1922 to 1943. 393 pages.

Sheridan, Sarah. Secretary to Alex Dow of the Edison Illuminating Company when Henry Ford worked there in the 1890s. Their acquaintance continued throughout the lifetimes of both Henry and Clara Ford. 7 pages.

Simpson, Mr. and Mrs. Howard. Howard Simpson joined the engineering staff of Henry Ford and Son in 1918 and worked as a design engineer until his resignation in 1939. He describes experimental tractor development, experimental transmissions, the Ford-Ferguson tractor, and working as an engineer for Henry Ford. 148 pages. (See biography in this book.)

Simpson, Mr. and Mrs. Lewis. Lewis Simpson assisted in the design of Henry Ford's residence, Fair Lane. The Simpsons speak of Henry and Clara Ford, W. H. Van Tine, the construction of Fair Lane, and its architectural features. Included are personal glimpses of the Fords. 25 pages.

Smith, Albert. Started with Ford Motor Company as an inspector at the Piquette plant in 1903. As a manufacturing superintendent, he describes production and personnel problems, including his relationships with Charles Sorensen, Peter Martin, Harry Bennett, and Mead Bricker during his thirty-nine years with the company. 108 pages.

Smith, C. J. Employed by Ford Motor Company from 1906 to 1949. During most of this time, he worked in the Experimental Department under direct supervision of Henry Ford. He was mechanic of the winning Model T in the Transcontinental Race of 1909 and was asked to test a great variety of experimental vehicles during his career with Ford. 57 pages.

Smith, Charles R., Jr. Tells of the work of his father, C. R. Smith, Sr., at Highland Park and the Dearborn State Bank, the banking crisis of 1933, Henry Ford, the children of Greenfield Village, and old-fashioned dancing. 32 pages.

Smith, Dr. F. Janney. Became a staff member of Henry Ford Hospital in 1915. He describes Henry Ford Hospital, its origins, administration, professional staff, patients, and personalities from 1915 until 1954. Ford's ideas on health, diet, and medicine are discussed. 28 pages.

Smith, Isabelle Gassett. Discusses the Greenfield Village Schools in theory and practice, Henry Ford's interest in children, his charitable activities, and his personality. 31 pages.

Smith, Robert A. Entered Henry Ford Trade School in 1926. After graduation, he worked in the Edison Institute Experimental Laboratory. In 1933, Henry Ford gave him his own farm laboratory, where he worked on the utilization of farm products, developing a series of soybean food derivatives. 33 pages.

Smith, Roscoe M. Entered Ford Motor Company in 1916 as a maintenance man. In 1919, he transferred to the Starter and Generator Department and became department head in 1925. He describes starter and generator manufacture at Ypsilanti, the Ford Village Industries, and B-24 production at Willow Run where he was plant superintendent. 78 pages. (See biography in this book.)

Snow, Clara. A longtime resident of Dearborn, she was an intimate friend of Henry and Clara Ford. She was a member of the old-time dance group and participated with Clara Ford in the Dearborn Garden Club and the National Farm and Garden Association. She describes the Fords in these various relationships. 64 pages.

Soli, Thorvald. Joined Ford Motor Company as a clerk in the Pequaming commissary 1927. His memoir tells of his meeting Henry and Clara Ford and their discussion of the overall plans for the development of Upper Michigan. 22 pages.

Stacey, Rev. Hedley G. As rector of Christ Episcopal Church in Dearborn, he was sometimes spiritual adviser to Clara Ford. He speaks of the religious life of the Ford family. 47 pages.

Stafford, John. Became a Ford dealer in 1907 and held the franchise until 1953. He describes dealer contracts and early problems in selling automobiles and tractors. 12 pages.

Stakes, Capt. Perry T. Licensed as master of steam and motor vessels of all oceans unlimited and first-class pilot of inland waters from Boston to New Orleans and of the Great Lakes. Stakes was hired by Henry Ford to captain the yachts *Sialia I* and *II*. He tells of trips taken with the Fords and their friends aboard the ships from 1919 until 1927. 27 pages.

Steinke, R. J. Joined the Accounting Department at Iron Mountain, where he worked until 1951. He describes Ford housing at Iron Mountain, the purchase of land in the Upper Peninsula, logging camps, the search for iron ore, and glider production. 40 pages.

Stout, William B. Describes his role in the early aircraft industry, the Stout Engineering Laboratory, and the Stout Metal Airplane Company and his joint venture with Henry Ford in producing the Ford Trimotor. 132 pages. (See biography in this book.)

Strauss, Frederick. Did not work for Ford but tells of Henry Ford's apprentice days at James Flower Brothers and the Detroit Dry Dock companies. He describes Ford's early gasoline experiments and the Ford workshop in 1899, the Park Place Shop, and the building of the 999 and the Arrow. The formation of Ford Motor Company and predecessor companies are also recounted. 92 pages.

Strielman, Joseph R. Principal of Big Bay School, he reports the benefits received by the town from Henry Ford's plan to improve the economic status of its people. 9 pages.

Stromquist, Eric. Was with the Land Department of the Ford Motor Company at Iron Mountain from 1920 to 1951. He describes company policy in the purchase and sale of land as well as logging and mining operations. 17 pages.

Sullivan, C. J. A professional educator, he gives his evaluation of the Pequaming School system operated in accordance with Henry Ford's theory of education. 8 pages.

Swanson, Mark. Worked for Ford Motor Company at Iron Mountain from 1923 to 1952. He gives details of the evolution of manufacturing and administrative changes during the period of progress from wood parts only to assembly of complete station wagons. 33 pages.

Tallberg, V. Y. Completed a student's course at Ford Motor Company and in 1928 was assigned to the Berlin, Germany, assembly plant. After serving as service representative, he became chief engineer of Ford of Germany. He describes German operations, manufacturing, engineering, purchasing, and political considerations. He returned to the United States in 1940. 170 pages.

Thompson, George R. Worked as a construction engineer for William B. Mayo on the expansion of the Highland Park plant and on early Rouge construction. He tells of working with Mayo, Albert Kahn, and Henry Ford. He left Ford in 1919 and later became city engineer for the city of Detroit. 76

pages.

Thomson, R. P. Became accountant and office manager of Richmond Hill plantation in 1936. He describes the renovation of Richmond Hill, Henry Ford, the schools and schoolchildren of Richmond Hill, and Ford's personality. 55 pages.

Thompson, W. W. Iron Mountain bank president, he recalls his efforts to purchase land for Ford Motor Company; his assessment of E. G. Kingsford, an agent for Henry Ford; and his impression of Ford's interest in the Upper Peninsula. 8 pages.

Tornberg, E. E. Associated with accounting activities of Ford Motor Company in the Upper Peninsula, he explains these procedures for the period 1923 to 1951. 9 pages.

Turner, Raymond. Legal counsel for Ford Motor Company in the Upper Peninsula. He describes agreements for the development of an iron smelter, deeds and contracts for the purchase of dolomite lands, and logging agreements for Ford. 14 pages.

Ukkleberg, H. G. An agricultural scientist, he recalls his employment by Thomas Edison at Fort Myers, Florida, to utilize goldenrod as a source of rubber. He later worked for Ford at Richmond Hill, Georgia, attempting to convert plants to industrial products. 28 pages.

Verner, William F. Joined the Power and Construction Department of Ford Motor Company in 1917 but left Ford to enter business for himself in 1921. He describes Eagle boat construction, the Rouge plant site and physical facilities, the conflicts between Ford executives, and Henry Ford as an engineer. 53 pages.

Vivian, Frank. Entered Ford Motor Company in 1913 at the San Francisco branch. He describes the Panama-Pacific Exposition of 1915, Henry Ford's interest in soybeans, labor relations on the West Coast, and Ford's interest in antiques. He retired in 1952 as power engineer of the Richmond, California, plant. 106 pages.

318 Voorhess, Charles. Employed by Ford Motor Company in 1910 and three years

later transferred to Ford Farms. In 1917, he became power engineer at Fair Lane and also at the Dearborn Engineering Laboratory, where Henry Ford kept him busy on a variety of electrical power projects. 194 pages.

Waddell, H. R. Joined the staff of the Dearborn Publishing Company in 1923 and in the following year was transferred to the office of Henry Ford as a secretary. In 1946, after the death of Frank Campsall, he became secretary to Henry and Clara Ford. He tells of Ford's daily routine. 10 pages.

Waggoner, J. M. A toolmaker, he joined Ford Motor Company in 1915. He describes employment practices and union activity 1915–1916; tool design 1915–1925; manufacturing, engineering, and styling of the Lincoln car 1930–1942; union activities 1941–1947; and the development of automation 1947–1951. 226 pages.

Wagner, John. Started in the Maintenance Department of Ford Motor Company in 1916. His responsibilities included safety devices, safety education, and other functions of the Safety Department 1916–1952. He discusses labor grievances and union activities 1930–1952. 41 pages.

Wagner, Walter. Entered Ford Motor Company in 1910 at the Piquette plant as draftsman and machine tool designer. He became chief tool designer for the Lincoln plant and presents a history of the Lincoln organization. He also tells of his involvement in the manufacture of aircraft engines in Poissy, France, as well as at Willow Run. 171 pages.

Wait, E. F. Worked with Goodyear and Firestone tire companies before joining Ford Motor Company in 1936. He describes the organization, operation, and administration of the Ford Motor Company tire plant, also the Ford rubber plantation in Brazil and the use of plastics by Ford. 88 pages.

Walters, E. A. Came to Ford Motor Company in 1912 after Ford purchased Keim Mills of Buffalo, N.Y. A press operator, Walters became superintendent of the pressed steel division of Ford in 1919. He describes the Keim Mills 1899–1912, the five-dollar day, the pressed steel division 1912–1941, and World War II union activities. 136 pages.

Wandersee, John. Hired as a sweeper in 1902 by Ford. He tells of the formation of Ford Motor Company, the metallurgical developments with which he became associated, and his impressions of Henry Ford and other executives of the company. 72 pages.

Ward, Willis. Hired as a vacation employee from the University of Michigan in the 1930s by Harry Bennett. He joined the Employment Office, where he supervised Ford's policy of racial integration. He tells of racial discrimination at the university, racial integration at Ford Motor Company, the rehabilitation of the village of Inkster, and how depression problems were handled. 115 pages.

Wasson, Harold W. Joined Ford Motor Company at the Rouge plant in 1919. He speaks of the beginnings of the Rouge, the dismantling of the 199 ships, and Model A development. In 1931, he traveled to Japan as adviser to a Ford parts manufacturer. 44 pages.

Watt, Burt L. An employee of the Lake Shore Engineering Company of Marquette, Michigan, who repaired sawmill parts for Henry Ford and formed a lasting friendship with him. He tells of conversations with Ford on vacations at the Huron Mountain Club. 13 pages.

Weber, Benjamin P. An employee at the Iron Mountain plant, he describes the manufacture of wood body parts, stock scheduling and distribution, and a glimpse of Henry Ford on his visits. 14 pages.

Weber, John J. Employed by the Michigan Iron, Land and Lumber Company at Iron Mountain in 1922. He tells of operations of the cashier's office, the Ford Investment Plan, commissaries, home construction, industrial relations, and the depression. 16 pages.

Westberg, Lars. Describes the manual training program at the Pequaming, Michigan, school. 6 pages.

Westman, Albert. Ford gardener at the Pequaming bungalow 1923–1951. He tells of Clara Ford's interest in flowers and the visits of the Fords to the town of Pequaming. 4 pages.

Wiesmyer, M. L. Joined Ford in 1918 as a lathe operator, advanced to the Factory Layout Department, and in 1923 was selected to work on branch assembly plant layout. In 1944, he had become director of manufacturing operations at all Ford branch plants. He describes branch assembly plant construction, equipment, and supervision 1923–1952. 149 pages.

Williams, John H. Became a member of the staff of Fair Lane as house boy in 1922. He describes Ford family routines, social entertainment, travel, recreation, religion, and other aspects of daily life. 50 pages.

Williams, Thomas H. Joined the Ford Motor Company at Highland Park and transferred to Iron Mountain in 1927. He describes his work in the Investigation Department at Highland Park and the men and manufacturing at Iron Mountain. 25 pages.

Wilson, Rufus. Henry Ford's personal chauffeur from 1919 to 1945. He reveals many facets of Ford's complex personality including Ford's own driving habits. 48 pages.

Winkler, Dr. H. J. Practiced medicine for Ford Motor Company in the Upper Peninsula and traveled with Henry and Clara Ford on their trips to northern Michigan. 34 pages.

Wolfe, A. G. From 1907, lived on the Ford Dairy Farm where his father was in charge. He attended the Henry Ford Trade School and was employed beginning in 1920 in the Experimental Department of Ford Motor Company. He describes Ford's interest in farming, construction of Fair Lane, experimental vehicle design and testing, the Ford family on vacations, and the Ford cemetery. 226 pages.

Wollering, Max F. Became production superintendent of the Ford Manufacturing Company in 1906. He tells of manufacturing and assembly methods at Ford Manufacturing 1906–1917 and at Ford Motor Company 1907–1908 and Ford's industrial philosophy. He also speaks of his experiences at EMF Company, Studebaker Corporation, and Hudson Motor Car Company. 56 pages.

Wright, Evan. A former employee of William B. Stout, joined the Aircraft Division of Ford Motor Company in 1926 and worked as a design engineer until

1932. He describes aviation in general and Stout's activities 1914–1923, the Ford Trimotor, and the Ford bus program 1938–1947. 14 pages.

Zarembski, Frank. Employed in Greenfield Village, where he made shoes for Henry Ford. 9 pages.

Zaroski, Joseph. Henry Ford's barber during the last ten years of Ford's life relates many anecdotes about Ford's attitudes toward money, politics, war, and religion. 29 pages.

Zoerlein, Emil. Mechanical engineer who worked very closely with Henry Ford on many problems. He was present during conferences between Henry and Edsel Ford and describes the relationship between father and son. 256 pages.

Titles in the Great Lakes Books Series

Copper-Toed Boots, by Marguerite de Angeli, 1989 (reprint)

Detroit Images: Photographs of the Renaissance City, edited by John J. Bukowczyk and Douglas Aikenhead, with Peter Slavcheff, 1989

Hangdog Reef: Poems Sailing the Great Lakes, by Stephen Tudor, 1989

Detroit: City of Race and Class Violence, revised edition, by B. J. Widick, 1989

Deep Woods Frontier: A History of Logging in Northern Michigan, by Theodore J. Karamanski, 1989

Orvie: The Dictator of Dearborn, by David L. Good, 1989

Seasons of Grace: A History of the Catholic Archdiocese of Detroit, by Leslie Woodcock Tentler, 1990

The Pottery of John Foster: Form and Meaning, by Gordon and Elizabeth Orear, 1990

The Diary of Bishop Frederic Baraga: First Bishop of Marquette, Michigan, edited by Regis M. Walling and Rev. N. Daniel Rupp, 1990

Walnut Pickles and Watermelon Cake: A Century of Michigan Cooking, by Larry B. Massie and Priscilla Massie, 1990

The Making of Michigan, 1820–1860: A Pioneer Anthology, edited by Justin L. Kestenbaum, 1990

America's Favorite Homes: A Guide to Popular Early Twentieth-Century Homes, by Robert Schweitzer and Michael W. R. Davis, 1990

Beyond the Model T: The Other Ventures of Henry Ford, by Ford R. Bryan, 1990

Life after the Line, by Josie Kearns, 1990

Michigan Lumbertowns: Lumbermen and Laborers in Saginaw, Bay City, and Muskegon, 1870–1905, by Jeremy W. Kilar, 1990

Detroit Kids Catalog: The Hometown Tourist, by Ellyce Field, 1990

Waiting for the News, by Leo Litwak, 1990 (reprint)

Detroit Perspectives, edited by Wilma Wood Henrickson, 1991

Life on the Great Lakes: A Wheelsman's Story, by Fred W. Dutton, edited by William Donohue Ellis, 1991

Copper Country Journal: The Diary of Schoolmaster Henry Hobart, 1863–1864, by Henry Hobart, edited by Philip P. Mason, 1991

John Jacob Astor: Business and Finance in the Early Republic, by John Denis Haeger, 1991

Survival and Regeneration: Detroit's American Indian Community, by Edmund J. Danziger, Jr., 1991

Steamboats and Sailors of the Great Lakes, by Mark L. Thompson, 1991

Cobb Would Have Caught It: The Golden Years of Baseball in Detroit, by Richard Bak, 1991

Michigan in Literature, by Clarence Andrews, 1991

Under the Influence of Water: Poems, Essays, and Stories, by Michael Delp, 1992

The Country Kitchen, by Della T. Lutes, 1992 (reprint)

The Making of a Mining District: Keweenaw Native Copper 1500–1870, by David J. Krause, 1992

Kids Catalog of Michigan Adventures, by Ellyce Field, 1993

Historic Highway Bridges of Michigan, by Charles K. Hyde, 1993

Henry's Lieutenants, by Ford R. Bryan, 1993